WHY QUANTUM PHYSICISTS PLAY "GROW A GREATER YOU"

LEARN HOW TO LIVE THE MOST TRULY FULFILLING LIFE HUMANLY POSSIBLE

BY

GREG KUHN

ISBN: 978-1500445850

Createspace Formatting by www.ebooklaunch.com

Table of Contents

Introduction

"The two most important days in your life are the day you are born, and the day you find out why."
   Mark Twain (1835-1910)
   American humorist, essayist, and novelist

How would you like an owner's manual for life as a human being—just like the one you have stashed in your car's glove box? A manual instructing you specifically, step-by-step, how to live as happily and successfully as you want, however you wish to define those things. A manual that teaches you exactly how to achieve and manifest any desire.

We've had versions of owner's manuals since ink was first put to paper. Various religious and spiritual practices, for example, have provided some of our most important and revered texts; philosophers have contributed their best ideas and created time-tested books; and physicians and scientists have used their knowledge and insight to craft valuable tomes—all of which have been used as human owner's manuals.

The wisdom available to us from these three groups has been a tremendously significant asset; their versions and iterations of human owner's manuals have helped millions of us live healthier, more aware, successful, and purposeful lives. In fact, they've created the modern world in which we live.

Yet, as the 21st century unfolds in earnest, you, like so many others, continue to seek a still more thorough and more accurate owner's manual for life. It's important to stress that I don't believe we're still searching because the previous efforts of religion, spiritualism, philosophy, medicine, and science have been inadequate. To the contrary, the tremendous and seminal contributions from these fields can't be adequately praised in regards to their scope and impact.

In that spirit, I hope you will agree that, no matter how advanced we become as stewards of this planet and architects of our own lives, we retain a naturally strong desire to grow and manifest into the greatest versions of ourselves we can dare to imagine.

Growing into our greatest versions of ourselves is not only our natural inclination, it is also our birthright. We were not born to play small. It is so essential to a fulfilling human life that we will continue striving for such growth and fulfillment even while living lives of health, wellness, awareness, and abundance that humans a century ago could only dream of. And why are we not satisfied? Because one of our most primal desires is to awaken our almost unbelievable potential and nearly limitless power.

As great as you've become, you still want to grow a greater you. Me too.

Well, I have wonderful news. You're on your way in earnest now to that blossoming of your immense creative power that you so rightfully desire. This book is your long-awaited owner's manual for life on this planet. And it comes to you in the form of an amazingly fun and tremendously effective game called "Grow a Greater You."

I realize what a bold claim that is, yet I am confidant you'll soon agree that I've melded the best insights, knowledge, and teachings of religions, spiritualists, philosophers, doctors, and scientists into a very precise and rather unique instructional guide for fully realizing your powerful creative abilities as the architect of your life. This owner's manual will make it possible for you to manifest your desires (large and small) and end your suffering. If you follow this owner's manual, there is little doubt that you will awaken into your greatest, grandest vision of yourself as a deliberate creator of your material reality.

"Grow a Greater You" combines insights from quantum physics and neuroscience with spiritual and religious teachings. I am neither a quantum physicist nor a neuroscientist nor a spiritual or religious leader by profession, however, and this book is not written to thoroughly teach you about those subjects. Rather, I am an author whose great interest in these fields helped him create new paradigms from their teachings, both independently and in context with one another.

To learn about quantum physics, I recommend the following books:

Brian Greene (*The Hidden Reality: Parallel Universes and the Deep Laws of the Cosmos*, New York: Vintage, 2011), Stephen Hawking (*The Grand Design*, New York: Bantam, 2012), Amit Goswami (*The Self Aware*

Universe, New York: Tarcher, 1995), Nick Herbert (*Quantum Reality: Beyond the New Physics*, New York: Anchor, 1987), John Gribbin (*In Search of Schrodinger's Cat: Quantum Physics and Reality*, New York: Bantam Books, 1984), William Tiller (*Conscious Acts of Creation: The Emergence of a New Physics*, California: Pavior Publishing, 2001), Richard Feynman (*Six Easy Pieces*, New York: Basic Books, 1998), and Michio Kaku (*Physics of the Impossible: A Scientific Exploration into the World of Phasers, Force Fields, Teleportation, and Time Travel*, New York: Anchor, 2009).

To learn more about neuroscience, I recommend the following books:

Joe Dispenza (*Evolve Your Brain: The Science of Changing Your Mind*, Florida: HCI, 2010), Harry Carpenter (*The Genie Within: Your Subconscious Mind*, California: Harry Carpenter Publishing, 2011), and Bruce Lipton, PhD (*The Biology of Belief*, California: Hay House, 2013).

To learn more about religion, spirituality, or philosophy, I recommend the following books:

Benjamin Hoff (*The Tao of Pooh*, New York: Penguin Books, 1983), Rick Warren (*The Purpose Driven Life: What on Earth Am I Here For?*, Michigan: Zondervan, 2011), The Dalai Lama (*Transforming the Mind: Teachings on Generating Compassion*, London: Thorsons, 2003), and Jon Kabat-Zinn (*Wherever You Go There You Are: Mindfulness Meditation in Everyday Life*, New York: Hyperion, 2009).

"Grow a Greater You" is created from the wisdom of these teachings. It shows you how to use that wisdom experientially—to put it into action. I am not simply combining the wisdom of empirically proven quantum physics and neuroscience with the noetic wisdom of religion, spiritualism, and philosophy. I am also an active practitioner of "Grow a Greater You"; I continue to live its brilliance daily and experience it vicariously through the lives of thousands of readers.

In fact, the amazing results of the people who play "Grow a Greater You" have allowed me to hone its instructions to razor-sharp efficiency. This game is what you came to Earth to play, and play it you shall—with power, wisdom, and authority.

I call it a game, by the way, not because it's a trivial pursuit (see what I did there?). To the contrary, this game may be the most important thing you'll ever do for the advancement of your efficacy as a human being. And playing it may be the single most satisfying thing you will ever do to imbue your life with joy, happiness, and success, because "Grow a Greater You" allows you to manifest your desires as well as make your suffering optional.

So without further ado, I give you the last owner's manual you may ever need, in the form of the most wondrous game you could possibly play: "Grow a Greater You."

Chapter One

How Evolved Are We, Really?

In my first book in this series, *Why Quantum Physicists Don't Get Fat*, I asked you to envision what life was like for humans prior to the first scientific revolution. I reminded you of the primitive understanding of the natural world that humans labored under and how it affected their ability to experience fulfilling lives in the manner we do today. Now, I want you to imagine some of our most primitive ancestry: Neanderthals, uncivilized and wild.

Neanderthals lived on Earth up to 45,000 years ago. They lived in social groups with a hierarchy. They had a language, they built dwellings, they fashioned advanced tools, and they may have even built dugout canoes. These abilities, combined with their significant physical strength, made Neanderthals an apex predator. We also know that they ate cooked vegetables in addition to their meat-heavy diet.

Yet, as much physical prowess as Neanderthals possessed, they were always at the mercy of many challenges stemming from their primitive existence. Larger, more powerful predators and even large animals upon which they preyed were a constant threat to their lives. Escaping disease and not succumbing to life's normal wear-and-tear on their bodies were largely insurmountable obstacles dependent upon their mere good fortune. Even the effects of weather and other uncontrollable circumstances of nature were threats that a Neanderthal could neither predict nor hope to greatly mitigate.

Imagine being a Neanderthal-era human. How would you understand life? What would be your paradigms to explain what was happening to you and what was occurring around you on this planet? How would your life "work"?

All you would have at your disposal for crafting your paradigms would be your senses. What you saw with your eyes, heard with your ears, tasted with your tongue, etc., would be the extent of the measurable, recordable data available to you. As such, I imagine you'd believe the following:

- Material objects and life experiences are external things, awaiting your discovery.

- The things and experiences that are pleasing (or even life-saving), like killing a healthy game animal or discovering a suitable and uninhabited rock outcrop under which you can sleep, are gifts bestowed upon you by an unknown source.

- You call such pleasing and lifesaving things "gifts" because they're not always assured.

- Not only is the giver of these gifts unknown, how you earn the gifts is also unknown.

- You revere the giver of these gifts and try to earn its favor, because you need the gifts it can bestow.

- You try to please the giver of these gifts by painting your face, making loud noises, dancing, sacrificing animals to it, building fires, etc.

- No matter what you do, though, a clear pattern develops: sometimes you get the gifts you want and sometimes you don't— and there is no way to discern how and why that decision is made.

- You fear the giver of these gifts because it has the power to deny important things to you.

- You are very often furious at the giver of these gifts because it regularly denies them to you, causing suffering and even death. But you are wary of displaying that anger, for you do not wish to alienate the giver of gifts and bear the brunt of its retribution.

- Life is frightening and uncertain. You feel unsafe, and your survival is not guaranteed from one day to the next. Surviving the threats of your daily existence takes luck and lots of help from the mysterious giver of gifts.

That is an existence none of us would enjoy or voluntarily return to. Aren't we fortunate to be living during our era? Although our primitive

Neanderthal predecessor had no basis to conceptualize how it could be accomplished, they surely longed for a life such as we enjoy today. Huddled together during a cold, torrential downpour, with a sick child in their midst, having not eaten for two days, a Neanderthal social group must have felt like your pet dog does when accidentally left in your backyard during an all-day rain: abandoned, for unknown reasons, by the giver of gifts.

As primitive as all that sounds, though, I propose that for most modern-day humans, understanding how life "works" hasn't really evolved all that much.

Yet.

Compare, if you will, modern humans' current understandings of how life "works" with a Neanderthal's. Certainly, for modern-day humans, you can take out the parts about "surviving" and replace them with references to "thriving" instead. Most of us do not have to wonder how we will stay warm, dry, or fed from day to day. Our ability to meet our basic physical needs is a challenge that has largely been solved and, for most people, the concern has shifted to simply being happier. We can swap out most of the examples of what might be most pleasing to us—replacing "killing a game animal" with "having a cool car," for example. And we can probably change out some of the rituals done to earn good fortune or favor—for example, "sacrificing animals" with "repeating positive affirmations." Most of us do not paint our faces and beat drums around a fire to summon blessings.

But, for most people, life is still a mysterious and painful guessing game of trying to somehow earn the favor of the giver of gifts. Many humans' understanding of how life "works" is still inhibited by a reliance upon their senses.

This book will not only teach you to play "Grow a Great You," it will also teach you how to live the most fulfilling life you're willing to grow into. It will even teach you how to make the world a better place for the rest of your fellow humans. And, best of all, this book actually introduces you to the mythical and mysterious "giver of gifts."

The giver of gifts, surprisingly, is not "you." Well, not exactly. You certainly do *possess* the gift giver. The giver of gifts is found *in* you; it is found in the very vessel that makes human life possible: your physical body. More specifically, it is found in your subconscious brain. And once you learn who, or what, the true giver of gifts is, you will finally be able to stop unwittingly keeping your primitive ancestry's limiting, misery-inducing paradigms alive.

The giver of gifts is your beliefs. Your material reality, your life experience, your unique, individual universe is always a perfect reflection of your beliefs. I know full well that for much of your life you have only experienced portions of those reflections as "gifts"; the rest of those reflections have left much to be desired. Me too. Through "Grow a Greater You," however, you will learn to see all the reflections of your beliefs as gifts, even the ones that displease you (as strange as that might sound to you right now).

You have greatly enjoyed the times when your beliefs have happened to be aligned with your conscious desires, because the reflections you experienced were always very pleasing. Those have been your happiest, most fulfilling experiences of human life, and, like everyone else, you have not only treasured those times, you also long for more of them. Until now, you may have felt punished or unworthy when your beliefs have not been aligned with your conscious desires, because the reflections you experienced were always very displeasing. Those have been your most unpleasant experiences of human life, and you have not only suffered during those times, but you have often been desperate to learn how to experience them no longer.

So do not feel pity for the primitive Neanderthal just yet; there are plenty of people in the 21st century just as much in need of enlightenment. How fortunate that you will now no longer count yourself as a member of that group. I feel the same gratitude, personally, and am very excited that one more of my fellow humans is joining me in the cadre of "Grow a Greater You" all-stars. Thank you for adding your energy to this game, to the growing enlightenment and evolution of our paradigms regarding how life on this planet "works."

The following are the beliefs created by playing "Grow a Greater You." I'm certain many of them resonate not only with your conscious, logical understanding of life, but also with the beliefs you desire and intend to use. Beginning now, these beliefs will no longer reside in the realm of "Wouldn't it be nice if..." or "This is how I think it ought to work, but it usually never does..." You will now begin to live yourself into *knowing* these beliefs; these beliefs will become who you are. And, as that happens, you will be growing a greater you than you might have thought possible.

1. The universe is a living, omniscient, omnipresent field of energy called the quantum field.

2. We are energy and are a part of the quantum field.

3. The quantum field becomes coherent with our energy and, thus, our own unique, individual universe is formed in context with us.

4. Our expectations are the vehicle through which our energy becomes coherent with the quantum field.

5. Our expectations are formed, unconsciously, from our beliefs.

6. Our beliefs are stored in our subconscious and, thus, we are not consciously aware of them.

7. Our beliefs are simply stories, inspired by trusted sources, that we've repeated to ourselves often enough to give them that power.

8. The stories we tell ourselves about every person, place, thing, or event that we experience give them a subjective, unique, and personal meaning and value for us.

9. The stories we tell ourselves both reveal and influence our beliefs.

10. Our life experiences are always an accurate reflection of our beliefs; our material reality is created in context with us.

11. We do not literally create every person, place, thing, or event, but we always contextually create our own unique, individual version of such—as well as add to their ongoing communal creation through the stories we tell ourselves about them.

12. We play "Grow a Greater You" to experience a unique, individual universe that is much more pleasing to us, one that is much more aligned with our dreams and desires.

Reading and cognitively embracing these beliefs with your conscious awareness is good. But do not harbor the misunderstanding that you must, in this moment, fully embrace them on a complete, subconscious level. And you don't even need to make a concerted effort to study them, memorize them, or internalize them. Agreeing with them or at least being open to their possibility is all that is required of you for now, because playing "Grow a Greater You" is not a metaphorical, conceptual endeavor; the power of this game is that you live yourself into *knowing* them. And it happens without having to exert any intentional effort to make it so.

I'm sure you can see that living according to these beliefs will create an amazingly abundant life full of freedom, yet you needn't wonder or worry about how you might acquire them. I will teach you exactly how to live your way into them. All you need to do is play "Grow a Greater You" as you're taught and these beliefs will become yours in all their glory. Thankfully, playing this game is not an intellectual, theoretical exercise.

You're done with theoretical musings. You're through with truthful yet esoteric explanations of how and what you ought to think and believe. You're finished with Band-Aids that cover up the wounds for a while, merely allowing you to forget they're there but never healing them. You're no longer going to be trying to talk yourself into a new way of living; you're now living yourself into a new you—a you who, from this point forward, is one of your choosing. A you who is as fulfilled as you dare to dream. A you who no longer must play small for fear of suffering. A you who can grow into her greatest vision and version of herself—and who creates real opportunities for others to do likewise if they choose.

I am in the "Grow a Greater You" Hall of Fame. There is space reserved for you there too. I don't play it perfectly; I stumble, I play small, and I emulate my Neanderthal ancestry from time to time. I mention this to highlight the important idea that there is no expectation for perfection and no need to strive for it. Your mistakes, your skinned knees and stubbed toes along the way, are actually an important part of this game.

This book was actually written for a classroom setting, for a course which might be called "How to Live the Best Human Life Possible," and I trust you can appreciate this—even if your classroom is your living room. While you may not be a novice regarding how our universe works and how we intentionally create our material reality, I ask your patience and indulgence.

Similarly, you will see some concepts and phrases repeated continually throughout this book. This is not done to insult you or to talk down to you. I in no way consider you a simpleton who needs things repeated in order to understand them. I do this intentionally so that someone who is a novice to these concepts will encounter them over and over. If you already agree with some of the concepts in this book and feel it unnecessary to read them repeatedly, although often restated and rephrased, I once again ask your indulgence and patience.

Greg Kuhn

Chapter Two

What Is This Place?

First, let's discuss the very nature of the playground you inhabit, our universe—the material reality you experience as a human being on this planet. The world we inhabit appears to us in the same manner as it did our Neanderthal ancestors; we see a physical realm full of things, solid and tangible objects that are separate from us and merely awaiting our discovery. These physical things with which we share our world seem to us to be pre-existing objects whose presence has nothing to do with us. In other words, to our senses the material world would be here even if we weren't and will be here long after we're not.

There is some degree of truth to these observations, which I'll go into later.

During the first scientific revolution, classical physics revealed almost everything about how this material world we see and experience through our senses operates. The birth of modern science, from the 16th through the 18th centuries, only served to reinforce the paradigm of a world of "things" that exist independently of us, awaiting our discovery. In fact, as late as the 19th century, the most promising science students were usually counseled to not go into the field of physics because it was thought that everything important about the way the material world worked had already been discovered.

And the entire world moved forward with creating paradigms based upon classical physics, the science that explains how the physical world works on an "eyeball" level, the world of the seeable and touchable. Certainly, there were always people who intuitively explored the more esoteric and noetic experiences humans share, seeking to answer philosophical and spiritual questions such as "What is the meaning of life?" "Why are we here?" and "What happens when we die?" But these were not questions scientists sought to answer, for two primary reasons. One, because almost all the mechanisms of how life works could be explained through classical physics. And, two, science is a discipline that concerns itself only with things that can be observed and measured.

The idea that physics had already explained everything about how our universe works underwent a change in the early 20th century when Albert Michelson and Edward Morley used classical physics to measure the speed at which the Earth was traveling through space (which, at that time, was called the universal ether). Classical physics had revealed the speed of light, so all Michelson and Morley needed to do was take measurements of the Sun's rays each day, which would readily reveal the Earth's speed.

The results of the Michelson and Morley experiment showed that the Earth was traveling at zero miles per hour. This finding sent the scientific community into a tailspin. While the failed experiment probably meant little to laypeople like you and me, scientists realized that there was much more to discover about the rules of the natural world than they previously thought. Their efforts to uncover these answers necessitated the creation of a new science: quantum physics. And quantum physics has ushered in a second scientific revolution, one that's far more powerful, accurate, precise, and impactful than the first.

Quantum physics explains the behavior of both the tiny and massive portions of our universe, the parts of it we don't experience with our senses on an eyeball level. Aspects of our universe that we didn't even know existed until scientists were forced to go back to the drawing board and create a science that seeks to observe, measure, and create methods of explaining it. Quantum physics has proven to be the most reliable science ever created; its findings, in many respects, supersede classical physics because it has consistently proven incredibly more accurate.

Classical physics still works very well to explain the portion of our universe we perceive with our naked eyes and, thus, is still very valuable. Engineers, for example, use classical physics to build airplanes. But classical physics should no longer be the basis for our paradigms. Classical physics should no longer be used to tell humans how life works, to define the reasons we do things the way we do them, because it is not the most accurate model for such. Classical physics, as a basis for understanding why we should do things the way we do them, creates inaccurate paradigms not all that different from the ones our Neanderthal predecessors used.

What, then, does quantum physics tell us about how our universe works—about this material world we perceive and in which we live? We now know that the universe is actually best described as an omnipresent, omniscient, creative, intelligent field of energy. Often referred to as the quantum field, this field of energy exists in a state of potential—the potential to manifest, or form, into any material object.

We now know that the material world, as experienced by our senses, is, in large part, a beautiful illusion. It's an illusion that is necessary for us to experience human life on this planet as we know and love it. It's an illusion that there are separate and distinct things that are not connected to each other. It's an illusion that these apparently separate things exist independently of one another. And, perhaps most importantly, it's an illusion that humans have no influence upon the creation of the material world we experience.

These are all illusions, you ask? How can it be an illusion if you can pick up a pen—feel it, hold it, manipulate it, and write with it? That pen is not an illusion, your senses rightfully scream, it's real. Don't worry, that pen and everything else is what we call "real" in the material world.

Yet that pen and everything else is made of atoms. And atoms are 99.999999999% empty space. If you blow an atom up to the size of a massive cathedral, the nucleus of that atom (a nucleus that constitutes 99.999999999% of the tangible mass of an atom) will be the size of a fruit fly. The rest of our cathedral-sized atom would be nothing but empty space. Thus, 99.999999999% of every "thing" in the material world is 99.999999999% empty space. The sensation of touch is merely the negative charge of the electrons, which are part of the atoms making the two things repulse each other. The negative charge of the electrons in the atoms will not allow any two things to pass through each other.

I share this not to assert that our material world is irrelevant. It's definitely not. It's very relevant because it's all we've got. It's wonderful, it's important, and it's how we experience life as a human being on Earth. And I don't know about you, but I happen to love being a human and living in this material world of ours.

I share this so you know more about what quantum physics has taught us, compelling us to adopt new paradigms that reflect the way the universe really works—daring us, if you will, to stop playing small as if we are unimportant footnotes in a pre-existing material world that has nothing to do with us and over which we have no dominion or power to influence. Quantum physics teaches us that, when it comes to our life experiences in this material world, we are not inconsequential.

For our purposes, the universe can be thought of as a vast, all-encompassing ocean of energy. And when things take form from the energy ocean, or the quantum field, those things are only temporarily abandoning their state of "energy with the potential to become anything." We can think of things in the material world as waves on the Atlantic Ocean. The waves are not the ocean itself, but they are what the ocean is "doing." Likewise, things in the material world are not the energy ocean, itself, but what the energy ocean is doing.

Things, or material objects, are excitations, or vibrations, of the quantum field. Like waves on the Atlantic Ocean or, on a smaller scale, ripples on a pond, things are not actually pre-determined objects and are not separate from the field of energy that gives birth to them. Material objects are a temporary deviation in form; things are temporarily deviating from the interconnected dynamic energy of the quantum field to take a definitive, but temporary, form. The things that make up our material world, however, retain their inherent connection to the quantum field and, thus, remain part of the vast, interconnected intelligence that gave birth to them.

How do we know this? Follow the logic here:

- All things are made of atoms.

- All atoms are made of subatomic particles.

- All subatomic particles are made of energy.

A human body, a tree, a piece of tinfoil, a turnip, etc., is made of energy.

Except there is one important distinction we need to add to that hierarchy. A subatomic particle is not *made* of energy. It *is* energy. So your body is not *made* of energy, it *is* energy. Your body's current time-space manifestation is that of a physical thing (your body is real, don't worry), but this is only so because the energy of the quantum field from which you are formed has temporarily deviated from its true state of pure potential and collapsed to form your body and any other material object.

How would we have ever known this without quantum physics? We will certainly never experience this on the level of our conscious, eyeball awareness. But the fact that we cannot experience this with our senses is merely a factor of our perspective—we are too large to see this. Think about trying to experience the world as a round globe by walking out into your front lawn. It is impossible for you to experience the Earth as a sphere from that perspective. Yet, of course, you know the Earth is a sphere because science (and, eventually, photographs) proved it a long time ago. Likewise, humans will eventually know that everything is energy, and utilize this knowledge in their lives, because science has proven it.

Fortunately for you, you do not have to wait until this has become intricately interwoven into the paradigms everyone uses to govern the reasons they do things the way they do them. By playing "Grow a Greater You," you are not waiting until this becomes a part of humankind's conventional wisdom to begin living a highly fulfilling life. And make no mistake: All humans will eventually live by some form of the new paradigms you are learning here.

Physicists have discovered that the quantum field is not merely omnipresent, it's also omniscient, and that all information is present in every portion of it at all times. Every single bit of the quantum field contains every possible kernel of knowledge, and that knowledge is shared, instantaneously, throughout it in every moment. Think of all the systems in your body. There are many, and they have important, unique functions. Medical science tells us that all your systems share information in real time; they all know what the others are doing, they know why they are doing it, and they respond accordingly. That's how the quantum field works, except it is a millionfold more efficient and intelligent.

It is so intelligent, in fact, that the quantum field can do or become any "thing" at any time.

How simple is it for the omniscient quantum field to form into a thing in general or anything in particular? It is as simple as drawing a breath is for you. Because, you see, every physical object in the universe is merely some unique combination of mostly four basic elements: carbon, hydrogen, nitrogen, and oxygen. Those four elements need only be assembled into some particular combination, and in a particular amount in relation to the others, to create virtually anything you can imagine.

Physicists call things, or material objects, time-space events. A time-space event is a portion of the quantum field that has abandoned its state of potential and become a concrete, physical manifestation. A thing is a part of our eyeball world even while it does not abandon its relationship with the quantum field. A time-space event is not the quantum field, yet it is what the quantum field is doing.

When the quantum field forms into a physical object, physicists call that act a collapse of the quantum possibility wave, because subatomic particles do not actually exist in a pre-determined form as we might imagine. Since subatomic particles are nothing more than a possibility wave, when they become a distinct object we refer to that as collapsing the wave (a "wave" in the vernacular of physics, not an ocean wave). In this manner, we now know that the creation of our material world is not what logic, our eyeballs, and conventional wisdom would have us believe; we know that the material world is not a pre-existing entity that simply awaits our discovery of it. The notion of a pre-determined material reality reflects the old, Neanderthal paradigms, where we are at the bottom of the creation pyramid, a material world in which we play no creative role and where we are merely the detached, uninvolved observers of pre-existing material objects.

Quantum physics reveals that the creation of the material world is, in fact, a top-down process. This is a paradigm that tells us that we are at the top of the creation pyramid.

Of course, this begs the questions, "If a human being is truly at the top of the creation pyramid, then how is our material world actually being created? Who is doing the creating, and how?" The answers to these questions form the basis for "Grow a Greater You."

People are time-space events just like every other thing in the material universe. But people are very special time-space events in two primary ways:

1. People have a consciousness, which may not be something any other time-space event in the material world possesses.

2. People, being at the top of the creation pyramid, are contextual creators of everything they experience.

One worthy addition to these two facts is that people do not actually "possess" a consciousness. It is more accurate to say that a consciousness inhabits, or utilizes, a person's physical form. This is because, while a person is a time-space event, a consciousness is not. A consciousness is not a collapsed part of the quantum field—it is still in an energy state. A consciousness remains a non-collapsed part of the energy ocean. And, as such, your consciousness is using your body to experience the material world in tangible form.

Let's call people "consciousness-possessing, time-space events." Because we possess this amazing and unique thing called a consciousness, we play the seminal role in creating the material world. People are responsible for the collapse of the quantum possibility wave; people contextually create our material world. More specifically, people contextually create their own unique, individual material world.

Physicists tell us that each person experiences her own unique, individual universe—and that is meant literally, not metaphorically. This is not to suggest that some of us experience purple grass in our front lawns or cows with wings. But it does mean that each consciousness is experiencing her own unique version of the material world.

There is also no longer any doubt about what this universe really is: intelligent energy. And you, being a very special portion of that omnipresent, omniscient field of energy, play the role of creator in it.

Greg Kuhn

Chapter Three
Why Are You Here?

We've examined what this place is. Next, let's expound upon something I touched on in that chapter: the role of creator you play in our universe.

Our role of creator can sound like a new-age, feel-good, wouldn't-it-be-nice-if-it-were true philosophy when weighed against a Neanderthal's paradigms. To the skeptic still trapped in the paradigms of her senses, this philosophy can sound like something that all of us "new-age, airy-fairy" types naively wish were true. There is precious little indication from our senses that we are contextually creating our material experiences. Who can be blamed for thinking that the material world is "out there" (outside of us, existing independently of us) and merely awaiting our discovery?

But because we now know how our universe really works, and because we now know that the creation of the material world is not a bottom-up process, those Neanderthal perspectives have a limited shelf life. That's fortunate for Neanderthals, because a bottom-up paradigm is pretty scary. In fact, some of us could say that we play "Grow a Greater You" not because we want to get to paradise but because we've been imprisoned by our misery and we don't ever want to go back to it.

This chapter title, "Why Are You Here?," is a trick statement of sorts. You see, if the answer to the question of "Who is doing the creating?" is "you," we are naturally led to discover who "you" are, and the answer to that question reveals why "you" are here.

There is another trick statement of sorts in this chapter's title, because the term "here" also helps answer the question of why "you" are "here."

"You" are not your body. Your body is finite, as far as we know; your body is a collapsed portion of the quantum field and, as such, is a time-space event. "You" are your consciousness. The "here" is your physical body. In other words, "you" are "here"; you are not just on this planet experiencing material reality; you are also inhabiting your physical body, which is the vessel allowing you this experience.

Do you, like me, think this is probably the noetic wisdom inspiring the age-old concept of your body being your temple?

So this chapter is actually answering the question of why you (your consciousness) are here (using your physical body to facilitate the experience of a human being alive on Earth). You are here to contextually create. Every person on this planet is contextually creating, at all times, in every second, whether or not she knows it or believes it. Every person on this planet is collapsing the potential of the quantum field, in every single instant of her life, because that is what people do. You can't stop collapsing the quantum field and contextually forming the material world if you try.

I don't mean to make fun of skeptics, by the way, as I make continued references to Neanderthals. Please bear in mind that I lived by those paradigms for the bulk of my adult life and I am still prone to falling back into them on any given day. These references are as much a gentle poke at myself as anyone else and I don't mean to make light of anyone's suffering.

Thus, I am making tongue-in-cheek references to myself when I write about such perspectives. I think of a modern-day Neanderthal as "someone who is still doing research about using old paradigms." Someone who still wants to cling to old paradigms, and suffer in the process, is actually doing the important work of becoming willing to play "Grow a Greater You." But in the meantime, whatever misery she experiences may be absolutely necessary to becoming willing to change.

It took every ounce of misery I experienced to get me willing to play "Grow a Greater You," and I'm very grateful for all that suffering (more about that later). Ever heard the story about the frozen bird that, almost dead, was pooped on by a cow? The warmth of the cow manure revived the bird. And the moral of that tale is that not everyone who poops on you is doing you a disservice.

The poop, or misery, a Neanderthal experiences is warming her up—and adding to the factors that will lead to her eventual surrender of her old paradigms. Once that occurs, she can finally open herself up to this new way of life and experience the freedom from misery she has long desired.

Although "Grow a Greater You" is rooted entirely in science and the new paradigms we can rightfully glean from it, the opening paragraphs of this chapter would fit right in with the most esoteric, non-scientific, new-age, mystical, philosophical book out there. Yet I am teaching you things that science tells us about the creation of the material world and your role in it. In fact, no matter how much this book would be right at home in Amazon's New Age section, all of "Grow a Greater You" is squarely rooted in science.

Throughout this book, I will occasionally make reference to a hypothetical skeptic, simply because I find it valuable to address possible reservations to these new paradigms. I know this hypothetical person all too well—I used to be that person. Since I was once just such a person, and I love myself (even the older versions of me), I prefer to talk about those perspectives in a lighthearted manner. So if you are a skeptic, or someone you love is currently one, please accept my heartfelt welcome.

One of the most important things that you, as an early adopter of paradigms that will eventually permeate our planet, need to know about why you're here is that consciousness manipulates energy. Consciousness is at the top of the creation pyramid. We can see this replicated throughout quantum physics, although most physicists are not intentionally describing it using those words. Not using those words, however, is changing through the work of many pioneers in the quantum world.

Even the most hardened skeptic must acknowledge that you have a consciousness (although you already know that stating it that way is backwards; your consciousness has your body and uses it as a vehicle). Someone could argue that your brain, and not your consciousness, collapses the quantum field and forms material objects, but the data does not support that. The data tells us that a consciousness is the commander and the time-space events are the results.

And the data also tells us what mechanisms are used by your physical body to enact the collapse of the quantum field's state of potential into concrete things. You will soon be learning how that happens and how to use these mechanisms intentionally with wonderful efficiency. But first, more discussion of why you are here.

The most reliable and dramatic evidence of your role as a contextual creator can be seen through quantum physics' most famous experiment, the Double-Slit experiment. Nobel Prize-winning physicist Richard

Feynman once referred to the Double-Slit experiment as "...the only thing you need to know about quantum physics." This experiment encapsulates a perfect blend of the mystery, beauty, and otherworldly strangeness of quantum physics.

There are a plethora of books and websites that can give you a description of the Double-Slit experiment because it is generally described as the most revered experiment in the discipline. In a nutshell, what the Double-Slit experiment shows us is that the observer is the agent who contextually creates the form and behavior of particles. When scientists watch, or observe, a particle pass through the two slits, the particle goes through one slit or the other. But if the particle is not observed it acts like a wave and goes through both slits at the same time. The particles' behavior, in other words, will change based upon observation.

And perhaps the strangest part of the Double-Slit experiment is this: Data tell us that it is not simply the act of observation that dictates whether there is a particle or a wave present, but it is actually the expectation of the observer that determines that. The observer is not really an observer at all but is an integral part of the experiment; her expectations, communicated via her observations, are, in fact, just as important as any other portion of the experiment.

The observer is a contextual creator of the results of the Double-Slit experiment.

To add to the weirdness and solidify the interconnectedness of the quantum field, it has also been proven that the same results will occur even if the observer is merely thinking about, or intending, a certain outcome from the Double-Slit experiment. The observer does not actually have to be physically present and literally looking at the experiment to influence the outcome.

The observer will not technically "see" a wave or a particle in the typical manner that we call "seeing" something, because, until the observer observes (whether in person or merely by thinking about it), there is, literally, nothing to see; what the observer is observing was, prior to her observation of it, only a potential—a potential for energy to become a particle or a wave until that potential was observed. It was the act of observing, whether by physically putting her focus on it or by merely thinking about it, that commanded the "potential" to become "something" (in this case a wave or a particle).

As Sir Martin Rees, the British Astronomer Royal and former President of the Royal Astronomical Society, states it, "In the beginning there were only probabilities. The universe could only come into existence if someone observed it. It does not matter that the observers turned up several billion years later. The universe exists because we are aware of it."

The observer is the action-agent who collapsed the quantum possibility wave. Without an observer, the quantum field remains in a state of pure potential. This idea that you, a consciousness-possessing time-space event, are commanding the potential of the quantum field to collapse and become things is still somewhat resisted by the scientific community. And there are valid reasons for that, based on long-held precepts about how science is studied. But other fields have been acknowledging the validity of our power to contextually create and influence material reality for decades.

The medical and psychological community, for example, have been making allowances for just such influences, and human contextual creation, for decades through their use of blinds and double blinds during research. A blind is an indispensable research safeguard where the subjects of the research do not know which portions of an experiment or study are active agents (i.e., the actual pharmaceutical) and which portions are controls (i.e., a placebo). A double blind occurs when neither the subjects nor the researchers are aware of which portions are the active agents and which are the control, or placebos.

Blinds and double blinds are essential for medical and psychological research because it is well established that human beliefs can virtually dictate outcomes. We all know about the effect of placebos, which leave no doubt that if a human merely believes she is being given a medicine or treatment she will command her body to respond to it.

What you may not have known about placebos, however, is that research also shows that humans' positive responses to them increase as society more fully embraces the medicine or treatment being researched. Studies of drugs and treatments find that people can respond to placebos up to 60% or 70% of the time. But, often, we find that the initial introduction of a drug or treatment does not produce such high responses from the placebo. Why? Because the public is not yet familiar with the drug or treatment and has not yet embraced or accepted it. Thus, the test subjects do not yet have a high level of awareness or belief in the drug or treatment.

The scientific community has, historically, almost never used blind or double-blind techniques, because the prevailing paradigm has always been that a researcher's preconceptions and intentions have no effect upon the outcome of an experiment. Nature, in effect, has been thought to already be blind, and such precautions have been thought unnecessary because nature cannot be influenced by such things as preconceptions and intention. How shocking to the scientific community, then, was the research, published in 2001, of William Tiller, PhD, Walter Dibble, Jr., PhD, and Michael Kohane, PhD, that clearly shows just how much influence we have.

Using the traditional scientific method, Tiller, Dibble, and Kohane conducted research on the effects of human intention on water, enzymes, and fruit fly larvae. Their research, published in *Conscious Acts of Creation*, clearly demonstrates that human intention produces large-scale, measurable effects upon their intended targets. The results are not only accurate and valid but reliable and reproducible. How the scientific community will incorporate these findings into ongoing research and theory remains a work in progress, but you and I can certainly proceed with confidence and aplomb as we expand our role as a more intentional contextual creator of our life experiences.

"Grow a Greater You" is already becoming a part of our conventional wisdom because of how deeply and accurately rooted in science it is. Playing "Grow a Greater You" is becoming a way of life for a growing number of people each month. As time passes and more of this incredibly accurate science permeates our culture and changes our paradigms, the day will come soon that this book is not simply being studied in groups around the world but is also being read by students in school classrooms.

And if you're reading this book in a high school or college classroom, thank you for manifesting that desire. How fortunate you are to learn this game as part of your curriculum.

Human eyeballs tell us that a thing in the material world exists independently of us, that it is there whether we're around to observe it or not. Of course, human eyeballs also told Neanderthals that the Sun revolved around the Earth so they, and many people after them, believed that very effective illusion until it, too, was dispelled by science. Contextually creating the material world is your job, a special role you have in this universe that no one else can perform. Remember the old philosophical question: If a tree falls in the forest and no one is around, does it make a sound? It turns out that if no one were ever around, there couldn't be a forest.

And while you may not literally and solely create that forest, you are most definitely contextually creating it on your own unique, individual universe.

So that your special role doesn't sound too fantastic, however, I want to tell you about communal creation. You are not literally creating every single thing in the sense that the things you're experiencing don't actually exist at all until you personally manifest them. It is true that a material object does not exist in your own unique, individual universe until you contextually create it through your observation, but most things have already been contextually created by other people prior to your discovery of them.

Additionally, remember that your mere awareness of something, your thoughts and ideas about it, contextually create things as well; you do not need to be in the physical presence of a thing to contextually create it. Simply because you know of something, you are participating in its contextual creation.

That is why both formal and informal organizations that explicitly teach people what to think about things and how the universe works are so powerful and important. Schools, religions, governments, families, businesses, television stations, websites, radio stations, advertising agencies, peer groups, book publishers, etc., are all teaching people ideas and concepts that cause people to contextually create every aspect of their material world. Even if we will never physically see or be in the physical presence of any of those things, we will contextually create all of them in our own unique, individual universes based upon what we've been taught by influential people and organizations.

And, while we sometimes have limited choice regarding the people and organizations to which we are exposed and from whom we're influenced, as adults we should be as discerning as possible regarding to what we lend our attention and focus. You are not solely responsible for the plight of the world and, thus, you are not given the task of only exposing yourself to uplifting, responsible information. Yet you are solely responsible for the content of your own unique, individual universe. And you also have a tremendous ethical responsibility to any young person you're influencing.

I asked you earlier to think of a thing like an ocean wave on the Atlantic Ocean. Another way to envision a material object is like a warm spot in the Atlantic Ocean. You're swimming and you pass through it, perhaps never contemplating the miracle of billions of atoms passing through that warm spot every second. The atoms enter that space and leave by the billions, yet they become warm while there and return to being cool when they leave. That's a great illustration of a material object that is manifest from the quantum field.

When you encounter a warm spot, a material object, in the quantum field, in almost every instance other humans have already been contextually creating it. In this manner, it is not entirely incorrect to say that it did pre-exist, just not in the way our old, classical physics' paradigms told us it did. You will always create your own unique, individual version of that warm spot, in your own unique, individual universe. And your creation of it, in this manner, adds to the communal creation of that thing.

Notice that when I answered the old question earlier about a tree falling in the forest, I did not say, "If you're not there, there is no forest." It's true that if you're not there and you have no knowledge of the forest, there is no forest in your own unique, individual universe. But if other people have been observing and experiencing that forest, it has been created contextually, independent of your observations, and exists in their universe. In this manner, that forest does pre-exist because it has been, and is being, created by other humans. The exception to this rule is when someone actually is a literal creator of a material object, such as an artist creating a painting or a craftsperson building a piece of furniture.

You will find me referring to you as a "contextual" creator and this is why. The law of attraction may lead some people to believe that they are literally creating every "thing", but you now know that you don't. I don't believe it's necessary to get bogged down in semantics because you are the literal creator of a "thing" in your own unique, individual universe. Just don't think of yourself as the sole reason that thing exists at all.

There is another important caveat, however, regarding your seminal role as a contextual creator of time-space events (the material world). There is one time-space event you never create: other people. Unlike almost every other time-space event, other humans do actually exist completely independent of you. This is because, just like you, other people have a consciousness. They fulfill the same role of contextual creator that you do and, thus, exist whether or not you observe them or are even aware of them.

Just as with every other thing, however, you do create your own unique *version* of other human beings. You will find that your ability to create a unique version of other people will be of immensely powerful assistance to you as you play "Grow a Greater You" at higher and higher levels.

Although quantum physics is helping to change this, most humans are still not fully aware of their role as contextual creators. How often do you hear people say, in a defeated manner, "What can you do about it?" or "That's just the way it is"? Lack of awareness does nothing to change a human's role in our material world's creation because there is absolutely no way she could stop contextually creating. But awareness of your role as creator can, and in your case will, give you a tremendous leg up regarding how powerfully and how intentionally you can play it.

Stick with me, read with your full attention and a completely open mind, absorb like a sponge, drink up what you discover like a woman stumbling upon an oasis in the desert, and practice what you learn with a heated passion. I promise you'll soon be playing "Grow a Greater You" at an all-star level and having the time of your life.

Greg Kuhn

Chapter Four

How Do You Play Your Role?

How are you, and all other humans, fulfilling your role? How are you communicating with, or commanding, the quantum field to create the material world we all experience with our eyeballs? How does that ocean of energy know what things to manifest in your own unique, individual universe? If you're like most people, you've undoubtedly been frustrated by some of the things you've been creating. And you'd like to exert more influence upon that creative process so that the things you manifest are more pleasing from this point forward.

To answer these questions and completely understand your role as the contextual creator of the physical world you experience, you now need to learn about coherence. Coherence refers to particles that are cooperating perfectly; they are in sync in such a complete way that they act as one, like perfectly choreographed and rehearsed dancers in a chorus line. When subatomic particles are cooperating with each other in perfect unison, a system of coherence is formed. Inside a coherent system, the energy of what were once disparate particles becomes one, unified whole.

Coherent particles are no longer unique entities. They are, in fact, more than in-sync chorus line dancers; coherence means that the paired particles are now one. Coherence means that the particles share all information within the system, in real time, instantaneously. There is no delay—coherent systems are of "one mind," completely and totally conjoined in every sense of the word.

Coherence is one of the most powerful phenomena in the universe. A light bulb, for example, would emit the force and power of a nuclear explosion if its atoms were in coherence. Thankfully though, light bulbs do not produce such power, because their atoms are all emitting photons of light at different times. The light photons of atoms from a light bulb are confused enough to illuminate only a room, not organized enough to level a city.

Coherence is the powerful methodology used by the universe to create time-space events. Time-space events, or things, are manifested from the quantum field when the energy of the quantum field becomes coherent with the energy of "you." It is your consciousness that gives you the unique power to form coherence with the field and collapse the quantum possibility wave. Your consciousness allows you to form a unique, individual, coherent system with the quantum field and, thus, command it to form your material world.

While it is natural to envision a traditional master/servant relationship drawn from standard human interactions when hearing terms like "command," the actual process of forming coherence between you and the quantum field does not unfold like a master commanding a servant. You do not tell the quantum field what things to form using anything like a verbal command one person would issue to another. In fact, the way coherence is formed between you and the quantum field transcends the gross limitations of verbal commands.

This is great news for all of us; because of the method through which coherence is formed, nothing the quantum field manifests in accord with your "orders" will ever be a mistake. What the quantum field manifests for you will always be a perfect match to your orders because they cannot be hindered by any misinterpretations or misunderstandings caused by conventional human communication. And neither will your orders be created from your whims and sudden bursts of desire caused by strong emotional responses.

In fact, the quantum field largely couldn't care less what you consciously say you want or even what your top-of-mind, conscious desires are. Although they are powerful, your words actually have far less effect upon the manifestations of the quantum field than you might have thought. Their power will be explained in more detail later, but your words are most certainly not the vehicle through which coherence is formed between you and the quantum field.

And, while you may be guessing that it is your thoughts that serve as that vehicle for coherence, you might be surprised to learn that is wrong also. Your thoughts are, indeed, powerful energy but they are also word-based. Thus, while the energy of your thoughts has the power to help you feel better in the moment and to elevate your mood, it does not play the primary role in forming coherence with the quantum field.

It's tempting to wish that your orders could be delivered by such conventional means of human expression (like Aladdin commanded the Genie in the lamp), but I trust you'll come to appreciate the actual way they are given. After all, it's not difficult to perceive the mess such a protocol could produce. The maxim "Be careful what you wish for because you just might get it" often proves true. The way you form coherence with the quantum field is perfectly designed to force you to play "Grow a Greater You" so that you can grow into your desires and manifest them, because, believe it or not, the journey toward the fulfillment of your desires is the actual reward—even more so than the attainment of your desires.

Rather than words and thoughts, you use energy to communicate, and form coherence, with the quantum field. Coherence, you see, is a phenomenon involving the communication and perfect synchronization of information on an energy level. That is why words and thoughts have a limited role in the coherence you form with the quantum field. Consciousness, not traditional forms of human communication such as verbal commands, manipulates energy in our universe. This is precisely the reason that positive thinking and positive affirmations do not work to manifest your larger, most important desires. When used as vehicles to intentionally manifest a material world aligned with your important desires, they are almost always being misused.

The actual vehicle you use to form coherence with the quantum field may seem simplistic and appear to be something you already have a significant handle on. The way you deliver your commands to the quantum field is through your expectations. But withhold any judgments about using your expectations. I make that request because you undoubtedly have an incomplete understanding of what your expectations truly are.

Your expectations are actually your most accurate form of energy communication. They are virtually, and thankfully, untainted by any immediate whims created through strong emotional responses. Because you use your expectations to form coherence with the quantum field, you can never fool or lie to it. You'll soon learn why your expectations' role in forming coherence means that growing into the greatest version of you is the only way to most powerfully influence your own unique, individual universe—and why the journey you're beginning now is required.

But first, let's take some time to examine exactly what your expectations are. And what they are not.

Chapter Five

Why Aren't You Already Manifesting All Your Desires?

At this point, it is important for you to fully understand what your expectations are if you are to begin realizing your amazing power to intentionally create a more pleasing and abundant physical reality. Do not dismiss the notion that a more complete understanding of your expectations is in order; your expectations are most likely not what you've previously envisioned them to be.

Your expectations are devices of energy communication formed unconsciously from your beliefs. And because they are formed unconsciously, you have no direct control over them. You cannot change your expectations; they are what they are. Think of your expectations as the juice you get when you squeeze an orange and think of your beliefs as the orange. You cannot get anything other than orange juice when you squeeze an orange because that's the only thing inside it. Likewise, your beliefs will always produce certain accompanying expectations, and there is no way to change that fact.

Your expectations are not your top-of-mind desires, nor are they usually even part of your conscious awareness. Because your expectations are unconscious, you are hardly ever aware of them. Your expectations are almost never your conscious wishes, thoughts, intentions, hopes, worries, plans, fears, etc. Those conscious feelings are important and powerful clues that guide your playing of "Grow a Greater You," but those top-of-mind feelings and thoughts are not your expectations and they do not form coherence with the quantum field.

It is a common and understandable mistake to label your top-of-mind

Greg Kuhn

wishes, thoughts, intentions, hopes, worries, plans, or fears as your expectations. For example, when you consciously form an intention to have a great day at your job selling cars, that intention will not necessarily reveal your true expectation. Likewise, when your mood suddenly turns sour upon seeing the forecast calling for all-day rain (knowing that this traditionally kills car sales), that negativity also will not necessarily be your true expectation.

You, like every human being, have conscious wishes, thoughts, intentions, hopes, worries, plans, and fears. And, if asked whether or not you truly want the things you desire, your answer will undoubtedly be a resounding "Yes! Of course I want them. Very much!" Conversely, if asked whether you truly want the displeasing things gone forever, your answer will undoubtedly be a resounding, "Yes! Of course I want them gone. Very much!" But, while those answers are true reflections of your top-of-mind desires and conscious thoughts, they may only occasionally reveal your true expectations.

Your wishes (your top-of-mind desires) are certainly a part of your conscious awareness. You think about the things you want—and the things you don't want—every day. But things you are consciously aware of and think about are not the vehicle through which you form coherence with the quantum field. Your top-of-mind desires and dislikes are not the commands that create the things in your own unique, individual universe.

Shouldn't you be able to create just about anything you want if you expect to manifest it? Yes you should. And, in fact, you are absolutely correct to develop this idea because your expectations will always, and without fail, deliver your material experiences to you in the form of reflections of your beliefs from the quantum field. The only problem has been your misunderstanding of what an expectation is.

A commonly shared misunderstanding results from not truly knowing what is, and isn't, a true expectation. When you confuse your top-of-mind desires with your true expectations, you naturally and logically begin to focus on thoughts that keep those top-of-mind desires on the forefront of your awareness. That's exactly what many law of attraction teachers instruct their students to do.

Yet practicing that methodology leads to a paradox. When someone doesn't know what their actual expectations are, they very naturally think that their conscious focus on their top-of-mind desires is how to use the law of attraction. And that doesn't work—unless, of course, their actual expectations happen to be the same as their top-of-mind desires. The paradox is that if their top-of-mind desires were the same as their true expectations, they would already be manifesting those desires and that person would never be trying to manifest them in the first place because those desires would already be present in her life.

Additionally, keeping your conscious focus on your top-of-mind desires and thinking they are your expectations only makes you feel good in the moment. That misunderstanding does not change your actual expectations so they are aligned with your desired outcome, because there is no way for you to alter your true expectations since they are produced unconsciously from your beliefs. There is no way to get anything but orange juice from an orange, after all.

You might be tempted to say, "But Greg, if I think that focusing my conscious awareness on my top-of-mind desires will result in their manifestation, isn't that an expectation? And shouldn't that expectation result in coherence between my energy and the energy of the quantum field?" And I will respond by saying, no, you are continuing the mistake of confusing your conscious wishes, thoughts, intentions, hopes, worries, plans, and fears with your true expectations.

It is vital to remember that your expectations are unconscious. That means you will almost never be consciously aware of them. And it is vital to remember that they are unconsciously formed from your beliefs. That means you will rarely, if ever, be consciously able to control or moderate them. In other words, if you are aware of any feeling or thought, you can almost always bet the house that what you are aware of is not your actual expectation.

The incongruence between your desires and your material reality is where pain comes from. And, as you know, this pain, unresolved, becomes suffering in rather short order. Thus, the reason so many of us suffer is that we are not able to manifest our desires because our true expectations are coming from beliefs that differ from them. Until you understand what your expectations really are, where they come from, and how they're used to manifest things from the energy ocean, your suffering is compounded by how thoroughly you focus on ineffective methods to manifest your conscious desires.

If you are suffering in any area of your life, it is almost assured that your desires and your beliefs in that area are not aligned. Any time they are not in alignment, your true expectations, stemming from those beliefs, will always triumph over your conscious, top-of-mind desires—since your expectations, and not your conscious desires, are the commands that form coherence with the quantum field. And because your true expectations are formed unconsciously, they are delivered to the quantum field before you're even actually aware of what has happened.

This is how the eminent physicist Dr. William Tiller, PhD, describes it:

"The information handling capacity of the human unconscious (the inner layer) is about a million times that of the conscious brain (the outer layer at less than 50 bits per second) which interfaces via our five physical senses with the physical reality aspect of our playpen classroom. Thus, we are only weakly conscious at this outer layer level of our personality level. It appears that the inner level does most of the work of accessing information from nature and, after fully processing and digesting that information, fashions small kernels of information to feed to the conscious brain so that it will be able to perceive and experience events occurring in the distance-time aspect of this playpen, however, it appears that the topic contents of these kernels of information are only those to which the conscious brain has heretofore given 'meaning'. Information not seen as meaningful to the conscious brain appears to be ignored, rejected or dumped. It thus appears that for the human conscious brain to become more conscious of this playpen (simulator) it needs to give things more meaning in its life so that the unconscious layer of the personality self can feed it more information about the multiple aspects of nature, both inner and outer, of the classroom environment wherein it is playing."

Because you have no direct control over your true expectations since they are formed unconsciously from your beliefs, you may naturally wonder how in the heck you are supposed to play "Grow a Greater You." If you have virtually no control over the commands you're delivering to the quantum field, what chance do you have to manifest a material reality that matches your conscious, top-of-mind desires? Although it is true that you have virtually no direct control over your expectations, you needn't fear. You actually have an even better option at your disposal than controlling or micromanaging your true expectations.

For although you have no real-time control over your true expectations, you do have complete control over the source of your expectations— your beliefs. Trying to control or micromanage all your true expectations would consume far too much of your time anyway, even if that were possible. Instead, you're going to play "Grow a Greater You" by altering the source of your true expectations. And having complete control over your beliefs allows you to turn "Grow a Greater You" into the most amazing, exciting, and rewarding game you'll ever play.

Greg Kuhn

Chapter Six

Why and When Would You Want to Change Beliefs?

We've spent five chapters describing how our universe works for you, a consciousness-possessing time-space event more commonly referred to as a human being. In this fashion, we have constructed the creation pyramid. Atypical for building a structure in the physical world, however, we built the top of this pyramid first. Because, after all, since we now know that the creation of the material world is a top-down process, it's only right that we build our pyramid in the same manner.

Starting at the top of this creation pyramid, we correctly identified you as the contextual creator. Having secured the most important part first, we next moved to the foundation of the structure, the ground floor, with the understanding that the universe is actually an ocean of energy with the potential to become anything. One level up, we've built another floor that tells you that you and all other things in the material world are waves on that energy ocean or warm spots in it. The next level of this pyramid is your understanding that you are a very special wave or warm spot, a thing that, because you have a consciousness, creates other things.

We created another floor of this creation hierarchy by exploring how you create things by forming coherence between your special creator energy and the rest of the energy ocean. And still another floor of this pyramid was built through the understanding that coherence between you and the ocean of energy is formed through a very specific delivery vehicle: your true expectations. And, nearing completion of this edifice, almost back to the top of the pyramid, you learned that your expectations are created unconsciously by your beliefs. The last floor before getting back to where we began is the knowledge that your expectations, being formed unconsciously, are often not synonymous with your top-of-mind desires.

Now we're ready to return to you, putting the finishing touches on the top floor of this beautiful creation pyramid. This top floor is the beautiful observatory from whence you will play "Grow a Greater You" with immense power, influence, and efficacy. It is where "you" are found. And head of this pyramid is where we find the fountainhead of those all-important true and unconscious expectations of yours—those very expectations that, even while you remain almost entirely unaware of them, are being used to form coherence with the quantum field and, thus, manifest a material reality for you. In this chapter you, the top of the pyramid, will get the finishing touches: You will learn about your beliefs.

As with expectations, do not suppose that you already have a complete understanding of your beliefs. I don't intend to insult your intelligence—as I'm sure you're at least reasonably familiar with beliefs—but staying with me here will pay large dividends as you play this game.

Why are your beliefs so vital? Imagine you are in charge of the water supply for your town. There is a large reservoir half a mile away from your quaint village. And the people who live in your town get their water directly from underground streams that flow directly out of that reservoir, running right to a series of wells all your neighbors use to get their water.

If the reservoir became polluted and unsuitable for consumption, would you try to fix it by cleaning up the water in the wells? Of course not, because your task would never end. Instead, you'd go right to the reservoir because that is the source of the water in those wells. Cleaning up the reservoir would automatically bring about the needed improvements in the well water.

In that analogy, of course, the wells represent your true expectations. And the reservoir represents your beliefs. And just as you would have gone to the reservoir to clean up the town's water, you will also want to "clean up" your beliefs to change your true expectations so that they are aligned with your desires.

In that last scenario, your desire would be stated as, "I want to clean up my town's water supply." As an intelligent human being, you probably would have confidence that there must be a way to accomplish this desire. You might incorrectly identify those thoughts as your true expectation for the outcome. But the only way that would be correct is if your actual beliefs about cleaning up the reservoir were the same as your conscious thoughts about them.

It is possible that you might have true, unconscious expectations in that scenario that communicated an improbability that the town's water problem could actually be solved. Perhaps, for example, you held a belief that polluted water was simply an unavoidable, unfortunate reality of life and there was nothing you could really do about it. Or perhaps you held a belief that, no matter how hard anyone tried, water would keep returning to being polluted because that's just the way things are on our planet as a result of the way we create and dispose of waste. In those cases, your true expectations, formed unconsciously from those beliefs, would be akin to "I will not be able to clean this water."

And, if that's the case, no matter how hard you worked, even if you followed expert instructions to the letter, the actions you took would always end up being trumped by your true expectations as they formed coherence with the quantum field. Even though your top-of-mind desire was to clean the water, your actual and unconscious expectations would always win. And if you didn't understand that your beliefs needed to be aligned with your desires, you might become as frustrated as a Neanderthal.

Thankfully, "cleaning up" your beliefs is not as challenging as cleaning a water reservoir. Your beliefs are, after all, only your most practiced thoughts, which means you can definitely change them. Although your beliefs are both important and powerful, because they form your internal rulebook for life and are the source of your true expectations, they are neither carved in stone nor are they true for anyone but you. The fact that many other people may share the same beliefs as you is based purely upon those people having had similar influences shaping their formation.

Almost every belief you have was formed when you repeated thoughts as a child. When you have a thought, it is actually energy traveling along a neural network in your brain. Those neural pathways became your beliefs as a child. And the more influential or trustworthy the source of a thought was, the greater the opportunity it had to become one of your beliefs.

Thoughts inspired by trusted sources in incredibly impressionable children anchor themselves into their subconscious brain, their belief storehouse, with superglue. And because beliefs are stored in your subconscious brain, you will almost never be able to consciously identify them. As an adult, you've become more guarded to such influence and your guardedness does more than prevent new ideas taking hold; it actually adds a layer of cement to the beliefs you created during childhood.

Believe it or not (see what I did there?), your beliefs are completely subjective. While many of your beliefs may very well conform to those of the majority of your fellow humans, you are still the one choosing to hold them. But since your beliefs are subjective, since they are nothing more than repeated thoughts that were inspired by trusted sources during childhood, any belief can be changed—anytime you wish, no matter how many other people insist you must retain and adhere to your current beliefs.

Many people assume their beliefs are unchangeable—that their internal rulebook simply "is what it is." Most adults, in fact, don't think they can do anything about them. Actually, they mostly have no idea that they have limiting beliefs at all and, even if they are aware, know of no reason to change them.

This unfortunate resignation stems from how your beliefs have been transferred to you by people and sources that had a God-like level of significant influence over you. To alter your beliefs, then, is to disavow, or turn your back on, a trusted and beloved source of influence upon which you've based your understanding of how life works. Also, changing your internal rulebook is uncomfortable. Even if a belief you hold is painful and makes your life difficult, there is a predictability and reliability in it that your subconscious brain clings to.

Adults cannot form new beliefs unless they truly understand how to change them in a manner their subconscious brain will allow. Your foundational and most important beliefs were formed during childhood; you were a belief-sponge as a young child and you gave the important adults in your life almost unfiltered influence regarding their formation. As adults, many of us mistakenly think that positive thoughts, positive emotions, and other forms of focusing conscious awareness on what we desire will change our internal rulebook.

Once you know how to change your beliefs, the prospect can still feel unnerving, like beating your father in basketball for the first time. To a young man, that might seem an exhilarating goal he can't wait to achieve. But actually doing it is a little scary because it means you have surpassed the physical prowess of this God-like figure. Beating him means that he is "weak" in ways you don't yet really want him to be on some level. (I used this phenomenon successfully, by the way, to beat my sons in basketball for years after they became skilled enough to defeat me on our driveway hoop. Hey, what can I say? I desire to win basketball games when I play.)

Of course, some people may be angry with their father, perhaps because he has not parented them with a lot of compassion, and relish this symbolic graduation from his seeming tyranny. Beating him in basketball is a huge relief for such a person if she's had enough of his clumsy guidance. If you've had enough misery in your life, perhaps you are now ready to look at your old, limiting beliefs in the same manner.

Many adults desiring new, uplifting beliefs are lured by the ease and simplicity of using positive affirmations in lieu of following an effective, formal protocol to change them. Since those positive affirmations make us feel good in the moment, we logically, but mistakenly, assume they are doing the trick. When our problems inevitably return, we can easily become jaded to the notion of intentionally changing them. The failure of positive thinking can lead some to reject the science of deliberately influencing their material reality.

The obstacle preventing the use of conscious, logical thoughts, no matter how positive, to change your beliefs comes from where they are stored: in your subconscious brain. Your subconscious brain only understands feelings and consequences, not language or logic, so it is the natural place for beliefs to reside. Your subconscious brain will not allow positive thoughts to gain enough access to change your current beliefs in the slightest.

Under what circumstances would you follow a formal protocol, if you knew one, to change a belief? Very simply—when you experience a continual bugaboo in your material reality, when you are unable to create time-space events that are pleasingly aligned with an important desire. When positive thoughts and positive affirmations have finally run their course, having made you feel good for the moment while predictably proving unable to manifest that deep, long-held desire you have.

Because your material reality is always perfectly coherent with your true expectations, you want to change your beliefs any time important desires remain consistently absent in your life experiences. In that scenario, the only thing you can do to manifest these most important desires is to change your beliefs, because improving your beliefs to match your desires will automatically and unconsciously improve your true expectations so that you're now giving commands to the quantum field that can become coherent with your desired outcomes.

Before you learned how to play "Grow a Greater You," you probably tried to alleviate the misery of having nonaligned beliefs by trying to dampen or kill off your absent desires. I'm sure you found out that trying to negate your desires or pretend you don't really have them simply doesn't work. In fact, doing this only adds to the misery of their absence.

Unlike the Neanderthal paradigms that tell you that you have no involvement in or influence upon the creation of your material universe, you now know that your physical reality is always a mirror-perfect reflection of your beliefs. I did not say that your material reality is always a mirror-perfect reflection of you. You are not your beliefs; your beliefs are the merely the tools you use to contextually create and assemble the physical experience of physical life on Earth. Thus you are not to beat yourself up for having beliefs from childhood incongruent with your desires.

You can also now release the idea that you must somehow do just the right things, in the right combinations, to earn the favor of an outside source. You are perfect just as you are. You are not broken, and you do not need to be fixed. And if you, like me, spent years treating yourself unkindly because you've developed a habit of blaming yourself for your displeasing material reality, start giving yourself a new, better-feeling, believable label: You are perfectly imperfect.

You're no longer held prisoner by those limiting childhood beliefs. Changing them does require some effort and does need to be done in a manner that your subconscious brain will allow. If it didn't, after all, we'd all be changing our beliefs on the fly to align with our latest and greatest conscious desires.

That effort is not based upon positive thought. Positive thoughts will still continue to feel better than negative ones and, thus, will always be preferable. But rest assured the protocols you'll follow for improving your beliefs to align with your desires are simple and intuitive. Belief-alignment is the seminal task for manifesting the "big stuff" that has eluded you. Having new expectations aligned with your desires will, with clockwork reliability, command the quantum field to form a material reality for you that is coherent with most of those long-held desires of yours.

It's hard to blame you if you think all that might sound too good to be true. Could manifesting your desires really be that simple? Yet I call your attention back to our beautiful creation pyramid and assure you that this is truly how our universe works. Aligning your beliefs with your desires is truly all the work you need to do and you'll soon be following the belief-raising protocols in "Grow a Greater You" with growing experiential confidence.

Greg Kuhn

Chapter Seven

You Were Born With a Picture-Perfect Feedback Loop to Guide Your Every Choice

Before moving into the instructions for "Grow a Greater You," let's have a vital discussion about your emotions. Your emotions are a very important component of finally manifesting your deepest desires and for playing "Grow a Greater You" at the highest levels. But perhaps they are not important in the ways you may have thought.

Emotions are powerful. They get our attention like a squalling baby and can actually frighten us. We tend to dread unpleasant emotions, which can scare us, while we cherish and luxuriate in the desirable ones. Most of us also use our emotions to define who we are. Yet the fear/fascination relationship we have all experienced with our feelings is largely due to a misunderstanding about their purpose.

Your emotions are actually nothing more than a feedback loop for you. Your emotions provide valuable and useful information that's designed to educate you about the alignment (or lack thereof) between your beliefs and your desires. Positive emotions signal that your beliefs are aligned with your desires in that area of your life. Similarly, negative feelings are information telling you that your beliefs are not aligned with your desires. Additionally, just how far in or out of alignment your beliefs are with your desires is revealed to you via the intensity of your feelings. Your emotions, therefore, serve as an incredibly accurate and reliable "belief thermometer."

Isn't this great news? You do not need to "get under the hood" and figure out what beliefs you hold. You do not need to undergo some intensive therapy so that you can identify your current beliefs and categorize them into lists of "Beneficial Beliefs" and "Limiting Beliefs." Thanks to your emotions, you already have all the information you need to play "Grow a Greater You" without all that work.

Emotions, therefore, are intended to provide you with unerringly accurate, useful, and helpful information that you can use to navigate and adjust your beliefs; your feelings tell you when your beliefs are not aligned with your desires, and you can then use that information to improve your beliefs accordingly, as a sailor adjusts a ship's sails to align with the wind.

Most people, however, misuse emotions. Who among us hasn't assigned them the leading role in determining our state of being, or who we are? For example, if you are experiencing sadness as information about a lack of alignment between your beliefs about having a soul mate and your desires for such, it would not be unusual for you to say, "I am sad," "I am alone," or "I am unworthy." Unfortunately, when most people say, "I am sad," what they are really saying is, "Sad is who and what I am."

This not only perpetuates "sadness" as a state of being, it also represents an abuse of your emotional feedback loop. When you don't understand that emotions are useful information, you naturally tend to identify with them. You make the logical assumption that your emotions are telling you who you are instead of giving you feedback.

Sad, after all, is not "who you are"; it is merely feedback that tells you that your beliefs about having a soul mate are not aligned with your desires for having a soul mate. And the intensity of your feelings of sadness is very precise information about how greatly out of alignment your beliefs and desires are on that topic. This doesn't make experiencing sadness pleasant, but it does allow you to benefit from the important information sadness provides you. It gives you direction to go to the source—your beliefs about your desire for a soul mate—and play "Grow a Greater You" on them.

Seen properly, isn't it possible that you could actually feel grateful to get this information? I'm not suggesting that you should ever feel overjoyed about feeling sadness, because it is a painful emotion. But, just as a pain in your foot is information alerting you to the splinter you just got while walking across your deck, the emotion of sadness is information alerting you that your beliefs are not aligned. How would you know you had that splinter, after all, without the valuable and useful information provided to you by the pain in your foot?

The proper way to use your emotional feedback loop, as it is intended, is to say, "I am experiencing sadness in this moment." In this manner, you step outside of the very personal and sometimes intense visceral experience your emotions can create and employ them as they were intended—as the very useful and valuable information they are.

Additionally, saying, "I am experiencing sadness in this moment" also removes your emotions from the job you have probably inadvertently assigned them of determining who you are at any given moment. After all, you are not, literally, sad—meaning "sad" is not "who you are." You are *experiencing* sadness.

Do you get mad at a thermometer when it tells you that you've got a fever? Of course not. You know that the thermometer is simply the messenger and you also know what the real source of its information is and how to address it. Do you get angry with your foot, or your central nervous system, when pain alerts you to the fact that you've picked up a splinter from your wooden deck? Certainly not. You are actually somewhat grateful for the pain because it's altered you to something you want to fix. And, yet, these examples probably portray exactly how you've often treated your emotions.

Remember the old saying "Don't kill the messenger"? That saying arose because in ancient times the messenger was often, literally, killed when he delivered bad news. But use that saying now as you learn to properly employ your feelings. They really are only the messenger, not the cause and not the solution.

Your emotions are not the cause of your suffering; they are not responsible for your pain. Your emotions are simply alerting you *to the cause* of your suffering and the root of your pain—beliefs that are out of alignment with your desires. Rejoice in that alert! How else would you know when and where you need to improve your beliefs so you can finally experience the manifestation of all your desires?

I mentioned earlier that feeling preferred emotions like joy, love, and happiness is a desirable state. And feeling undesirable emotions like loneliness, fear, and sadness is a state we often actively avoid. The very act of calling emotional states "desirable" and "undesirable" speaks to another very common misuse of them: chasing an emotional state or running away from one as if the emotional state, itself, will manifest or keep away your desires.

Chasing or avoiding emotional states, instead of using them as information about the alignment between your beliefs and your desires, is like trying to find the absolute coolest jogging suit if you want to be a great runner. To manifest your desire to be a runner, you go to a sporting goods store and purchase the most expensive jogging outfit available. You put it on and merely sit in your living room every day after you get home, but after a while you realize that the outfit is not accomplishing your desire. Undaunted, you go to a specialty store that sells only running gear and buy the best suit there, on the recommendation of the owner. You put your new outfit on and, once again, merely sit in your living room every day after you get home, but after a while you experience the same phenomenon as before.

When you finally revealed what you were doing to your best friend, she would correctly tell you that you are crazy. The right jogging outfit will never be responsible for turning you into the healthiest runner in your city. And the wrong jogging outfit will never be responsible for keeping you from being the healthiest runner in your city. The jogging outfits are not responsible for manifesting or keeping away your desire.

Yet how many times have you tried to manifest a desire by chasing the emotions associated with it, as if the emotions, themselves, are the things responsible for manifesting it? Conversely, how many times have you desired to end your suffering by masking or denying the emotions associated with it, as if the emotions, themselves, are the culprit?

Your emotions are information-rich byproducts of alignment and misalignment. They are not the source. I've encountered many law-of-attraction teachers who say that you should focus on holding desired emotions as a way to intentionally manifest a more pleasing physical reality. There is nothing wrong with feeling desirable emotions; if your beliefs and desires are aligned, facilitating an appropriate emotional state associated with your desires is powerful. But that technique should not be used in lieu of employing your emotions in their proper role of providing you with important information.

Just how essential is the feedback your emotions provide? You have learned how important your beliefs are in contextually creating your material experiences—they are the source of your unconscious expectations, which create coherence with the quantum field and command it to form a physical universe for you that mirrors those expectations. Consider how impossible it would be to constantly monitor and analyze your beliefs. How would you have time to do anything else in your life while tackling the Herculean task of continually inventorying, identifying, ranking, and cataloging your beliefs? Thankfully, you do not need to expend all your energy combing through your beliefs, because your emotions tell you everything you need to know about them.

Consider the Neanderthal paradigms of personalizing your emotions and not using them as helpful information. Within this paradigm, what is the logical response to feeling negative emotions? Of course, you must change the thing that is causing them. In the sadness example we've been using, the logical response is to take actions like getting a new hairstyle, trying to lose weight, joining a dating website, asking your friends to set you up with someone, etc. But you now know those actions never addressed the true source of your displeasing material reality that was causing your feedback loop of sadness: your misaligned beliefs.

Because you have built-in thermometers for telling you how in or out of alignment your beliefs are with your desires, all you need to do is stay aware of your emotions. Your emotions will do all the heavy lifting for you. Whenever you feel negative emotions, on a regular basis, regarding a topic or issue, those negative emotions are sending you a huge, flashing, neon-red message: "Attention! Your beliefs about this part of your life are not aligned with your desires for it!" Thus, your emotions will identify for you, with little to no effort on your part required, exactly when and where to raise your beliefs.

Even though your emotions are not who you are, make no mistake: Your emotions are real. They're there, you feel them, and they shouldn't be denied or stuffed. And your emotions are powerful because they're supposed to be. Your emotions are designed to get your attention like being slapped in the face.

Negative emotions are so discomforting, in fact, that people are prone to either deny them or to do things that change how they feel simply to avoid feeling them. We know about the destructive, self-abusive things people do, but even seemingly healthy behaviors, such as exercise or work, can become harmful when abused to avoid feeling your emotions.

While it is important for you to depersonalize your emotions and reassign them to their essential and proper role, it is also important that you allow yourself to feel them. Denying them, stuffing them, and trying to change them is dangerous and adds to the power your emotions hold over you. Additionally, denying, stuffing, and trying to change your emotions causes you to lose touch with them and build up your tolerance for ignoring them. Acknowledging them and seeing them as something you are experiencing in the moment rather than who you are, will allow your emotions to perform their intended function without taking you hostage.

This illustrates the old saying "Until we agree to suffer, there will be no end to the suffering." While that might sound like a negative sentiment to someone convinced (as I used to be) that positive thought must be maintained at all cost, it couldn't be truer. That saying might also sound extremely negative to someone who worries that acknowledging negative emotions fuels them and creates a powerfully destructive monster. While dwelling and fixating on your negative emotions can certainly feed them, now that you have the tools to depersonalize them and utilize them in their proper and vital role, you needn't worry about unleashing a monster by allowing yourself to feel them.

Trying to deny, stuff, or change your negative or undesirable emotions is like trying to fix a noisy car engine by cranking up your car stereo. For the moment you will not be bothered by engine noise and, perhaps, during this interlude you may even forget that your car's engine is having trouble. Yet, because your ears will quickly adjust to the loud music, you'll soon to able to hear the engine noise again. Eventually you will either blow out your car speakers or make yourself deaf. But, all the while, your engine trouble will undoubtedly be growing worse.

And so it is with denying, stuffing, or trying to change your feelings. Your negative emotions will never go away under those circumstances because the reason they're present is unchanged. They're not supposed to go away unless your beliefs in that area come into alignment with your desires. Until your beliefs are aligned with your desires, emotions will continue to do what they're designed to do: tell you, "Hey! Here is an area where your beliefs are not aligned with your desires. Don't you want to improve your beliefs to address this pain?"

Many people eventually try to stop desiring something to escape the painful feedback of their negative emotions about it. Stopping the desire seems like their only way to escape the misery. This is a worst-case scenario for a human being because your desires will never go away. You can rationalize not having the thing you want so badly, you can vilify those who do have it, you can get angry about not having it, and you can start to actively convince yourself that you don't really need it and are better off without it. But none of that works.

I have continually used the phrase "negative emotions" and will do so throughout this book. I do that to more clearly discern between emotions that are often pleasant and desirable versus those which aren't. No emotion, however, is inherently negative, because it is simply providing you with accurate information about your beliefs.

My father is a retired psychiatrist, and one of his areas of expertise was helping people lower stress. Most of my Dad's patients blamed something or someone outside of themselves as the cause of their stress. Nothing, however, causes you to experience stress; stress is a response to something we experience, not "caused" by something we experience. Just as my father taught people to stop trying to change the "outside world" to alleviate their stress, I am teaching you to stop denying or sublimating your emotions in an effort to prevent yourself from feeling them.

None of the ways we misuse our emotions are valid because they're not based on how our universe really works. Your painful emotions will remain until you raise your beliefs to match your desires. Why? Because, just like a splinter will not stop hurting until you remove it, your undesirable emotions will never stop giving you information until you alleviate the source of the pain. You desire what you desire and you will continue to desire those things until you are able to manifest them.

Greg Kuhn

Chapter Eight

Why Embracing Everything as Information is Your Key to Freedom

Now I want to take you on a quantum leap with the concept of using your emotions as information, for there is even more freedom to be found in expanding this into every aspect of your material experience. Knowing what we do about how our universe really works, we are now free to call every single thing and experience "information." Anything you experience, desirable and undesirable alike, is helpful, useful, and valuable information that guides you and alerts you to any area of your life where your beliefs are in or out of alignment with your desires.

For example, do you take it personally when you receive the following information: sniffles, chills, and a fever? Those symptoms are really just valuable and useful information that tells you that you probably have a cold and need to rest and recuperate if you wish to be well.

You don't let that information dictate the meaning and value you ascribe yourself, right? You don't take that information personally. The sniffles, chills, and fever are not who you are; they are merely symptoms of, or information about, something you probably want to change. You're even actually somewhat grateful for the information. Who would wish to be informed that she had a problem with her health by dropping dead from a cold that ravaged her body because she had no information about it before it was too late?

It's not difficult to see your cold symptoms as information and it's not a challenge to not take that information personally by letting it define who you are. But there is some information you probably take personally almost every time you receive it. In fact, there is some information that you probably never even thought of as feedback at all—as if there were no other option than using it to define who you are.

Your knowledge about how our universe works and how you play the role of creator in it frees you to see everything as information. After all, since every "thing" is a reflection of your beliefs, every "thing" is valuable and useful information about your beliefs. When anything in your life is displeasing, you are being given important information about the nonalignment of your beliefs and desires.

I don't blame you if you're saying, "Greg, I'm with you on seeing emotions as information because that makes sense and I see the value there. But every 'thing' being information? I'm not so sure about that one." After all, until now, you could only rely on your senses and on conventional wisdom to discern between what is "information" versus what is "who you are."

What information falls into the category of things you've only used to define your worth and state of being instead of information? In my experience, these are the top three:

- Your weight

- Your money

- Your relationships

Is it insane to say that those things are "information" akin to the sniffles, chills, and fever alerting you to your cold or to your emotions alerting you to beliefs that are not aligned with your desires? How can weight, money, relationships, and everything else be information?

Yes. It is absolutely crazy to call those three things, and everything else, information—but only if you have no desire to become the most powerful intentional creator of your life possible. And if you have no desire to play "Grow a Greater You" at the highest levels of fulfillment possible, you should stop reading this insane chapter right now. But if you do have a desire to make the "Grow a Greater You" Hall of Fame, hear me out.

Here's some logic I'll bet will resonate with you. I first heard Dr. Wayne Dyer turn an old Neanderthal homily on its ear by restating it as "I'll see it when I believe it." If that statement is true, and I'll bet you do agree with it, then the opposite must also be true: "If I don't see it, that means that I don't believe it." And if I am not seeing something that I desire to see, what information does that give me? Not seeing something is information that I don't believe it.

And there's something about this concept that might just blow you away. Do you realize that learning to play "Grow a Greater You" does not actually involve doing things you don't already know how to do? Because you are already contextually creating your material reality each moment of your life, that is not something you have to learn how to do. You're simply learning to be more intentionally influential regarding the contextual creation you couldn't stop doing if you tried.

Learning to see everything as information, even weight, money, and relationships, follows the same principal. You've undoubtedly already been using these things as feedback your entire life; you're not actually learning to do anything you haven't already always been doing. You've simply been using these things as information to define your self-worth instead of to tell you where your beliefs are in or out of alignment in those areas. And, in the process, you've been using them as weapons to demean yourself and beat yourself up.

For example, if your weight feedback displeases you, you chastise yourself with "I'm fat" or "I'm ugly."

If your money feedback displeases you, you berate yourself with "I'm poor and unworthy" or "I'm a loser."

If a relationship feedback displeases you, you rail on yourself with "I'm lonely" or "I'm unlovable."

Those are examples of using the feedback of weight, money, and relationships as information. But you've been misusing that information like you previously misused your emotions. That information's role is not to define who you are, it is to provide you feedback regarding whether your beliefs in those areas are in alignment with your desires. That information, like all else, is merely a thermometer reading, because *your material reality is always and without fail a reflection of your beliefs, not a reflection of you*. You are not your beliefs. Your beliefs are subjective and changeable. They are not who you really are.

So when you're displeased with your current manifestation of your body, it is improper and self-harmful to say, "I am fat and ugly." Instead, tell yourself, "My current beliefs are reflecting a displeasing body back to me.

This is not pleasant or enjoyable. This information alerts me to the fact that, if I want to experience a more pleasing body, I need to raise my beliefs about food and about my body so that they are more aligned with my desires."

And when you choose to see feedback about your weight as information, you can even eventually add, "Thanks, displeasing body, for the information. Now I know what to do." And, just as with your emotions, you can tell yourself this while still acknowledging the unpleasantness of the experience. Seeing everything as information doesn't immediately resolve the painful reflection, but it does direct you to the source of that reflection and the most important thing to improve if you want to change it: your beliefs.

After all, what happens when you use the Neanderthal paradigms, where your displeasing information about weight defines you, rather than playing "Grow a Greater You" and using the information to alert you to beliefs that are out of alignment with your desires? You already know the answer: If your weight feedback is painful, you go on another diet, you start another exercise regimen, you weigh yourself constantly, you appraise yourself in the mirror, you stare enviously at the models on the cover of supermarket magazines, you question your value as a human being, you assign the self-worth you desire to a number on a scale, etc. And do these things work? Of course not. Why not? Because, while they are all logical, action-oriented responses designed to remedy your painful material reality by trying to alter the outside, they are never going to address the source of your material reality: your nonaligned beliefs.

It's the same thing as the Neanderthal painting his face, banging bones together, and dancing around a fire. You're performing all of these actions to earn favor with the "giver of gifts," hoping that, somehow, you'll get it right this time and become worthy of the things you want so badly.

I know you're probably saying, "But Greg, that doesn't make sense. A lot of those actions are exactly what I should do to manifest the change in my weight that I desire." And I agree that some of those actions are good logical choices that can effectively assist your manifestation of a more pleasing body—but only if your beliefs are aligned with your desires when you perform them. Without that alignment, the quantum field cannot manifest a material reality that corresponds to your top-of-mind desires for weight, because the quantum field can only form coherence with your true expectations, which are arising unconsciously from your beliefs. And, remember too, that your top-of-mind desires may very well have little in common with your true expectations created unconsciously by your beliefs.

While that may sound a little discouraging at first—especially if you've been in the habit of taking this type of information personally—look at the freedom it gives you. Do you need to worry about which "magical" diet or exercise plan to follow? Do you need to fret about whether or not to eat carbohydrates, protein, fat, or fewer calories? No, because none of these things actually matter unless they are things you're doing because you're inspired by aligned beliefs. All you need to do, actually the only thing you need to do, is align your beliefs about your body and food with your desires for it. The rest will take care of itself, because the quantum field will always, and without fail, form coherence with your beliefs.

Thus, learning to view everything as information doesn't place blame on you. In fact, learning to see everything as information actually releases you from blame because it allows you to remember that you are not experiencing displeasing manifestations because you are doing something wrong—and that "you" are not wrong. Your displeasing manifestations are not punishments, nor are you experiencing them because you are somehow unworthy of experiencing your desires.

Is anyone really unworthy in the first place? I don't believe they are—primarily because a human's worthiness has little to do with the material reality she creates—except, of course, as her beliefs about her worthiness are reflected back to her by the quantum field.

As you play "Grow a Greater You," I want you to view everything as information, just as you're viewing your emotions. I want you to see everything as feedback about how aligned, or misaligned, your beliefs in that area are with your desires for it. Because, as weird as your neighbors might think you are for doing this, you can rest assured that this practice is a correct one and corresponds to the blueprint given to us by science for how our universe really works.

Greg Kuhn

Chapter Nine

How Can Bad Things Happen to Good People and What Can You Do About It?

Now I'd like to answer a very common question that can inhibit people from embracing becoming influential architects of their own life experiences. If we create our material reality, how can horrible things happen to good or innocent people? Here you will find solutions, in addition to explanations, that can allow you to be a more thoughtful contextual creator from this day forward.

You, like me, have personally experienced suffering that seems not only unjust but also incongruent with your character and good intentions. And, in the same vein, we've all witnessed the suffering of innocents at the hands of others. In addition to explaining how bad things like those could occur in a world where humans are the creators of our material reality, I will teach you to powerfully and contextually create my greatest desire with me: making suffering optional for every human.

It can, indeed, be miserable to watch other people achieve and enjoy the very things you so long for, to see them be happy and enjoy the things you dream of having. And more maddening still is that you're truly a good person who tries very hard to do the right things in your life; you're diligent about being caring, nice, kind, generous, and helpful. Not only do you look for opportunities to help, you are even careful not to take more than your share of what life has to offer. And you don't capitalize on others' weaknesses, as it appears so many have no qualms about doing.

Let's be completely blunt here: You quite simply feel you deserve the things you desire. In fact, anyone who wants something as badly as you want these things, and works as hard as you do to be a good person, should be able to have them—especially when your intent is to share your abundance with those around you, uplifting your corner of the world. You have suffered from the absence of your greatest desires.

I'm glad you now know that your material reality is a reflection of your beliefs and not you. Yet, especially if you're new to the science of deliberate contextual creation, it's natural to question if your role as a creator means that you are responsible for all the misery you've experienced. Being told you're a creator, when you've experienced misery, can sound like incrimination, blame, and accusation.

And perhaps even more troubling, yet still as natural, are the questions that arise concerning genuine victims: innocents such as abused children, someone killed by a drunk driver, a person who gets murdered during a mugging, people born into abject poverty, people in developing countries without access to modern healthcare, or people living without adequate food and water. Does being told that people are creators mean that such victims created these circumstances themselves or that we created them?

Like all of us, you've experienced personal misery firsthand and you have encountered the misery of innocents. Here is what the science of deliberate creation has to say about the answer to those two seemingly incongruent things.

Regarding your personal misery, the beliefs that are being reflected back to you by the quantum field were not chosen by you, they were chosen for you. You did not select your beliefs a la carte from a buffet. Your beliefs were given to you as a child, so it is completely incorrect to say that you create unpleasant, even horrific, experiences. Blaming yourself is a gross mischaracterization and a blatant misunderstanding of how the material world is created. Bad things, and the misery you've experienced through the absence of your desires, have been created by limiting beliefs. And, until now, you have not been responsible for your beliefs.

When I write, "You contextually create your material reality," I am *not* saying that "you" create your material reality. Semantics? Perhaps, but I want you to burn this into your brain: *You* are not the engine of creation; your *beliefs* are. Thus, you are not to blame yourself or beat yourself up for your displeasing experiences. You are perfect just as you are. You could never be unworthy. You are never being punished, and you are now being empowered to craft beliefs of your choosing.

Regarding the misery of innocents, you also know that your beliefs do not, literally, create other people. Because of her consciousness, another person does not need you to observe her for her to manifest; she exists whether or not you even know about her because she is a creator like you. Thus, you cannot actually ever control another person's actions, attitudes, or ideas. Because you are not creating another person, the control of her actions, attitudes, and ideas will always be her sole domain. And because you cannot control another person's actions, ideas, and attitudes, you cannot control her decisions to take actions, foster ideas, and hold attitudes that might cause great harm to you and others.

Another explanation for both your personal suffering and the suffering of innocents is found in your collective beliefs. When enough people hold similar beliefs, collective expectations unconsciously arise and are reflected by the quantum field. And, just as with your individual expectations, the communal expectations that arise unconsciously from communal beliefs may be far out of alignment with everyone's commonly shared top-of-mind or conscious desires.

For example, most humans have conscious top-of-mind desires for never experiencing violence personally and never seeing it inflicted upon others. Yet despite the undesirability of violence, we all acknowledge that it is a regrettable inevitability based on what we've been taught and upon our life experience. Based on the communal belief that violence is an inevitable reality, there is a corresponding expectation for it unconsciously formed. Thus we will continue to communally create violence through our collective beliefs about it.

We can say similar things about poverty, disease, starvation, subjugation, exploitation, crime, brutality, drug abuse, etc. No one consciously desires these any of things to occur, personally or globally. But even as you mourn a tragedy born from such things, isn't there a part of you that is resigned to the inevitability of their occurrence? That nagging feeling of the regrettable inevitability of such things is an echo of your unintentional participation in communal beliefs about their unfortunate reality.

In this manner our life experiences are greatly affected by our communal beliefs. Even by the beliefs of those whose time has passed because their contributions to our communal beliefs are part of their legacy. And, of course, our life experiences are also often greatly affected by the actions, ideas, and attitudes other people chose to take, foster, and maintain.

You personally affect the life experiences of other humans with your participation in communal beliefs and with your personal actions, ideas, and attitudes. You could decide, for example, to drink a twelve pack tonight, drive your car, and, in your drunken stupor strike a minivan— instantly killing a mother of three. It would be incorrect to say this woman desired her death or made it happen since she did not, literally, create you, nor did she have any control over your actions. And we must also acknowledge that there is a communal belief that people will, regrettably, drive drunk and great tragedy often results. In the early 1990s, my uncle was killed in a car accident under similar circumstances as the hypothetical one I just described.

I hope you've never been the cause or the recipient of such tragedy, yet I'm sure you've chosen actions, ideas, and attitudes that, though unintentional, have impacted other people in ways they didn't desire and wouldn't have chosen. An obvious example of this could be found in parenting decisions you made during times of anger. A subtler example could be your lousy mood after waiting in a long line at the Department of Motor Vehicles. Whether any of those people affected by your actions, attitudes, or actions desired the effects they had on them was irrelevant.

In addition to the actions of other people, everyone is strongly affected by the communal beliefs of past and present humans. Not only are you personally affected, your participation in the harmful ones is almost unavoidable. For example, do you personally believe that war is a good way to resolve conflicts and disagreements? Even if war has no place in your personal beliefs, no matter the circumstances, don't you harbor at least a small belief that it is inevitable? No matter how vehemently people consciously desire it to stop, won't dictators, governments, warlords, and despots always be the regrettable initiators of war?

Even if you have no place in your personal belief system for war, it is almost impossible to completely divorce yourself from communally held beliefs about its inevitability that almost all of us hold. From poverty, disease, suffering, lack, servitude, exploitation, and corruption to peace, love, joy, giving, health, freedom, and abundance, almost every single one of us is participating, on some level, in fostering collective beliefs regarding their unfortunate and regrettable inevitability. And by doing so, helping manifest coherent material experiences from the quantum field.

You will continue to be affected, and continue to affect others, through even your most benign participation in collective beliefs because it is virtually impossible to not participate in them. Take a communal belief such as disease. As a child, you were taught about the inevitability and tragedy of disease. As an adult, no matter how greatly you want to believe in wellness as opposed to disease, those beliefs from your childhood cannot be supplanted by your conscious, top-of-mind desires.

To illustrate how powerful and virtually inescapable your participation in communal beliefs is, imagine a world without disease right now. What a beautiful vision. But is a world without disease really possible? I'll bet your answer is a resigned "no" because you, like me, believe that disease, while unfortunate, is a displeasing part of human life that always will be.

Most people would laugh at the idea that disease could be alleviated through anything other than medical research. Yet our scoffing at this notion is not the result of it being impossible. Aligning our collective beliefs about health with our desires for it is not only possible, it is the only way our desires for health could be completely manifest. You know how the creative pyramid is constructed. And you know that all the actions taken to eradicate disease will be Band-Aids on a broken leg until they are undertaken in conjunction with beliefs aligned with the desire for its disappearance.

The same can be said for any actions taken to eradicate any undesirable manifestation on our planet. This does not mean we shouldn't participate in social justice efforts, victim relief efforts, charities, etc. It is imperative to understand, though, that those actions will not eradicate a problem from our world unless our communal beliefs are aligned with that desire. In fact, if you participate in charitable or altruistic activity with personal beliefs about the inevitability of the issue you're trying to resolve, you are actually inadvertently contributing to the growth of the collective belief that caused the suffering in the first place.

Let's illustrate that with an example of a common activity: saving money. Socking away a good portion of your paycheck in a savings account can be a very positive action if it's done in accord with beliefs about abundance. But if you're building your savings because of a limiting belief about scarcity, your logical actions regarding accumulating a healthy savings will actually be reinforcing and empowering your beliefs about scarcity.

We have all contributed to, as well as suffered from, painful and tragic manifestations because of the coherence that is automatically formed between collective beliefs and the quantum field. Not because you want to be sick. Not because you desire that a child be born with a rare form of cancer. And not because you intend a little boy's mother in Rwanda to be shot by guerilla soldiers. But you do acknowledge that such tragedies are an unfortunate part of life on Earth. And through that acknowledgment, you have inadvertently added to collective beliefs about their occurrence.

Unfortunately, there are some people so imbued with negative beliefs, primarily about themselves, that they choose to harm others intentionally. When someone's beliefs are negative enough to produce miserable self-worth, she may choose to take actions, or foster ideas and attitudes, that intentionally cause harm. While you often cannot stop someone from purposely harming you or others, you do have the power to contextually create your own unique version of that harmful person. For example, I have a friend who was physically abused by her father as a child. As an adult, she is now physically distanced from her father and safe from his harm.

My friend understands she did not "ask" for his abuse and had no control over her father's tragically harmful actions during her childhood. Now safe from his harm, she has created a new version of her father in her own unique, individual universe. She describes her new version thusly: "My father is a wounded, scarred, and scared man who hates himself on a deep level. He transferred his self-hatred to me, his daughter, by hitting me and calling me bad names. His abuse was not personal; any child who happened to be in his life would have received it. It did not happen to me because I deserved it, nor did I want it. I was a helpless target for a wretched man whom I can now choose to keep at a distance from me— one who can no longer harm me without my permission. And as sad and angry as those experiences make me feel, I can now heal."

That version of her father does not, literally, change him. He is still the same man he was before my friend started creating her unique version of him. Since he has a consciousness and is a creator, my friend's father is still completely in control of his actions, ideas, and attitudes. If he so desires, he can change those things by changing his beliefs, but my friend's new version won't do that for him.

There is great power in creating your own version of someone. Although my friend's new version of her father won't change the man, himself, she now has a new version of him in her universe that aligns her with her desires to heal rather than feeds her anger and self-blame. This new version of her father does not erase the tragic wounds he inflicted upon her but does put her focus onto her greatest opportunities for healing. And, in this manner, my friend really did "create" a new person in her own unique, individual universe.

There is, however, one person whose harmful actions, ideas, and attitudes you can always control: you. People who cause harm to others, even unintentionally, are almost always causing the greatest degree of harm to themselves. Your most limiting beliefs have undoubtedly been causing you even more harm than you've ever inflicted upon anyone else. Fortunately, you are already addressing this by playing "Grow a Greater You."

You now know how to mitigate the harmful actions of others by removing yourself from their presence, whenever possible, and by creating your own, more aligned version of that person. But what can you do about the harm created by collective beliefs? Should you be expected to harbor no beliefs about the unfortunate inevitability of tragedy and suffering? That seems like an almost ridiculous proposition, because we've all grown up believing that war, violence, poverty, disease, abuse, inequity, subjugation, exploitation, etc., while deplorable and horrific, are an unfortunate reality of human life.

Because inevitable tragedy is a part of our collective beliefs, we are always incorporating allowances for its occurrence, and it is nigh impossible that we won't contribute to the communal expectations that form coherence and manifest it. Did you intentionally cause a tragedy to happen through your participation in communal beliefs that even our innocent will sometimes suffer horribly? Of course not, yet you do hold beliefs about the reality and inevitability of such suffering.

So, even if your personal actions, ideas, and attitudes inflict no suffering, understand that you are still participating in collective beliefs that ensure such tragedy will continue to manifest. Even if an innocent child born with cancer dies too young to truly hold any beliefs of her own, all of us, including her family, her doctors, her family's friends, and even those who merely read about it on social media, have contributed to collective beliefs that unconsciously form expectations for the manifestation of such a terrible event.

Because we know that our material world is contextually created through our beliefs about it, it would be improper to say that we play no role in keeping tragic things a viable and expected part of our experiences as human beings. No matter how ridiculous it is to consider holding someone accountable for inadvertently adding energy to communal beliefs, we cannot deny that the world would be different if we did not participate.

So, if our participation in communal beliefs virtually guarantees great suffering, how can you possibly help stop bad things from happening to good people? How can you help make suffering optional?

There are some ways you can truly make a discernable difference, and they involve you never downplaying your role in the contextual creation of every aspect of your material world. Your contextual creations imbue meaning and value upon every "thing" in your own unique, individual universe. And when you contextually create a thing, you also influence the meaning and value that thing is assigned while being created by other people. As you imbue each material experience with a meaning and value of your choosing, you are actually pushing the material world in a specific direction.

Does it matter that the push you can give to the material world, by intentionally creating things that are more pleasing and more aligned with your desires, seems rather insignificant? After all, you're just one of over seven billion humans who are all contextually creating the material world. What difference will your decision really make? But what else can you contribute except that which is yours to contribute? Your contribution is one only you can make and to doubt its importance is to doubt your own.

You are always adding to the collective meaning and value of every aspect of the material world as you contextually create it in your universe. Work toward holding beliefs about a thing that serve you and align you with your desires and, in so doing, you will also be pushing the collective meaning and values of that thing in those directions. And the most exciting news about this is that you can do this most powerfully simply by continuing the journey you started back in Chapter One. All you have to do is play "Grow a Greater You" to make the greatest contributions toward uplifting and enlightened communal beliefs.

Could manifesting your personal desires by playing "Grow a Greater You" really be your most important contribution to making suffering optional for all humanity? Playing this game truly is powerfully altruistic because you are not only making suffering optional for yourself but for others too. Remember that beliefs are the engine of creation. All the actions you take are important, but the most important thing for contextually creating a more pleasing material reality is making sure your beliefs are aligned with your desired outcomes. So, as you raise your own beliefs, you will be contributing those raised beliefs to communal beliefs. As self-serving as it might sound, aligning your personal beliefs with your unique desires is truly your greatest tangible contribution to making suffering optional for every human. Actually, adding your positive energy to communal beliefs is the *only* thing you can do to influence them and is the only contribution to them you'll ever have complete control over.

On a practical note, playing "Grow a Greater" will also make you much better equipped to have a positive effect and influence on the life experiences of those around you. Your actions, attitudes, and ideas will be more enlightened, creative, and inspiring. Who cares if you play "Grow a Greater You" to manifest a BMW? Your journey to grow yourself into beliefs that will reflect that BMW back to you requires you to contextually create a universe where your individual beliefs, now raised, add to the energy of communal ones.

You will be turning on your own light each day, as brightly as you are able. Playing "Grow a Greater You" is the single most important thing you can do, because it adds one more enlightened beacon to this planet. Have you seen the movie "The Rise of the Guardians"? In this movie, Santa Claus has a huge globe with a dot of light for each person who believes in him. As long as there are enough lights shining, the Boogeyman is kept at bay. The light of your enlightened beliefs is an incredibly important contribution to our collective beliefs that only you can make.

If you don't make your contribution, it will never be made. How much more important could you be? Want to leave an inheritance for your heirs? No amount of cash could supersede the value of leaving your contributions to beautiful, empowering, and humane collective beliefs. So, thank you, in advance for playing "Grow a Greater You" and adding your light to mine.

As your personal beliefs grow and you become more equipped to freely give your time and money, actively assisting others by helping Habitat for Humanity build a house or sending money to Oxfam are to be applauded. Just make sure your beliefs are aligned with your desired outcomes before, while, and after. That way, you'll help ensure you're not inadvertently adding your energy to a collective belief that what you're helping overcome isn't an inevitable reality on our planet that can never truly be abated.

Tell yourself a story like:

"Although I can't, honestly, envision myself able to believe, completely, that this suffering will vanish or is not inevitable and, although it's even more challenging to imagine the majority of people on our planet believing likewise and, thus, creating a collective manifestation where this suffering does not exist, I can, at least, authentically acknowledge that the possibilities do exist, however unlikely they seem. And, furthermore, although my actions are important, valuable, and useful, I can also acknowledge that if this suffering is to be abated, it will be done through aligning my beliefs with my desires that this suffering is alleviated. In this manner, I choose to continue growing my beliefs toward those aligned desires and I can rest assured that I am doing everything within my locus of control to manifest my desire that this suffering ends.

Furthermore, I can also authentically believe that my one 'small' current contribution to communal beliefs is just as important as the final contribution that pushes them past the tipping point. When collecting a million dollars, the first dollar manifested is just as significant as the last dollar manifested. So, too, can I honestly say that my small contribution is just as important as every other, even the final one."

So play "Grow a Greater You," end your suffering, manifest your dreams, and experiment with the expanding influence you can have on making suffering optional for everyone. Isn't it wonderful to know that you can be of such immensely important and powerful service all while intentionally manifesting your personal desires in your own unique, individual universe?

Chapter Ten

Is Influencing Your Reality
a Pseudoscience?

One question that arises periodically from critics and skeptics alike is whether or not deliberately influencing your material reality, or life experiences, is a pseudoscience. Is this concept real? Can it be verified by science? After all, if the idea of being an intentional creator of your life can be proven, if it is real, shouldn't it be taught in our schools? Shouldn't it be in textbooks?

Before discussing this topic, I want to make clear that I am not solely a law-of-attraction teacher. I say "solely" because I do not mind being given that label; I love the law of attraction and I like reading, writing, and speaking about it. I did not, however, set out to write books solely about the law of attraction, because, as "Grow a Greater You" shows, you don't actually *attract* things *to* you. While the law of attraction has become a permanent part of our culture, the concept probably might have been more accurately called "the law of alignment."

The law of attraction is a cool name, though, so let's stick with it. That name not only encapsulates what people want it to help them do but also helps market the concept of deliberately influencing your material experiences. The catchier the name, the more people will explore it, and that's a great thing if it allows more light to be added to our planet. Of course, one of the side effects of calling this concept by that catchy moniker is that it encourages some people to be skeptical. It's hard to blame people; the idea of having intentional and deliberate influence over your material reality, of being able to create things, runs counter to everything we thought we knew about how the universe works.

Since we don't really attract things to us, the law of attraction, as it is often discussed and taught, is a bit of a misnomer. We grow into our desires, by growing our beliefs into alignment with them, instead of actually attracting desirable things to us. But that is really only semantics. While, technically, I teach people to use new paradigms from quantum physics, I would never discourage anyone from calling what I teach "the law of attraction."

Instead of attracting a desire, what you're really doing is becoming it in order to manifest and experience it. You're not a magnet attracting things to you; you are more like a person growing into a new pair of clothing (the clothing, in that metaphor, being your desire). So, when you want to use the law of attraction, you do actually have some work to do. You need to grow into, or become, the things you desire. But that is *all* you have to do. The quantum field will take care of the rest.

There is one aspect of the law of attraction, as it's commonly taught today, that is most certainly true. You don't have to take any specific actions to realize and fulfill your greatest desires other than aligning your beliefs with them. As you align your beliefs with your desires, things, experiences, opportunities, and possibilities virtually appear right in front of you where there were none before. That is because you are, literally, living in and seeing a different universe with each uptick of your beliefs about something. You couldn't see them from the perspective of your previous universe because your limiting beliefs could not form the necessary coherence.

However, whether you call "Grow a Greater You" a game that teaches you how to use the law of attraction or a game that simply teaches you how to powerfully utilize your actual role in how our universe works, there remain questions from some about the validity of this concept. Is it a real science or is it a pseudoscience? Can intentionally influencing your material reality be proven?

To respond to skepticism about the science behind deliberately influencing your material reality, there are some important things we need to understand. We need to first understand what it means to prove something and how that is done. You're probably readily aware that there are many things we accept as facts that we can, literally, never actually prove. Here are some things we know that never can actually be proven:

- We cannot prove that our brains are capable of understanding or knowing what reality is.

- We cannot prove that language is capable of conveying adequate meaning.

- We cannot prove that numbers exist.

- We cannot prove that any scientific facts have been present in the past or that they will be present in the future.

- We cannot prove that any scientific fact is uniform across the rest of the universe.

- We cannot prove that reality is rational and knowable.

- We cannot prove that we inhabit one small section of a much larger, vast universe.

All science and all knowledge rest on assumptions of uniformity and rationality. Now you may say, "Greg, don't give me that bunch of silly examples; we do 'know' those things are true. They are real." And I agree that there is no reason to not call those things "true" even though they cannot be proven. But that still does not negate the fact that they truly cannot be proven.

There is another aspect of the science of intentionally influencing your reality that we need to examine to resolve skepticism about it: how things are proven to be true or real. Science can only do two things—observe and measure. Science observes what can be observed and measures what can be measured. And even though those measurements are taken by highly trained professionals, recorded measurements do not, literally, prove anything. It is not the observed and recorded measurements, themselves, that make anything true.

The test of whether we'll call science "proven" or "true" is when those measurements are put to use to see if they work. In the field of engineering, engineers use the measurements of classical physics to design airplanes and spacecraft. If the field-level applications of those measurements prove them to be useful and valuable, if they work when applied, then we say the measurements are true. Yet even in this case, nothing has been proven except that the measurements are useful and valuable.

Does this mean scientific facts are not true? Of course it doesn't. They are true because they have been found to be so via the litmus test of usefulness and value we use—through the only method, in fact, that humans have available to call anything proven. Yet it's important to know that while we rightfully call useful and valuable measurements true, it still doesn't mean that those facts have been, literally, proven.

Semantics, you say? I can understand that reaction. Yet those distinctions are very important for anyone wishing to be a more discerning consumer of ideas. Being that you are playing "Grow a Greater You," I believe it safe to put you in that category.

For you see, the source of the measurements being put to our litmus test of their usefulness and value—not the value and usefulness of the measurements, themselves—is often what people are responding to when they throw around terms like "pseudoscience." The source of any measurement is not the most important factor in determining whether or not it is real or true. In fact, the source of the measurement is often irrelevant.

Bear in mind that science, itself, was once seen as an immoral and unacceptable discipline unless it was being conducted in the name of God. Pursuing scientific knowledge with the aim of merely discovering how the universe worked put someone in danger of being labeled a heretic and being persecuted. Science, as a source of finding evidence and clues about the operation of the material world, was not only distrusted and dismissed in certain circles, if you were a part of that source you might have found your life in danger.

Yet we now understand that those who embraced science when it was considered dangerous and heretical were actually early adopters with great foresight. And, in retrospect, those who sought to discredit or persecute science practitioners were wrong to do so. But we only see that after the fact, which is why you'll often hear that new ideas actually don't triumph by winning over their critics. New ideas eventually triumph because their critics finally all die.

Some people, as you know, are quick to huff, "Pffft! The law of attraction? That's a pseudoscience!" And, in my experience, that response is very often prompted by a prejudice against the source of that concept. They don't like that new-age, "artsy-fartsy, beads-and-incense, moonbeam" stuff. It rubs them the wrong way for some reason and, thus, when they attribute the source of an idea to "new-age" thinking, they automatically dismiss it out of hand.

This method for dismissing a new idea or theory is not only improper, it will also cheat you out of some potentially valuable new ideas. Dismissing ideas because of their source, rather than because they actually don't prove valuable or useful, reveals ignorance about how something becomes true for humans. Doing so will also, eventually, turn you into a curmudgeon: you know—one of those crabby, cratchety cranks who groan about how the world is "going to hell in a handbasket!"

Does such a crank ever stop to consider that her grandmother and great-grandmother once said the very same things when confronted with all the new ideas of their time? America's transformation to an urban society, automobiles giving teenagers the ability to spend time alone and unsupervised, female suffrage, slavery's abolition, the theory of evolution, psychiatry's rise to prominence—the list of new ideas that have caused people to cry about the "end of the world" as they know it is too long to print. And our progeny will be tempted to say similar things someday about whatever new ideas they're encountering.

But we know the world never really went to hell. I'm sure there are valid reasons for anyone to pine for the "good old days" because they don't like the new ways of doing things, but have you ever heard a young person doing that? That's because young people are actually trying out all the new ideas, discerning for themselves if they are valuable and useful. Young people don't concern themselves nearly as much with the source of new ideas as older people do—which is why you don't meet young curmudgeons. And, in this manner, we should use young people as our role models for discerning the value of new ideas.

From a certain perspective, becoming a curmudgeon could be called an appropriate reaction. Because the world as a curmudgeon knows it really is changing completely; new ideas are being found useful and valuable by discerning experimenters and, thus, those ideas are not only spreading because of their value, they are becoming the new conventional wisdom of the next generations. Of course it is normal and expected for some to be naturally inclined to call our familiar ways of doing things the "truth" and the "way things ought to be" because we have found them to be so and we are often suspicious of new ideas.

Why does a curmudgeon, after all, think the world is going to hell and why is she so angry? Rather than discerning whether or not new ideas are valid by personally examining their usefulness and value, as the younger generation is doing, the curmudgeon is reacting to the people who are using the new ideas. Thus, her annoyance at the people engaging the new ideas joins her dismissal of their source and acutely reinforces the misguided method she's using to determine whether something is true or not.

Why are there so many curmudgeons? Why does it seem that so many of us to become curmudgeons as we age? Because we are absolutely 100% guaranteed to be bombarded with new theories and data throughout our lives. If we're not discerning consumers of theories and data, we all run great risk of becoming a grumpy, cranky cynic.

But before we patronizingly shake our collective heads and chastise these sometimes annoying critics of deliberate creation, let's make sure we're not being hypocritical. After all, how many of us reject theories and data simply because of prejudices we hold against their source? Do you ever pull the curmudgeon act when the source is a religion, government entity, a large corporation, or a talking head with a political outlook you disagree with? Do you dismiss something simply because you learned about it on Fox News or Last Week Tonight?

I'm not suggesting that every new idea or theory should be called true, nor am I suggesting that you should accept and adopt every new idea or theory you encounter. What I am strongly recommending, though, is that you don't fall into the very trap that skeptics of intentionally influencing your material experiences often do. Learning to evaluate new ideas by personally and authentically testing their usefulness and value will keep you from devolving into a grumpy old lady who shakes her fist, from her front porch, at those annoying teenagers.

And knowing how new ideas are proven can also help you even if you decide not to test their usefulness and value. Even if you decide not to test new ideas personally, which is your right, you can avoid calling it a pseudoscience or rubbish based on their source, the people practicing them, or solely on the fact that they differ from what is familiar to you. That, alone, can save you from becoming a grumpy old woman.

"Grow a Greater You" may be a pseudoscience to someone. I know those people are wrong, however, because it is immensely useful and valuable. So if someone calls this game a pseudoscience I will be very suspicious that she is doing so simply because she does not like these new ideas, whether that prejudice stems from not liking the source or not appreciating its practitioners. I will be amazed, in fact, if she calls it a pseudoscience by claiming to have put these ideas to an authentic and thorough test and finding them ineffective.

I, and thousands of others, have put "Grow a Greater You" to the test, in the proving ground of our daily lives, and unabashedly determined it to be "proven" and "true". Not necessarily because of the source of the ideas or who is practicing them, but because of their usefulness and value. This game works, repeatedly and reliably, so I have no reservations about calling it proven. "Grow a Greater You" is not a pseudoscience because it passes our actual litmus test for what is true.

Greg Kuhn

Chapter Eleven

Is it Okay to Desire a BMW?

How, then, do you play "Grow a Greater You"? By creating beliefs that are aligned with your desires, you will exert more influence over what you are manifesting in your material reality, because your expectations will automatically be raised into alignment with them when you improve your beliefs.

Before moving forward, let's discuss something that you may not have thought you needed to: your desires. Since it's been said that our focus on desire is the root of all suffering, are you certain beyond a shadow of a doubt that it is okay to desire the things you do? Additionally, is each of your specific, individual, and unique desires okay for you to have, align your beliefs with, and manifest? In other words, is it okay for you to want what you want?

What if your desire is mostly self-focused and, perhaps, even driven primarily by a seeming need for self-gratification? Are some desires not okay for you to have, while other, more enlightened and altruistic ones, are? Should you be ashamed of desiring things that some would label base or materialistic? Is it wrong to desire a convertible BMW, $500,000 in the bank, and vacations in the Caribbean?

Are you even worthy of such things? Are you worthy of manifesting the best material reality that life can offer you? Are you being greedy to contextually create your ultimate dreams for a successful and fulfilled life while so many others suffer? Many of us have been told some version of "Who are you to think you deserve to live your dreams?" and "How dare you be so concerned with yourself while so many are miserable?"

Those are important questions to answer, especially considering that playing "Grow a Greater You" is about finally manifesting some of your greatest, most important desires. So let's dispel some myths and misconceptions about desires right now. You were born to desire; desiring is not only what you're supposed to be doing, it's what you came here to do. You came here to play this game, to expand into the greatest, grandest version of you possible.

I have a Buddhist friend who recently told me that suffering, according to his beliefs, is caused by inherent, fervent focus on your desires. Losing desire is, in his view, the key to happiness, serenity, and fulfillment. I disagreed with him and told him that, in my experience, it's not human desire that causes suffering but humans' *inability to manifest* their desires. Yet I understand why our desires have gotten such a bad rap. Until now, most people have not understood how to grow into them and manifest them in a reliable, repeatable manner.

Until now, if you wanted to manifest or achieve something, you repeated the actions that a qualified expert taught you. Those action-focused Neanderthal paradigms have the best of intentions and make perfect logical sense to our eyeballs, but we now know why that method never works reliably for the vast majority of people: because it is based on the Neanderthal paradigms of a giver of gifts, separate from you, who bestows things upon you or withholds them.

Many people haven't learned that what's really happening when those Neanderthal paradigms work is they are taking the prescribed actions while just happening to have beliefs that are aligned with their desires in that area. In fact, many of the people who teach you to follow their actions in this manner also do not understand that, while their actions are cogent and valuable, it is their aligned beliefs that are primarily responsible for making them so. Yet the ingredient so often missing for us—not having beliefs aligned with your desires when you take those prescribed actions to manifest them—causes repeated failure within that paradigm. And that leads people to blame themselves, start considering themselves unworthy, or to try in vain to stop desiring those things that remain elusive.

Your desires are intensely personal and your manifestation of them is essential for your growth and expansion as a spiritual being, yet you've been encouraged to actively sublimate them. Why? To save yourself from suffering, of course. Your subconscious brain is undoubtedly infused with the belief that you will simply not be able to achieve, or manifest, many things most important to you. The people who passed those beliefs on to you were doing so from their perspective regarding that painful "reality"; the adults in your life taught you to not expect to manifest important things because they couldn't.

Thus manifesting big dreams has come to be seen as the domain of special, anointed, lucky, or immoral people. How else could it be explained through the perspective of the Neanderthal paradigms? To not frame the manifestation of big desires this way, without an understanding of how the material world is truly created, the only other option is to blame ourselves in some way. Thus, within the old paradigms, which teach us that your actions are the sole agent for manifesting your material reality, people are virtually forced to vilify those who achieve their greatest desires.

Thus, due to our seemingly universal inability to manifest them, desires have become a cruel temptress beckoning us to seek the unattainable— and then laughing all the while at our futility and impotence. Throughout human history a belief has grown that says that you shouldn't desire the biggest, grandest, most fulfilling life experiences because such desires will only bring you misery. We have been taught, by those who thought they had no other option but to believe it, that we're better off playing small. Playing small saves you from suffering, people taught us, since you're never going to get those things anyway.

But at what cost have you been saved? Do your desires ever really go away? The demonization of your desires, while understandable as a defense mechanism, creates a dangerous fallacy when we adhere to conventional wisdom and question their value. And when we inevitably question whether we're worthy of manifesting them, some people have even grown to feel ashamed for wanting the things they dream of.

These attempts to save us from misery, as well-intentioned as they are, have created collective beliefs about scarcity, lack, and limits. We have been taught that the good things in life are finite in number and if we try to take more than our allotment, we are being greedy. We have been taught to accept our small allotment like a good person should and simply learn to be okay with it. We have been taught that if we seek more than what we've been allotted, we are stealing from others' piece of the pie.

Who are you, you've been taught to believe, to think you deserve a fit body? Or a healthy savings account? Or a soul mate? Or health? The list goes on and on.

For example, who among us didn't have some version of the homily "Money is the root of all evil" pounded into us throughout childhood? Hasn't that phrase, along with many other similar sentiments, been used to teach you that desiring money is base, materialistic, evil, and wrong? Even that money, itself, is evil and bad? And, if you're like me, you may have even been told that phrase comes from the Bible—a book held in such high esteem by some that many people unquestionably adopt any belief that they are told comes from it.

Money is the perfect thing to illustrate how we've been taught to sublimate or demonize our desires. It is a fascinating desire to analyze because so many of us have such a dysfunctional love/hate relationship with it. We desire it madly, yet we're often ashamed to admit that—even to ourselves. We love it because it is so important to us and affords us access to so much of what we want, yet we hate it because we never get as much as we want. We've been taught beliefs about the immorality of seeking it, making it a priority, and possessing a lot of it. Such beliefs are so directly opposed to our very natural desire for money that we are schizophrenic about it.

There is absolutely nothing wrong with not making money a high priority in your life. Money is not necessarily a key to a happy, fulfilled life. But as Zig Ziglar said, "Money won't make you happy, but everyone wants to find out for themselves." As long as your lack of desire for money is authentic and not the practiced results of avoiding misery about your unfulfilled desires for it, that's wonderful.

Because of beliefs like scarcity, most of us are encouraged to believe that desiring money is not a proper spiritual or enlightened thing to do. This belief was given to you with the intent to protect you by alerting you to "the way things are," because the people who taught you that money is evil had great personal desires for money that they could not manifest. Yet, regardless of the amount of shame you have towards your desire for money, has that desire really ever left you? Not completely—and it's not supposed to.

The actual quote people have modified to validate their beliefs in scarcity is "The love of money is the root of all evil: which while some coveted after, they have erred from the faith, and pierced themselves through with many sorrows." (King James Bible, 1 Timothy 6:10). I'm not quoting the Bible because I consider it an authoritative source of information for beliefs about money; I'm quoting the Bible to illustrate how conventional wisdom will twist the meaning of a passage from a revered text to propagate what has become an important and powerful belief in scarcity. Obviously, the original passage is not calling money the root of evil, nor is it even condemning someone for desiring it or manifesting it.

Money as the root of all evil? Hardly.

And let's debunk some of those myths about money right now. Is money really scarce? Is there a "money pie" of predetermined size from which we're all allowed a slice? Money is simply an idea. For example, I'm sure I'm not alone in hardly using tangible currency, cash and coins, anymore. Money is electronically deposited in my accounts and I pass it along to others electronically. What I possess is just an idea of money, represented by numbers in databases. And what I'm receiving and passing along, in the vast majority of cases, is merely the exact same idea of value.

We're all aware that it's been a long time since physical currency has been a tangible representation of a corresponding amount of gold stored in some heavily guarded vault. The modern world is no longer on the gold standard; our currency has no intrinsic value. A dollar bill in your wallet or a number on your bank account ledger only has the value that we all choose to believe it does.

Additionally, let's discuss the illusion that the amount of money, even as an idea, is finite. To illustrate money's abundance, consider if you own 1,000 stock shares of Google and the price of that stock rises $10 during one day of Wall Street trading. You now possess $10,000 that you didn't have the day before and you can see that money on your brokerage's website. Did our government suddenly print more money or did someone just discover $10,000 worth of gold? No. That money appeared out of thin air.

You might counter by saying that the $10 price jump reflects a tangible, discernable rise in the value of Google. Since Google sells goods and services, its rising stock value mirrors Google's rising market share and profitability. And there is truth to that statement, yet stock prices are not directly correlated to a company's sales; stock prices are a result of consumers' beliefs in a company's value. Yes, those beliefs are influenced greatly by a company's success and analyst's predictions, but the new $10,000 of value on your ledger is definitely a one-day manifestation of money that corresponds to consumer beliefs. It wasn't there the day before.

And what about the belief that people who have lots of money are evil? In my experience, nothing could be further from the truth. I've been fortunate to spend quite a bit of time with two gentlemen whose net worth each exceeds 100 million dollars. These men are two of the most giving and generous people I've known; their fortune is a joyful reflection of their beliefs and embodies the thoughtful people they are. Sure, we've all seen the Enron scandal, Imelda Marcos, and Bernard Madoff used to propagate the myth of rich people being evil, but the reason such examples are so public is that those folks fell back to Earth when their limiting beliefs finally began to be reflected back to them in their material reality.

Let's return to my adaptation of the Buddhist saying. Now that quantum physics has revealed how humans create their material reality, I trust you feel inspired to join with countless others who are intentionally learning to manifest their desires and updating their personal beliefs to align with my rephrasing of that Buddhist belief. For why do people experience misery, except for desires they cannot manifest? Whether that desire is for money, personal happiness, health, freedom, food and water, or anything at all, we suffer when we repeatedly experience the inability to manifest important desires.

Another protective adaptation humans have created is to pretend, in some form or fashion, that we don't desire those things we can't manifest. Unable to manifest a long-held, important desire and having reached the end of your rope with your suffering over its absence, you actively attempt to dampen or sublimate your desire. Perhaps you tried justifying your desire's absence by demonizing those who've attained it and labeling them shallow, vain, evil, or corrupt. Maybe you've tried to talk yourself out of wanting it anymore, telling yourself that you're actually better off without it. You may have attempted to dull your desire's attraction, perhaps going so far as to self-medicate your suffering with behaviors or substances that alter your mood and allow you to temporarily forget about them.

Whatever you've done to dampen your desires or pretend you no longer want to manifest them, however, I am fairly certain of one thing: none of your efforts worked. Your desires can only be temporarily forgotten; they never go away permanently. Why is that? You were born to desire because you were born to contextually create. How could you be a creator if you had no desires? Without your desires, after all, how would you know what to create? And what motivation would you have to create without your desires as you guide?

Are you supposed to reach your pinnacle of creative power and be able to deliberately manifest a material reality completely aligned with your utmost desires overnight? Of course not. You are here to grow into that power, in steps and stages, by going on a journey. The journey to become your desires by aligning your beliefs with them is the real treasure of human existence. You are here to unfold and expand into full enlightenment of who and what you really are—a part of the quantum field who is learning to more intentionally align her beliefs with her desires so she can contextually create a more pleasing material reality.

The key words for the purpose of aligning your beliefs with your desires are: grow, step, stage, blossom, unfold, expand, and learn. You are not here to wake up, snap your fingers or wave a wand, and instantly have everything manifest in absolute grandeur and perfection. That would be an experience; you came here to have a journey. In fact, you'll soon learn that the lion's share of your rewards is found in your journey and not in your actual manifestations. The view from the mountaintop is not what makes you a mountain-climber; it is the climb itself.

This is all precisely why it is not only okay to desire whatever it is you desire, it is also vitally important to manifest those very specific, personal desires. Growing into the desires you hold right now, no matter how self-aggrandizing, egotistical, or self-centered they may be, are vital steps in your journey of personal evolution. Manifesting your current desires, regardless of whether or not Mother Theresa would approve of them, is akin to the pedals of a flower slowing unfolding to greet the warm spring sunshine.

In this manner, you can look at your desires like a carrot on the end of a string hung just out of reach of a stubborn horse's mouth. The horse, attached to a cart, walks forward to eat the carrot and the cart gets pulled along. And the cart will move as long as the tasty meal the horse desires remains hung in front of it. In this metaphor, you are the cart, the horse is your beliefs, and the carrot is your desires. Except, when playing "Grow a Greater You," you actually get to eat the carrot every time. Don't worry, though, new carrots will always take the place of the one just consumed.

Manifesting your current desires is how you grow. It's how you expand. It matters not what those desires are; there are no "right" nor "wrong" desires, because the desires themselves are a means to an end. Your desires are merely a vehicle that facilitates and motivates your growth; your desires give you direction and inspiration for this journey. The manifestation of your current desires fuels the "Grow" in "Grow a Greater You."

That is why you hear successful people attribute their success to seeing opportunities where others see dead ends. We hear that and we smile approvingly, agreeing with this sentiment but perhaps thinking patronizingly, "How nice for her." We know that possibility exists and we've experienced it in some areas of our lives, but where we've suffered, the idea of seeing opportunities instead of roadblocks seems far-fetched, because you, literally, can't see the opportunities those successful people do until you see the universe as they do.

You will be always be gifted with more desires to grow into, and your new desires will be even greater than the ones you've just manifested. That's one of the most exciting things about playing "Grow a Greater You"; this game never ends and it's always just as exciting to play as it was on day one. The 1,000[th] desire you intentionally manifest by playing "Grow a Greater You" will actually be more fun and fulfilling than the very first desire with which you grew your beliefs into alignment.

Additionally, as you manifest your desires exactly as they are in the moment, without altering them to what you imagine you "should" desire or what other people would find more acceptable, appropriate, or altruistic, you'll find that your desires become more mature and less self-focused on their own accord. You're going to find out that the things you manifest are truly not the reward; your personal growth and the feelings you've probably imagined attaining that desire would give you are the true rewards.

Your particular desires are, in many ways, actually irrelevant—except for the fact that you desire them, of course, which makes them very important to you. Your pain or suffering motivates you to become those things you desire, and your becoming and growing is the vital, indispensable part of "Grow a Greater You" that cannot be replaced by anything else. The manifestation, or fulfillment, of the things you desire is not the game, you see, but the fruits of it. In fact, you already know, logically, that possessing or manifesting a thing will not make you happy. Manifesting a desired thing gives you permission to let yourself be happy and feel free.

So if you don't embrace your current desires and grow into them with a shameless, childlike abandon and gusto, you are virtually saying, "I am not worthy of growing into a greater me." Isn't it simply fantastic that the universe gives us something so spectacularly fun to use as our vehicle for growth and enlightenment? And the fun of manifesting our desires is exactly why I call "Grow a Greater You" a game.

You're almost being "tricked" into enlightenment by the strength of your desires. All you have to do, in fact, is follow your dreams and manifest your desires just as they are, and, before you know it, you've grown into a greater, grander version of yourself.

This game reminds me of one way I tricked my sons into going to bed when they were very young. Rather than go through a typical "I don't want to go to bed yet" debate, I learned to ask them: "Do you want me to carry you up to bed like a sack of potatoes or do you want me to chase you up to bed like I'm a monster?" My sons were so enthralled by the game that they made a choice, had a blast playing it with me, and, before they realized what was happening, were in bed. I tricked them into doing something that was very beneficial for both of us. Your desires play the same trick on you, and all of the outcomes from this trick are wonderful.

The things you desire, therefore, are not necessarily independently, or objectively, vital; while you may desire a soul mate and, thus, manifesting a soul mate is incredibly important for your expansion and personal growth, manifesting a soul mate is not universally important for every human being. Just for you.

In that example, manifesting a soul mate represents your particular chosen vehicle for your expansion into the next greatest version of you. Manifesting a soul mate is the delivery system for your next stages of personal and spiritual growth as an incredibly powerful and influential contextual creator. Manifesting a soul mate will deliver to you the exact experiences you need to continue fulfilling your destiny to expand into your greatest vision of yourself. It won't be your last expansion fulfilled through "Grow a Greater You," but it is something you need to manifest right now in order to play.

Manifesting your soul mate is, of course, not just wonderful simply because it facilitates your ongoing journey of expansion and fulfillment. It is also wonderful because having a soul mate is divine and rewarding.

There is a good reason you desire it—having a soul mate is awesome. You win on both accounts, and that is one of the most magical aspects of "Grow a Greater You."

The importance of manifesting your personal desires, just as they currently are, can be illustrated by my wife's painting. As of this writing, my wife has achieved a breakthrough with her painting that is eliciting some dramatic critical praise. In fact, my wife actually says that when she now looks at some of her earlier paintings, she almost doesn't even like them anymore.

The new paintings my wife is manifesting are not only very different from her earlier ones, they are also much more beloved by the people who view and collectively create them. Yet those older, less desirable (to her, anyway), paintings were incredibly important for her to create. My wife doesn't look back and say to herself, "I should've been painting in this new style all along, I can't believe all the time in my studio I wasted!" She understands that manifesting those older paintings were essential stepping-stones that allowed her to grow her beliefs about her ability to create beauty with oil and canvas. Thus, painting what she desired to paint, back then, was exactly the desire she needed to grow into.

By manifesting her desires, just as they were then, she was able to grow into her current greater, grander version of herself. What if she had denied her desires to paint back then? She was free to choose that option, of course, but if she had she wouldn't have been able to grow herself into the painter she is today.

My wife's earlier paintings were the vehicle for her to grow her beliefs into alignment with her current, more desirable paintings. Thank goodness she gave herself permission to paint what she desired to paint back then, right? And isn't it fun to know that her current paintings, although so much more aligned with her desires as a painter, are also vehicles for future, even grander paintings?

Your current desires are just as important for you to manifest as my wife's earlier paintings were for her to create. Manifesting your current desires will be amazingly fun and fulfilling. So embrace your current desires without reservation, whatever they are right now (unless they are illegal, immoral, or harmful). Even if it's something as base or completely self-centered as wanting to manifest some "eye candy" for your right arm at your upcoming high school reunion so all your old friends will eat their hearts out. Even if your desire is something as self-focused and globally irrelevant as wanting to fit into your favorite little black dress so your former partner realizes what he missed out on by breaking up with you.

Even if the first desires you manifest serve no one but you, even if they could be called childish, what will happen is you will get excited, inspired, and invigorated upon their manifestation. And as you revel in the satisfaction of your manifestations, which you are hereby given a mandate to do by the hearty bucketful, those fulfilled desires will quickly be replaced by new ones.

Don't fret or second-guess what you manifest now. I am confident you'll eventually be manifesting desires more altruistic and beneficial to your neighbors. If nothing else, I am absolutely sure you'll be doing one thing that is undoubtedly one of the most globally beneficial and altruistic things you can possibly do—you'll be adding your energy to my greatest desire of making suffering optional.

Even when manifesting your most self-centered desires, you'll be adding fire to the fast growing collective beliefs about our influence over our material reality and about how life doesn't happen "to" us. You're helping spread the communal beliefs of humans' inherent power to intentionally manifest our life experiences. And in so doing, you'll be lending your energy to help other people replace Neanderthal paradigms that foster perspectives of victimhood and powerlessness. What could be more important and what could be a greater gift?

Greg Kuhn

Chapter Twelve

Spring Training for Playing "Grow a Greater You"

The first order of business for playing this supreme game, "Grow a Greater You," is to familiarize yourself with your desires. That might sound a bit silly. "I'm already quite familiar with my desires," you might say to me, "because they're what I want and I typically think about them a lot each day." Yet what I'm referring to is categorizing your desires into three specific types.

The main goal of playing "Grow a Greater You" is to manifest your dreams and desires and stop your suffering. What is suffering, after all? Suffering is caused by your desires not being manifest for an unacceptable or untenable amount of time.

Let's make an important distinction: The goal of playing "Grow a Greater You" is not to stop pain. Pain is a natural part of life. Although it's not often a fun or desirable part of life, we can expect to always experience pain because we will always experience the unwanted. In fact, by the time you are done with this book and playing "Grow a Greater You" on a daily basis, you may actually begin to celebrate your pain.

Pain is important. Suffering is optional, yet pain is a gift.

What is pain, after all? Pain is information like everything else. Pain is feedback that your contextual creations in your own unique, individual universe are displeasing, which alerts you that your beliefs are out of sync with your desires. Pain is, therefore, value, useful, and indispensable information and your cue to grow and expand.

Not only is there nothing wrong with pain, you can actually celebrate it if you learn to see it as information saying, "Okay, time to grow your beliefs in this area or, at least, time to start telling yourself a better-feeling, believable story about it." (Those are tools you'll learn to use soon, by the way). And you can respond with, "Thank you, pain, for alerting me to that. Although you are a displeasing experience, now I know what to do so that I can start contextually creating a more pleasing material reality."

Why will you never stop feeling pain, even after you are inducted into the "Grow a Greater You" Hall of Fame? Because, quite simply, you'll never be done playing "Grow a Greater You." You can count on regularly feeling pain alerting you to your beliefs being unaligned with new desires. Thank goodness for that gift, because it means you're not done growing and there is more pleasure to experience ahead.

There is no "end zone" in this game. And, since you'll never be done, you can be assured that you'll always be gifted with new, greater, grander desires to grow into alignment with and manifest. No matter how long you live and no matter how many of your desires you align your beliefs with and manifest, you are assured that you'll always be gifted with pain, because that is how you'll know that your desires have expanded and it's now time to grow your beliefs into alignment with them.

If you stop experiencing pain, that means you are finished. You are completely grown and evolved. Your desires manifest instantly because you authentically hold beliefs at the top of the chart regarding every aspect of your life. I don't know about you, but I don't want to be finished being Greg just yet. Since I now know exactly how to remedy pain, I no longer fear and dread it so much. And, in this manner, I am often excited by my pain because I know that, before long, my material reality will be even more pleasing.

Suffering, on the other hand, is different from pain. Suffering, something we have all experienced, is optional rather than inevitable. Suffering is also information, but it is a severe and intense form of information you will experience much less, if at all, after you've been playing "Grow a Greater You" for a while.

Suffering is unaddressed and unrelieved pain that has grown over time. The only way to stop suffering is by playing "Grow a Greater You," even if someone doesn't call it by that name. Think about it for a second. Whether your experience with suffering has been physical, mental, psychological, or spiritual, even if you've previously alleviated it through professional help, you were playing "Grow a Greater You," even if you weren't calling it by that name.

While I will absolutely, 100% never recommend that you eschew qualified professional help in areas such as medical, mental, business, financial, legal, health, and fitness, by learning to play "Grow a Greater You," you will soon be learning how to address and alleviate your pain and suffering without always needing professional assistance.

Having clarified the distinction between pain and suffering, and having identified that the main goal of playing "Grow a Greater You" is to manifest your desires and, in tandem, stop your suffering, let's identify the three categories your desires will fall into. The distinction between these three categories is relatively simple, yet also very important. I believe you'll intuitively know which of the three categories each of your desires should fall into, and you will then also know how to manifest each type of desire as you play "Grow a Greater You."

I'm going to use baseball analogies to label each of the three categories of desires. You're playing a game here, after all, so continuing the sports metaphor is logical. And, just as you're bucking conventional wisdom by using new paradigms from quantum physics to become a more intentional architect of your life experiences, I'm using this terminology because baseball bucks the conventional wisdom of every other sport. You may not have realized this, but baseball is the only major sport where the defense has possession of the ball. Baseball is also the only major sport where there is no clock, and where the game doesn't end until every player has fulfilled his requirement to contribute.

The second reason is simply because I love baseball and, in fact, have greatly enjoyed playing "little league for old men" in a 38-and-over men's baseball league.

Category One—Home Run Desires

A home run in baseball occurs when the batter hits the ball over the outfield fence. It's one of the most exciting events in a baseball game. It's exciting because it's a spectacular outcome of a batter's turn at the plate and it is almost always the most desirable. A home run is an automatic run for the team batting and it's also the most powerful and emphatic way to score a run in baseball. Thus the phrase "home run" has become synonymous with virtually any huge success.

A Home Run Desire is one you are manifesting regularly and at levels that please you. You probably don't even pay much attention to this type of desire because you've undoubtedly gotten used to manifesting it and you may often take it for granted. This type of desire is rarely a problem for you to manifest; it's a desire you've got almost on autopilot. A Home Run Desire rarely frustrates you, so you most likely hardly even think about it. And why should you, except to relish in your enjoyment of it and your gratitude for it?

The key characteristic that defines a Home Run Desire is ease. You get to trot unobstructed around the bases, smiling, and touch home plate to the cheers of teammates and fans.

You may occasionally experience pain or frustration around a Home Run Desire, but it's more like a pothole on a smooth highway than it is a challenging detour. Navigating around a brief rough patch or bump in the road, you're quickly back on your way, enjoying your Home Run Desire with your accustomed level of ease. Manifesting a Home Run Desire is something you're very confident about and you often don't even have to think about it because you manifest it so effortlessly.

If your life were a game of darts, a Home Run Desire hits the bull's-eye more often than not. If you stop and assess yourself, I'll bet you have more Home Run Desires in your life than you might think at first blush. Like most people, you are probably more used to thinking about and focusing on what you don't have. "Grow a Greater You" will improve even these desires.

Category Two—Ground Rule Double Desires

A ground rule double in baseball occurs when a batter hits the ball really hard, it strikes the ground deep in the outfield, and then flies over the outfield fence after bouncing off the field surface. The batter is then awarded second base, automatically, but not allowed to advance any further on the hit. A ground rule double, then, is not quite the same accomplishment as a home run, yet it is still a mighty hit with a wonderful outcome. A batter puts himself in easy scoring position when he gets to second base. So a ground rule double is exciting and desirable, yet still shy of a home run from a batter's perspective.

The key characteristic that defines a Ground Rule Double Desire is pain— but not suffering. You didn't hit the homerun you desired, and you're disappointed about that, but you did still get a productive and satisfying hit.

A Ground Rule Double Desire is one you've generally manifested with a reasonable or acceptable level of success. You're not necessary overjoyed with your manifestations of this type of desire but you're not in despair about them either. You manifest a Ground Rule Double Desire in your material reality in a pleasing manner, although not to the point where you don't sometimes wish it were manifesting in a much more grand and complete manner. You probably even occasionally get frustrated by how poorly or incompletely a Ground Rule Double Desire manifests, but not enough to think of this area of your life as an ongoing failure.

A Ground Rule Double Desire is one where you regularly encounter pain. Not debilitating, untenable, or unmanageable pain that stops you in your tracks, but pain stemming from occasional absences of this desire that frustrate and confound you—sometimes causing you to doubt yourself or temporarily lose confidence. You probably enjoy your Ground Rule Double Desires on a regular basis but you often have to work at them. It's not a second-nature type of manifestation for you like a Home Run Desire, and you're used to having to remind yourself how to get back on track with it. Pain, not suffering or agony, is a familiar companion with a Ground Rule Double Desire.

If life were a game of darts, a Ground Rule Double Desire rarely hits the bull's-eye but often lands pretty darn close to it. In other words, you're not missing by much—certainly not enough to get really discouraged and not enough that the possibility doesn't exist of hitting a bull's-eye with each throw. And certainly not missing in a manner that makes you feel like throwing in the towel.

If you're like most people, you have a lot of Ground Rule Double Desires, and by playing "Grow a Greater You," you're going to turn them into Home Run Desires in relatively short order.

Category Three—Strikeout Desires

A strikeout in baseball occurs when a batter fails to make contact with a pitch and returns to the dugout after three strikes, recording an out for the team. A strikeout is the worst type of out for a baseball team, by the way, because there are many productive things a batter can do, despite making an out, as long as he puts the ball in play. Thus, a strikeout is universally despised in baseball, and the term "strikeout" has become synonymous for failing at almost anything.

The key characteristic that defines a Strikeout Desire is suffering or misery. You walk dejectedly back the bench, to great disappointment, and may even begin to dread your next at-bat for fear of it happening again.

A Strikeout Desire is one you pine for but never, or only once in a blue moon, manifest. This is a desire you've wanted to manifest badly for a long time, yet have almost exclusively had to settle for watching other people enjoy. You may occasionally catch a snippet of a Strikeout Desire, but you've mostly spent your time vilifying those who manifest it, denying the magnitude of your desire for it, justifying its absence in your material reality, and otherwise rationalizing its non-existence in your life. There is almost always some degree of anger, resentment, and suffering around this type of desire.

The key symptom of a Strikeout Desire is suffering. These are absent desires from which you don't just feel pain, you have prolonged, sustained, regular, or acute feelings of agony, anger, loss, or worthlessness. Strikeout Desires cause pain that crosses your threshold for "normal" and acceptable levels. This is an area of your life you may even feel ashamed of, try to cover up, or avoid being honest with yourself and others about.

Strikeout Desires may even be hard to identify at first, because you're used to lying to yourself about them. Your habit of pretending you don't want them, or distracting yourself from them, is natural. But you are now free to be honest with yourself about your Strikeout desires because you've got their resolution in your hands.

If life were a game of darts, a Strikeout Desire mostly strikes the wall upon which the dartboard is hung and only sporadically hits the dartboard at all. And you haven't experienced enough success to have much hope, outside of blind luck, for hitting anywhere close to the bull's-eye. It seems so unfair to have to watch other people hit the bull's-eye with seeming ease and without appearing to deserve it any more than you. I'm sure you have at least one or two Strikeout Desires, if you're like most people.

But don't worry. Playing "Grow a Greater You" will elevate your Strikeout Desires into Ground Rule Double Desires and, eventually, Home Run Desires with continued practice.

You're going to place your desires into these three categories so you know what to do with every desire you have, so you can play "Grow a Greater You" most effectively and efficiently. This game teaches you how to align your beliefs with each category of desire so you'll never have any guesswork about what you should do. Don't fret or sweat over which category any of your desires should go into if you're not sure or you don't think about it in the moment.

And now that you know the three categories, you're almost ready to start playing "Grow a Greater You." There are just two more topics, both vital, that we need to cover in the next two chapters first.

Greg Kuhn

Chapter Thirteen

Mother Goose is an Amateur Compared to You

The first concept I'm introducing to you may sound simple, or even strange, if this is your first time hearing it. You are such a prolific and persistent storyteller that even a combination of Aesop, the Brothers Grim, Scheherazade, and Mother Goose couldn't hold a candle to you. You were born to tell stories and you do so almost every moment of every day you're alive.

What do I mean when I say you're a prolific storyteller? I'm referring to the way you assign meaning and value to each and every person, place, thing, and experience in the material world. That's how you discern whether any aspect of your material reality is pleasing or displeasing. Telling yourself stories about every "thing" is how you assemble and make sense of the material reality you are contextually creating every second of your life.

You may say to me, "Duh, Greg, that's no revelation! I have preferences. There are things I like and things I don't like. I enjoy some things and others I don't. There's nothing special about doing that; there is no need to call that 'telling stories' nor make a big deal out of it." While you could be correct to say that, allow me to illustrate the value of thinking of your preferences and judgments as stories you tell yourself. There are many things of immense value to you that you are in the habit of taking for granted, correct? Your virtually automated breathing, your heart beating without you having to consciously manage it, your responsive immune system working 24 hours a day, your ability to be a good friend, the sun rising this morning—the list could go on and on.

But, just because you never take time to think about these experiences as gifts, does that mean you can't do so? Just because you're not in the habit of feeling grateful for incredibly pleasing blessings that you manifest with ease, is there a rule that you shouldn't? There is immense value in making a concerted effort to cultivate gratitude for these kinds of manifestations. Gratitude is powerful, it feels good, and it builds beliefs that reinforce a confident awareness that you are already abundant and blessed in many ways.

And, additionally, the value of building such beliefs, by cultivating gratitude for manifestations you've habitually taken for granted, is an untapped pot of gold that conventional wisdom says you're probably silly to employ. I'll bet some of your friends and family would roll their eyes if you started talking about how joyful you feel about your ability to breathe. But, just as there is no imperative that states that you must feel joyous gratitude for such things, there is also no rule that says you can't.

So given the choice between taking something for granted versus celebrating it, when celebrating it is a genuine and authentic response to its unparalleled value in your life, which choice would you make? You are certainly "allowed" to go on taking it for granted—there will be no Gratitude Police showing up at your door to arrest you and you'll probably go on experiencing those manifestations anyway. But, if you make the choice to follow conventional wisdom and not cultivate gratitude for these often forgotten Home Run Desires, as poker players say, you're leaving money on the table.

As Einstein is reported to have written: "There are two ways to live your life. One is as though nothing is a miracle. The other is as if everything is a miracle." Why would you choose the former? And aren't you glad you have that choice?

Telling stories can be thought of in the same manner. There are two ways of looking at how you give meaning and value to things. One is that your preferences and judgments are merely ordinary and pedestrian methods everyone utilizes that should not be thought of as special or made a big deal out of. The other is that the stories you tell yourself about every "thing" create their meaning and value for you, in your own unique, individual universe and are special and important. Given the choice between those two perspectives, why would you choose the former?

There are two amazing gifts inherent in looking at how you give meaning and value to all things as subjective stories you tell yourself. One is your understanding that you, and you alone, are the author of your stories; you are completely and solely responsible for the entire content of every single story you tell among the thousands you're telling every day. Another is realizing that you have complete, total, and unreserved freedom to tell any story you choose; no one, and nothing, has the power or authority to dictate any story you tell unless you surrender that power.

You may be in the habit of thinking that you're "telling it like it is" when you assign meaning and value to every one of your experiences. But that is not so. You are definitely "telling it" every second of every day, but there is no such thing as "like it is." There is no "like it is" except what you decide "it is" or how other people have told you "it is" if you agreed to go along with their stories. You are actually never really "telling it like it is"; you are always "telling it like *you're choosing to tell it*." How you choose to tell it becomes "how it is" for you. Just know that the "thing" to which you're assigning meaning and value is not "how it is," except for the story you told yourself. Because "it" does not have a pre-existing meaning and value.

This is true because there is no thing in your physical universe with inherent meaning and value, no pre-existing "is" that awaits your discovery in a pre-formed state of "good" or "bad." You are the entity who imbues all the things you experience with the label, meaning, and value of "good" or "bad"; you, and you alone, create the "is" in "tell it like it is." And you create the "is" almost exclusively for you and you alone. The meaning and value in your own unique, individual universe is yours alone, except in how that meaning and value contributes to that "thing's" ongoing communal creation.

What makes something good or bad for you is not the thing, itself, but the story you choose to tell yourself about it: the subjective and personal meaning and value you assign to each thing, event, and circumstance in your life.

Want an example? Let's say you get a new boss at work. She's been on the job for a month as you gather in the break room to eat lunch with a co-worker who shares your new supervisor. Neither of you has had much personal, one-on-one, contact with your new boss. Yet you've both participated in meetings she's led, you've read her reviews of your department, and you've adapted to her new policies and procedures. Suffice it to say that both you and your friend have had the same amount of exposure, in almost the same context, to your new boss.

As you bite into your roast beef sandwich, your co-worker lets out a long sigh. It's obvious something is bothering her, so you oblige her passive request and inquire as to what's the matter. As if she had been waiting for your permission, your co-worker begins to unload a stream of complaints and gripes about your new boss. According to your co-worker, your new boss is controlling, manipulative, ego-driven, and untrustworthy—and you hear a litany of evidence for these qualities.

The surprising thing to you is that you feel just the opposite about your new boss. You find her to be relatively open-minded, collaborative, and inspiring; you are actually glad she is on the scene and have been looking forward to working under her supervision. Because, as far as you're concerned, the changes she's ushering in have been needed for some time.

In this example you and your co-worker have had the same exposure to your new boss and you're both basing your stories off the same information that has come via her memos, department meetings, and new policies. The only qualitative difference between you and your co-worker are the stories you told yourselves about your new boss and the things she's doing. You told stories about your new boss that made her "good," while your co-worker imbued your boss with meaning and value that made her "bad."

So which is the truth? Is your new boss good or is she bad? Are you wrong or is your co-worker? You already know the answer—you are right, your new boss is good, in your own unique, individual universe. Because of the stories you're choosing to tell yourself about your new boss, the meaning and values you're assigning to her, she is "good" in your material reality. And your co-worker is also right, your new boss is bad, in your co-worker's own unique, individual universe. Because of the stories she's choosing to tell herself about your new boss, the meaning and values she's assigning to her, she is "bad" in your co-worker's material reality.

It is correct to say that you and your co-worker probably told different stories about your new boss because you both have had different life experiences and have different criteria for what makes a boss "good" or "bad." Each of you most likely also believes that your assessment is the more accurate one because of your familiarity and comfort level with the criteria you used to form it. You may hear your co-worker's story about your boss and say, "She is wrong about our new boss. She is forming that opinion based on criteria that I do not consider valid. Her beliefs are creating a universe I do not see and do not agree with. And I, in turn, am forming my opinion based on mature, principled criteria that are aligned with a real-world understanding of how to best manage our workplace. My beliefs are forming a universe that is pleasing to me."

The stories we tell about every "thing" are not only subjective, but they can differ from others' because of our reasons for telling them the way we do. There is nothing unusual about this. In fact, it illustrates perfectly how we contextually create a universe that is entirely and uniquely ours to see. Even when we are contextually creating the same thing as another person, this is how two people can see and experience it completely differently in each of their own unique, individual universes.

Let's use another example: food. Let's say I love Limburger cheese and you deplore it. To you, Limburger is stinky and yucky. I, a person who in your universe has horrible taste in food, can't get enough of it, however. Am I wrong? Does Limburger cheese await my discovery every day in a pre-existing condition of "bad," yet I am unable to recognize that? Or does Limburger cheese await your encounters each day in a pre-determined state of "good," with you being unwilling to acknowledge it? Limburger has no inherent meaning or value except that which you decide and bestow upon it via the stories you tell yourself about it. You, alone, make Limburger "good" or "bad."

How about your assessment of a movie? When you watch a movie, you tell yourself a story that defines that movie's meaning and value as "good" or "bad." And, of course, your story is based on your personal criteria for what makes a movie "good," such as humor, plot twists, romance, special effects, dialogue, etc. You and I can watch the same exact movie, sitting next to each other in the theater, and leave assigning a completely different meaning and value to it.

You don't ever have to call my favorite movie "good." And there is no rule that says you must call our new boss "good" either. There is never an imperative for you to change the story you tell yourself just because it doesn't agree with someone else's. But, now that you know your stories are subjective and told only because you choose to tell them, you will always have that option available to you. The manner in which you've been deciding the meaning and value you assign to things is a normal method that every human uses.

Because calling your personal stories "the way it is" is simply a learned behavior, you can now unlearn it. Since there is actually no pre-existing "way it is," and since things have no meaning or value expect those that you choose to assign them through the stories you tell yourself about them, you are no longer trapped in the Neanderthal prison of contextually creating displeasing material experiences as if you're powerless to do otherwise. You can alter your stories anytime you choose or see fit.

And, you will soon see, there are many important reasons for you to choose to alter your stories. Changing the habitual manner in which you've decided to assign meaning and value, as well as changing the meaning and value itself, is immensely important for playing "Grow a Greater You." Don't worry, you will not need to become a robot and tell stories that I choose for you. And you definitely won't always have to tell "good" stories about every "thing"—because you wouldn't want to, and never should, label everything "good." In fact, I will insist that you acknowledge and honor when you really feel "bad" about a thing, even as you're exercising your right to tell a story of your own choosing about it.

Let's continue our movie example to illustrate how you might employ your right to change any of your subjective and personal stories. Suppose you grew up in a home with erudite, highbrow parents who eschewed popular comedic movies as "low brow" and vulgar. During your upbringing, you were taught to believe that the only movies worth watching were deep, intellectual ones like "My Dinner with Andre" or "The Remains of the Day." But while in college, a friend who you greatly admire takes you to see a campus showing of "Dumb and Dumber."

Since "Dumb and Dumber" violates every single one of your personal, learned criteria for calling a movie "good," you definitely label it "bad." You hate it, in fact. When you tell your friend how much you despised "Dumb and Dumber," however, he frowns. Then he thoughtfully explains why ridiculous, goofy movies with no agenda but to make you laugh are actually wonderful. He espouses the delightful pleasure of forgetting about your problems for two hours and being reminded not to take yourself so seriously. In other words, he explains his criteria that makes non-intellectual, "low brow," comedic movies "good"—for him.

Because you think so highly of your friend, you are open to considering his criteria. He is a very happy person, after all, whom you and many others admire. And his criteria for the stories he tells himself about movies seem logical, plausible, and reasonable. For these reasons you are willing to give his stories a try by watching some movies you would have normally called "bad" with a mind open to telling stories similar to his. To your surprise, by telling yourself new stories gleaned from the criteria he shared, you are able to experience a completely different movie when you watch "Dumb and Dumber" for a second time. All of a sudden, simply because you told yourself new stories about "Dumb and Dumber," there is a brand new movie in your universe. Before you know it, you're actually laughing and enjoying "The Nutty Professor," "Animal House," and "Caddyshack" in your new universe, where these movies have become "good."

And, in this new universe, you discover that your admirable friend was correct in how useful and valuable such entertainment is. Did you also notice, harkening back to Chapter Six, that you were a discerning consumer of new ideas and used the appropriate criteria to determine whether your friend's theories were true? You are now experiencing a different material reality. Even when sitting in the living room with your parents and watching the same movie together (you bring home "Bridesmaids" to share with them), you manifest a different movie than they do through the stories you tell yourself about it.

And now you actually feel sorry for your parents. Simply because they choose to keep telling their same old stories about movies, which you now know to be completely subjective and arbitrary, they are cheating themselves out of a small slice of a more enjoyable life. They are missing out on some free opportunities to forget about their worries, the seriousness of life, and lose themselves in the simple pleasures of laughter for a couple of hours. What a high cost simply to retain old stories that they are unwilling to see as changeable.

Those examples are usually easy to digest because we're accustomed to thinking about our unique preferences in regards to movies, food, cell phone plans, politics, clothing, etc., but every single thing, event, or circumstance in your material experience, in your physical reality, follows suit. And just as you can learn to tell a new story about a boss, movie, or food, if you learn information that encourages you or you have a compelling reason to do so, you can learn to tell a new story about anything at all.

Even things that 99.99999% of us would call "good," like a loving act of charity or kindness, or "bad," like genocide, are "good" or "bad" because of the stories we choose to tell ourselves about them. Simply because 99.99999% of us choose to assign them the same meaning or value does not mean that those things have an inherent, pre-existing meaning and value—nor does it dictate the stories we choose to tell ourselves. We tell stories about things that are similar to other people's, not because those things are inherently and independently imbued with those values, but because we respond to them in a manner similar to everyone else.

You don't need to stop telling stories. You don't have to call anything "good" that you don't want to and, likewise, neither will you ever have to call something "bad" that you find you don't want to feel that way about. You only have four goals right now:

1. To embrace the idea that you're telling stories of your choosing, thus assigning meaning and value to every "thing" in the material world. All the time. Every second of the day.

2. To understand that your stories are how you create, for you alone, the meaning and value of every single thing or experience. You contextually create no person, place, thing, or experience that has a pre-existing state of "good" or "bad"; you create the meaning and value of every experience you have through the stories you're choosing to tell yourself about it.

3. To know that your stories are completely subjective because they are based upon criteria that you've been taught or decided to use—criteria that undoubtedly serves you well at times and, as you'll learn, sometimes doesn't serve you well at all.

4. To accept that you can change any story you're choosing to tell yourself. At any time. You will learn that labeling some things "bad" or "good," just because you have been taught to do so and just because everyone else seemingly expects you to, is an unnecessary habit that has been inhibiting your ability to contextually create a more pleasing material reality.

Here's an illustration of how subjective our stories and how unique our criteria for telling them are:

An old farmer had only one horse to help him with all his work, and one day it escaped the corral and ran away. When the neighbors heard this they thought, "What a tragedy; this will destroy our friend!" Yet when the neighbors came to console the farmer over his terrible loss, the farmer said, "What makes you think it is so terrible?"

A month later, the horse came home, with two beautiful wild horses in tow that followed her back from the mountains. This time, the neighbors became very excited at the farmer's good fortune and rushed over to express their joy. "Congratulations!" they proclaimed. "You now have three lovely, strong horses!" To which the farmer said, "What makes you think this is good fortune?"

The following week, while training the wild horses, the farmer's only son was thrown from one of them and broke his leg. All the neighbors were very distressed, as they couldn't imagine how the farmer would make due during his son's convalescence. "Such bad luck! We are so sorry for your misfortune," the neighbors said as they came to mourn with their friend. Yet the farmer said, "What makes you think it is bad?"

Three months later a war came. To the villager's dismay, every able-bodied young man in the community was conscripted and sent into battle, where all ultimately died. The only boy who escaped this fate was the old farmer's son, because, of course, he had broken his leg and was unfit for combat. Because of his accident on the horse, the old farmer's son remained behind and lived.

Would you have blamed anyone for telling the stories the neighbors did at every turn in that tale? Of course not. And, in fact, might the meaning and value the farmer ascribed to those events be seen by some as at least a little strange? Some might be tempted to call him naïve or tell him he had his head in the clouds. Some would expect him to label those experiences "bad" and worry about him for not doing so. Some people might even be angered by the farmer choosing not to call those things "bad." Yet this tale illustrates how incorrect the stories conventional wisdom says we are supposed to tell can be with time and perspective.

We've all had many experiences where something we felt compelled to call "bad" turned out to be a blessing in the long run. You simply may not have considered how useful and valuable intentionally making use of such an experience in the very moment you're contextually creating it can be—rather than waiting for the long-term perspective to develop.

Here are some examples of common life events and stories no one would blame you for telling about them:

1. Having your friend send you flowers is "good," because it means she really cares a lot about you.

2. Getting your credit card bill in the mail is "bad," because paying it will almost completely deplete your checking account.

3. Being told you're getting a big tax refund is "good," because it means you're getting a big infusion of money.

4. Learning that your daughter got caught smoking marijuana at her prom is "bad," because it means that she might be headed down the wrong path.

These are all reasonable stories. No one would blame you for telling them about each experience. And, perhaps, there is no reason to tell stories any different than these.

Yet, what if, like the tale of the old farmer, any of them could be shown to be inaccurate initial stories. What if your friend sent you flowers because she feels so guilty about having an affair with your partner? In that light, you might have called receiving the flowers "bad." What if your large credit card bill inspires you to finally start saving for your purchases in advance instead of buying on impulse? If that is the case, couldn't you just as easily call the invoice "good"? What if the euphoria of your big tax refund causes overspending on some impulse purchases and it's all gone before you got to do what you really wanted with it? You might then call that refund "bad." And what if your daughter's prom trouble facilitates some deep, important discussions that bring the two of you closer and help redefine your relationship? Couldn't you, then, call the prom incident "good"?

One of the most common objections I hear when people first encounter this concept is, "But this is just how it is; this is what anyone (or everyone) else will always call it. This 'thing' is inherently bad (or good) because that's just how it is." I promise you this: No matter how many other people tell the same story you're telling about something and no matter how many people assign something the same meaning and value you do, you are still making a choice to tell that particular story. You are never compelled or forced to tell any story, to define any event, thing, or circumstance with any other value than what you decide.

Another common objection to this concept is a worry that it allows people to call things "good" which we find deplorable. Does this mean that my philandering neighbor can now call her extramarital affairs "good" and feel happy about them? On some level, that could be true. And anyone's fears about this concept's validation of "situational ethics" could be accurate. Yet, if someone truly wants to try using this concept to validate harmful actions, she will only be fooling herself. And, while someone could attempt to do just that, she will only be reinforcing beliefs which cause her, and others, to suffer. Authentically playing "Grow a Greater You" will not allow such abuse of this concept to go on for long without painful and, eventually, untenable consequences.

Whether or not you ever change the stories you tell (spoiler alert: you will and you will love the results), from now on your stories can rightfully be seen as "telling it the way you're choosing to tell it." The stories you tell yourself will always be entirely subjective and entirely your choice. And, as you'll soon discover, embracing this premise will help make playing "Grow a Greater You" the most rewarding thing you will ever do.

Greg Kuhn

Chapter Fourteen

Are Your Beliefs True?

As a human, you need beliefs. You couldn't function without them, in fact. Beliefs are how you form coherence with the quantum field because they unconsciously form your expectations. Since your expectations are the vehicle through which coherence is formed between you and the quantum field, you couldn't contextually create your physical universe without your beliefs. In the creation of your own unique, individual universe, your material world, beliefs are the engine. Your expectations are the spark plug. And your desires are the fuel. Take away any of them and you're no longer going to be able to experience life, as we know it, as a human being.

Let's look at why your changing beliefs is where all the work of playing "Grow a Greater You" occurs. You don't ever have to manufacture desires because you, like every human, will always have them. And you can't manufacture expectations because they arise automatically and unconsciously from your beliefs. But your beliefs are subjective. And since beliefs are changeable, that's where all the treasure is found for a person wishing to form a more pleasing material reality.

Because you were born without beliefs, you soaked them up as a child like a dry sponge in a pail of water. You, like every child, were a belief-creating machine when you were young. Yet, as a child, you had no way to discern whether the beliefs you absorbed and assembled in your subconscious brain limited or served you. You collected them and adopted them not because they were the perfect beliefs for contextually creating your most pleasing life experiences, but because they were given to you by your most trusted sources of influence.

The overwhelming majority of your beliefs, stored in your own personal belief warehouse called your subconscious brain, were not chosen by you. They were given to you, passed on to you both implicitly and explicitly, by people and organizations you trusted. In other words, you have precious few beliefs that you have intentionally adopted.

I know you're tempted to debate that, because as an adult you're now enamored with beliefs like abundance, empowerment, and possibility. But I'll also bet that you haven't truly adopted those beliefs and they remain in status as wouldn't-it-be-nice-to-believe-this thoughts. Because if many of those beliefs you've now come to covet as an adult were truly now your real beliefs, you'd already be manifesting a life of your dreams. Even with a great deal of focus upon them and giving yourself constant positive affirmations inspired by them, you most likely haven't gained access to your subconscious brain in the manner necessary to truly change the beliefs you were given as a child. Because conscious, top-of-mind thoughts won't ever get access to your subconscious brain, where your beliefs are stored.

Your parents were your first contributors to your belief warehouse, passing along to you what they believed—their rules for living and how life works. Your schooling, particularly your early education, was undoubtedly also an important contributor. If you were taken to church or were exposed to religion as a child, that, too, contributed greatly to the beliefs currently stored in your subconscious brain. Additionally, the media you were exposed to as a child, the books, magazines, television, movies, music, or websites you saw, no doubt also added beliefs that are currently in your warehouse.

You assimilated the overt lessons and teachings that your influencers told you and showed you and, perhaps more importantly, you adopted their covert lessons and teachings by watching how your influencers behaved and what they did. Remember the old command "Do as I say, not as I do"? You learned from what your influencers said, but what they did cemented beliefs just as readily into the rulebook you built in your subconscious brain. Actions, indeed, often speak louder than words.

Of course, another reason you absorbed and adopted beliefs so completely during childhood is that you had such unreserved trust in the sources of those beliefs—even when, sometimes, your influencers didn't deserve that trust because they were flawed by normal human frailties like self-interest, self-absorption, or fear. You did not yet have the filters of cynicism and jadedness to "protect" yourself from beliefs that were limiting. And you did not have the maturity to discern whether or not your influencers were teaching you beliefs that served your contextual creation of pleasing things. You viewed your parents, and the other sources of beliefs to which you were exposed, as the end-all, be-all of life knowledge. To a child, such influencers have complete authority to teach them exactly how life works.

It is correct to label a child a belief-building organism. You were a blank slate. You were in need of and eagerly sought out beliefs. And you were under the absolutely unfiltered influence of your parents and other sources of influence who transferred beliefs to you with almost God-like authority. And you learned well.

In most cases, I'm sure the sources of your beliefs did their best to expose you to helpful, beneficial ones. And I'm sure that many of the beliefs you hold as an adult do serve you well. Your parents and the other sources of your childhood beliefs were only human, however, and were flawed and influenced by their own fear and their Neanderthal paradigms.

You should remember that most of our sources of influence lived within the paradigms of a Neanderthal where life happened "to" them and an unknown "giver of gifts" arbitrarily dispensed gifts and punishments in the form of displeasing and pleasing material experiences. Therefore, much of what they taught you was designed to protect you and spare you from the suffering of expecting to have many very pleasing manifestations of your most important desires. "Don't expect too much out of life; you're not usually going to get what you really want and that's just the way it is" is a common refrain explicitly and implicitly passed along to children.

Unfortunately, a lot of those beliefs designed to spare and protect you have wound up limiting and often harming you during your adult life. An example of such a belief is teaching a child that she has to be physically beautiful to earn someone's love and to get ahead in life. Or teaching a child that life is full of disappointment, so the sooner he resigns himself to the fact that he shouldn't really expect to have his desires fulfilled in the manner he hopes, the less suffering he'll have to endure.

I want to call your attention to my use of the word "intentional" because changing a belief is not as simple as you might first assume. Once a belief becomes rooted in your subconscious brain, as happened throughout your childhood, it will not be supplanted simply by learning new information you encounter as an adult—no matter how logical or pleasing that information is to you and how much conscious focus you spend on it.

You may consciously be aware of uplifting, enlightened beliefs such as abundance and say, "Yes, I want to believe in abundance; I do, in fact, believe in abundance." You may also have consciously and actively sought to have that belief as an adult. Yet, unless you have followed an intentional protocol for changing your beliefs, designed to actually allow access to your subconscious brain, your old beliefs are still there. No matter how many positive affirmations you've given yourself, no matter how much wishful thinking you've done, and no matter how much you've consciously focused on more enlightened beliefs, your subconscious brain will only allow you the access to change your beliefs if you do it in exactly the right manner.

But you can change them, because beliefs are completely subjective; beliefs are not independently true. For every belief you hold, whether it limits or serves you, the exact opposite belief would work just as well and could be equally true for you. Any belief, whether positive or negative in nature, will contextually create your material reality for you just as reliably as any other. As you already know, your beliefs do not have to be aligned with your conscious desires to contextually create your material reality. Serving the manifestation of your conscious, adult desires is not a requirement for a belief to be true for you.

Our subconscious brain only understands the language of emotions and consequences. Those two modes of communications form the perfect recipe for a belief. Our subconscious brain does not understand, does not use, and is not influenced by logic or language. Our neomammalian brain is the part of us that understands and utilizes language, logic, abstract reasoning, and all the other functionalities that make us such an advanced species. Yet, as logical as we might like to be, we can never change our actual beliefs through wishful thinking, positive focus, or positive affirmations, because conscious, logical thought has no effect on our subconscious brain. Our subconscious brain does not even understand logical thought and gives no credence to our conscious thoughts and desires.

Our subconscious brain is a primitive adaptation from our ancestors. While it may seem frustratingly stubborn, it actually serves humans incredibly well in terms of our basic survival. This concern for our safety and well-being means that our subconscious brain will not jettison an established belief and replace it with a new one unless we use an intentional, gentle, deliberate, and believable process— a process designed to speak its language of emotions and consequences.

Is it easy to see why most of us have spent our lives feeling like victims of some cruel joke? Thinking of our conscious, logical neomammalian brain as the primary commander of our mental faculties, we have put a great amount of energy into thinking and acting in positive ways designed to manifest our most important desires. That never happened for most of us, of course. And, all the while, we never knew that the true commander of coherence with the quantum field was operating completely cloaked and under our conscious awareness.

Thus, most of us find that in adulthood we have many enlightened thoughts and intentions about ourselves and our desires. We love money, freedom, romance, happiness, and good will. And we consciously think these things are good for us as well as extremely desirable. If you ask most people whether or not they want such things out of life, you will hear a resounding "Yes!" If you also ask most people whether or not they are focusing on positive intentions, outcomes, and thoughts, you will also hear "Yes." Even if you ask most people if they believe in those things, you will hear a great big "Yes!" And those responses will reflect the activity of our neomammalian brain, where logic, abstract reasoning, and language rule the day.

Precious few people stop to consider that their internal rulebook was created long ago, during their childhood, by people and sources who were flawed and scarred by fear and self-serving behavior. Thus, they have never considered that much of the internal rulebook they were given was unintentionally limiting and often keeps their greatest desires at arm's length throughout their lives. Perhaps they've never even considered that they have an internal rulebook at all, or known anything about its absolute authority to command the quantum field.

Most of us harbor beliefs like lack, scarcity, guilt, shame, unworthiness, and victimhood in our subconscious brain. These were the beliefs we were given as children. They were the beliefs transferred to us to explain life within the Neanderthal paradigms our predecessors used to explain their material reality. These beliefs were necessary to rationalize the endless anger, frustration, and suffering those Neanderthal paradigms manifested.

It's not that our subconscious brain doesn't want us to be happy. Our subconscious brain has no problem with us being happy, but only if we're safe while we experience that. And it can only form coherence with what it knows; forming a material reality that pleases us is merely a fortunate coincidence before we start playing "Grow a Greater You." Our subconscious brain has a job to do: store our beliefs and keep us safe via reliability and predictability. It will not allow your beliefs to be changed unless you speak to it in its language, so our logical, adult thoughts and desires will not alter its contents.

Your subconscious brain does not make decisions about what you "should" believe to align them with your conscious desires because it doesn't understand your logical thoughts and wishes. We have tried to talk to it logically our entire adult lives, in fact, and its lack of understanding our conscious desires is not its fault. It is up to us to learn how to communicate with it and properly mold it. If we desire more pleasing reflections from the quantum field, that is our responsibility.

For example, many people hold deeply ingrained beliefs that money is evil or that desiring more of it is immoral. Those beliefs will not be replaced simply because we, as adults, now find we desire money greatly. No amount of wishing or desiring, alone, will make it so; to change a belief you actually must retrain your subconscious brain. Positive affirmations will not change beliefs and retrain your subconscious brain.

What does it mean to retrain your subconscious brain? The answer to that question is found in how you build your beliefs; I use the term "retrain" because your subconscious brain learns to hold a belief like a dog learns to walk on a leash. You can't train a dog, after all, by sitting it down and logically explaining every nuance of how to walk on a leash, can you? Training your dog requires you to communicate with her in a way she will understand, nudging her gently and slowly toward the behavior you desire from her.

And if your dog takes a while to learn how to walk on a leash, you wouldn't expect that another round of logical discourse about your desires for her behavior would have any effect, right? You would simply return to your patient training, utilizing appropriate emotional and physical communication and consequences. It would be incredibly easy to train a dog if she understood logical, sequential instructions shared verbally with her. But she doesn't, so you know you really have no other alternative to training her that way—except deciding that you no longer desire to train her to walk on a leash.

Does that last option sound familiar, by the way? Doesn't it sound like how many of us have handled our most important desires after trying to manifest them through logical, conscious thought and focus? When many of us finally tried to no longer desire the things we couldn't manifest, we allowed our "dog" to go untrained.

Even though it may frustrate you, you don't get angry with your dog for requiring her to be trained in a more subtle and nuanced fashion, eschewing your normal and preferred use of language and logic. Why would you be angry about that, since there is nothing you can do about it? She didn't intentionally choose to require those forms of communications simply to frustrate you.

So why doesn't positive affirmation work to change beliefs, since that technique is a repeated thought? Why can't you simply repeat a positive affirmation often enough for it to become a belief? That would have worked when you were a child and you were actively absorbing beliefs into a relatively empty subconscious brain. But now, as an adult, your subconscious brain is "full." It has the beliefs it needs and will not allow new thoughts to form a new belief in opposition to any current beliefs. And, of course, all your positive affirmations have been in opposition to current beliefs. After all, you wouldn't have needed to give yourself positive affirmations if your beliefs were in line with your desires because you'd already be manifesting the very things you started doing the positive affirmations to influence.

Repetition and trust in the source of the new idea are two of the four keys to building new beliefs. The other parts of the recipe, though, are so vital that, without them, mere repetition and trust in the source are almost meaningless. And these two remaining components are concepts that many personal growth experts fail to teach. You must speak to your subconscious brain in the language it uses and you must lead it toward new beliefs in a gentle and deliberate manner that it will actually follow and allow.

What beliefs, then, would be beneficial for someone with such desires to hold? To name a few, a deliberate creator like you would soar with beliefs such as:

Greg Kuhn

- The material world is ceaselessly abundant.

- My accomplishments take nothing away from anyone else.

- I am an extremely worthwhile person and bring value to others' lives.

- There is no scarcity; lack and limitations are illusions.

- I am lovable, I am beautiful, and I am perfect.

- People are lucky to have me around.

- I am no less special or important than anyone on this planet.

- Health is my natural state.

- Wealth is my birthright and it flows to me freely in many forms.

- Inspiration is effortlessly provided to me.

- Energy, love, goodness, and serenity are given to me ceaselessly.

I'm sure that you recognize those beliefs as ones to aspire toward. I'm also sure that it's not hard to imagine what a wonderful life will accompany such beliefs as they automatically form coherence with the quantum field, through the expectations they naturally and unconsciously create. I'll also bet that, logically, you know it's possible you can have those beliefs.

Many of those beliefs are assuredly ones you know you ought to have even if you're not consciously seeking them. But when it gets down to the nitty-gritty, when the rubber hits the road, are those the beliefs you really hold in your subconscious brain? Are they the beliefs you were taught as a child? Or are they things you'd like to believe but that remain trapped in your logical, language-based, conscious neomammalian brain?

You can answer those questions for yourself right now by looking at the reflection of your true beliefs. You know I'm not asking you to hold a mirror up to your head; simply put down your book and look around you at the material reality you are experiencing. Look at the reflection of your beliefs by looking at your material experiences in your own unique, individual universe. Are your material experiences reflecting all your desires back to you?

I know there are many aspects of your beliefs' reflection that are incredibly pleasing. You have many Home Run Desires that you manifest with ease. Yet how many components of your reflection are displeasing you? This is how you know not necessarily *what* your true beliefs are but whether or not your true beliefs are aligned with your desires.

I am not placing myself in a different category, by the way. I, too, do not hold those beliefs wholeheartedly. How can I say that with assurance? I can unequivocally state that I don't completely and fully believe those things at the level I truly want to, because I am not manifesting all of my desires at the level I truly dream of.

My reflections still displease me on a regular basis. But looking at your reflections provided by the quantum field should not make you discouraged, because being displeased by your beliefs' reflection is something you should expect will continue for the rest of your life. Not only is there nothing wrong with being displeased, but you're actually supposed to feel that way as your cue to keep playing.

When you begin playing "Grow a Greater You," though, the displeasure you feel with your beliefs' reflections may certainly be acutely discouraging. You do not yet have a history of growing your beliefs to resolve your Strikeout Desires and you do not yet have a strong confidence built through years of intentionally manifesting your desires with this game. If you're just beginning to play this game, the displeasure you just experienced when you took time to examine your reflection might feel like another link in an unbreakable chain.

Just because the beliefs you hold right now have been there a long time doesn't mean you can't change them. When I first began playing "Grow a Greater You," I had lots of beliefs that were way out of alignment with my desires. My self-worth, finances, career, and marriage were all examples of reflections of my beliefs that caused me a lot of displeasure. The manifestations of those Strikeout Desires induced misery that I suffered with regularity.

By playing "Grow a Greater You" according to the rules you're now learning, I have systematically and methodically changed all those beliefs. And as my beliefs improved, my manifestations became more and more aligned with my desires. It happened as reliably as the sunrise, and I have no doubt the same will happen for you. You will see and experience a different, unique, individual universe with each gentle uptick of your beliefs because that is how our universe works.

Here are some of the beliefs we have found essential for your new life of being a more powerful contextual creator of a more pleasing material reality. In fact, the following are, in my experience, beliefs that playing "Grow a Greater You" will naturally imbue you with.

1. Mistakes are good.

2. Pain is good.

3. Suffering is optional.

4. No person, place, thing, or event arrives into our life experience with a pre-established meaning or value.

5. Each of our beliefs is true for us alone.

6. We may change our beliefs at any time.

7. Our feelings are information, not who we are.

8. There is no authority, force, or power separate from us who grants or denies our desires, wishes, or requests.

9. We don't attract things to ourselves; we grow into them and become them.

10. We have a consciousness, which makes each of us a creator.

11. Each of us is a creator whether we are aware of it or not and whether we believe it or not.

12. We all, collectively, create and contribute to communal beliefs.

13. We all, collectively, create and contribute to communal manifestations.

14. Each of us experiences our own unique, individual universe, even though we share communal manifestations, because we contextually create our own unique, individual version of every person, place, thing, or event through the stories we tell ourselves about them.

15. By changing our beliefs, and, thus, our manifestations, we not only play "Grow a Greater You," we contribute to changes in communal beliefs and communal manifestations.

You now know that the beliefs you hold, from this point forward, can be ones of your choosing. You are under no obligations to retain beliefs that don't serve you—even if everyone you know holds those beliefs. You are free to be the "crazy person" who believes in abundance, for example. And, additionally, you never have to change any of your beliefs if you don't want to.

Does all this information mean that you can really come to believe things that run counter to foundational aspects of the human experiences? Can you believe, for example, that humans can fly (without assistance) or could live forever? Perhaps you can, yet I can't imagine any circumstances where I could authentically believe fantastic things like that. And, honestly, I have no desire to even try it because I imagine doing so would take complete seclusion from society and a lifetime of meditation.

I am open to believing that I don't have to "grow old" as everyone expects. As I have aged, I have authentically refused to believe that my body gets fat, doesn't work like it used to, and loses virility and vitality. So far, so good and I don't expect that to change. But my participation in our collective beliefs about aging, and the unconscious expectations those produce, may eventually have effects upon my material reality. For example, I've noticed lately that it's more challenging to read small type, but I'm actively attempting to resolve that by aligning my beliefs with my desire to not use reading glasses.

I do go to my doctor for appropriate and regular exams, I do seek medical help for issues I notice, and I do get colds and take care of myself properly when they occur. But I always choose to remain consciously aware that I might contextually manifest illness when I am around doctors and health care professionals. It is their job to find health problems, after all, so if they look and I'm not being vigilant, there is no doubt they'll manifest some problems in their own unique, individual universe. In this manner, I am a much more discerning consumer of health care and am able to exert influence over my material reality regarding my health.

I'll bet you will be motivated to take on some very established collective or personal beliefs that have manifested a material reality for you that is rather displeasing. And I recommend that identifying areas of your material reality that displease you should remain your litmus test for when and where to play "Grow a Greater You."

To that end, you can feel comfortable and confident to simply let your desires, and the information your feelings and your pain give you about them, guide your game of "Grow a Greater You." They won't steer you wrong, and you'll never have to wonder or guess how and where you should grow. Your beliefs can now serve you in the manifestation of your desires and, in fact, your subconscious brain will be very happy to form a more pleasing coherence with the quantum field. As long as you train it properly, it will cooperate with any alignment of your beliefs you seek.

Chapter Fifteen

How to Play "Grow a Greater You" With Things That Are Already Pleasing You

You have areas of your life about which you are happy. No matter how many desires you can currently list that you've yet to manifest, you still have much to celebrate. While I don't know you personally, I am quite certain that you can fill up at least an entire page by listing things you effortlessly and marvelously manifest. Quite a lot of these manifestations, if you are like most people, are things you've been in the habit of taking for granted.

In addition to sharing how to play "Grow a Greater You" with your Ground Rule Double and Home Run Desires, I'm also going to heartily encourage you to stop taking your Home Run Desires for granted. Why should you discount them? Who made the rule that you can't feel great about the things that you're manifesting with ease and power? Who told you that you must focus primarily on the areas of your life where you're not manifesting your desires? Those perspectives are not helpful for an intentional creator; they don't allow you to play "Grow a Greater You" with the power you were born to play it, and they also don't feel good.

Many people treat their Home Run Desires the same way they treated their mother's compliments about how good looking they are. If your mother says you're good looking, it doesn't count, right? After all, you say, it's my mother saying it, and what else is she going to tell me? But why decide that your mother's appraisal doesn't count?

I don't want you to ever discount the things in your material reality that you effortlessly manifest in a supremely pleasing fashion. You are not guaranteed any of them. Who cares if "everyone else" takes them for granted, treating them like a mother's compliments? In fact, I want to help you celebrate all the things you manifest with little to no effort on a daily basis:

- Your marvelous heart, which beats roughly 35 million times a year, pumping about 2,000 gallons of blood through your body every day (about one million barrels of blood in your lifetime), and creating enough pressure to squirt blood at a distance of 30 feet.

- Your amazing eyes, which distinguish up to one million color surfaces and take in more information than the largest telescope known.

- Your awesome brain, which is more complex than the most powerful computer and has over 100 billion nerve cells. Your subconscious brain, in fact, remembers every single thing that happens to you in your entire life, and the only reason you do not have easy access to each memory is merely a byproduct of our recall process.

- Your incredible hearing, which is so sensitive it distinguishes between hundreds of thousands of different sounds.

- Your astonishing nose, which remembers 50,000 different scents and even smells while you sleep.

- The fact that you never have to expend any conscious effort to coordinate any of your body's remarkable characteristics; you never have to command your body to perform any of the countless functions it does so beautifully.

And this list of incredible things you manifest each day with ease and aplomb, which fulfill your desires so perfectly, doesn't even include things like:

- What a great listener your friends consider you to be.

- How loyal you are to the company for which you work and how willing you are to go the extra mile, even when you're not specifically being paid for the extra effort.

- You are your nieces and nephews coolest, most favorite aunt because you're so willing to have fun and play with them.

- The way you've always adopted your pets from the animal shelter.

- How you always pick out something special for your kids' school lunches when you're at the grocery.

- The fact that no one ever wonders whether you'll keep your word when you make a promise.

- Your habit of committing random acts of kindness, especially to other drivers.

- How willing you are to give people the benefit of the doubt, choosing to believe the best about them at every opportunity.

Let's face it, although you may be in the habit of taking them for granted, there is a huge list of Homerun Desires you truly knock out of the park each and every day. You are truly an amazing creature. The physical experience you are having, this wonderful adventure the energy of you is experiencing called "living on Earth as a human being," is imbued with so many fantastic things you're already creating, allowing, and experiencing with abundance and joy.

You have so many Home Run Desires already present in your life. None of them are promised to you, each of them is a miracle, and they are all reflections of wonderful, uplifting beliefs that serve you mightily.

So how do you play "Grow a Greater You" with these, your Home Run Desires? What you'll do with your Home Run Desires is the same thing you'll do with you Ground Rule Double Desires. Your Home Run Desires will upgrade spectacularly, creating even more pleasing fountains of pleasure. And your Ground Rule Double Desires will also be raised and strengthened, eventually growing into Home Run Desires with practice and patience.

What you do with your Home Run Desires and Ground Rule Double Desires is this: always tell yourself the best-feeling, believable story you can muster about every person, place, thing, and experience you have. Additionally, always use the best-feeling, believable words you can muster to tell your stories. There are no exceptions to this set of instructions. And, in fact, you will also follow them as you play "Grow a Greater You" with your Strikeout Desires. These instructions simply won't be the only thing you do to play this game with your Strikeout Desires.

Here you begin to take full advantage of your new understanding that your stories are subjective, that you create the meaning and value of everything you experience via the stories you tell yourself, and that nothing is inherently "good" or "bad" independent of your stories. This technique of reforming your storytelling will apply universally. In other words, these instructions are the bedrock foundation upon which all else you do for personal growth and intentional self-fulfillment are built. What you are about to learn to do is the very core of playing "Grow a Greater You"; it is the very "ball" in "baseball."

Always telling the best-feeling, believable stories you can muster is an absolutely ideal way to take greater control of how you are contextually creating your own unique, individual universe. It is the perfect method for contextually creating, manifesting, and allowing things and experiences that are much more closely aligned with your desires and even more pleasing than you may have initially envisioned. And this foundational tool for playing "Grow a Greater You" and intentionally creating a more pleasing life is a blast to use because of how amazingly effective it is.

Before you roll your eyes at the simplicity of this instruction, let's take a moment to examine each component of it by breaking it up into five parts. It is supremely important to thoroughly understand each portion. So you can employ this technique in a manner in which your subconscious brain will allow your stories influential access to the beliefs stored there.

Part one of the instructions we'll examine is the term "story." You've already read a chapter about how you tell yourself stories about every "thing" and how those stories assign meaning and value. It's important to reiterate, though, just how subjective the value and meaning you assign is. Even though it can sound crazy, I want to remind you that nothing arrives into your own unique, individual universe with a pre-established meaning and value. You are only one assigning meaning and value to anything.

You are truly the author of each "thing's" meaning and value, which means you really are the author of your life. It makes no difference whether or not every other person on this planet agrees or disagrees with any of your stories; you are still the only person responsible for any story you choose to tell. And you always have a choice about the stories you decide to tell.

Consider the following. I was recently driving in downtown Louisville with a good friend whom I've helped start a non-profit organization that transitions ex-convicts back into society. At a stoplight, we both noticed a man leaning against a building with a handmade sign asking for money. We saw two pedestrians stop and give him some cash. "That's really cool," I commented. "It's nice to see people taking notice and lending a hand." For me, the event we had both just contextually created was definitely "good," which was an easy and natural story for me to tell myself.

"Hold on a minute," my friend countered in a corrective tone. "The Coalition for the Homeless discourages giving money to people on the streets. That's actually not cool." He pulled the Coalition for the Homeless' local director's business card from his pocket and, sure enough, right on the back was printed: "Please do not give money to people asking for it on the street. Doing so reinforces learned helplessness; there are many free sources of food, shelter, education, and other assistance available to them."

For my friend, that event we both contextually created was "bad." It was easy and natural for him to tell that story based upon his beliefs that were different from mine. For him, a "good" event would have been someone giving that man directions to the Salvation Army.

My friend and I each communally created the same event and experienced it in our own unique, individual universes. And we each told two divergent stories about it that created two completely unique things, with divergent meaning and value, in our own unique, individual universes. Although completely different, each story told by the two of us was correct and appropriate. For ourselves.

Should one of us change his story? No one ever has to change her story. The main importance behind this part of your instruction is reminding you that you are merely choosing a story to tell yourself rather than "telling it like it is." Your stories are subjective and only true for you, even if everyone else would agree with them.

The next part of your instructions for playing "Grow a Greater You" with your Ground Rule Double and Home Run Desires we'll examine is the term "best-feeling." You are instructed to tell the best-feeling story possible. Let's emphatically highlight something you are _not_ instructed to do—tell a good-feeling story. This is very important.

Always telling a good-feeling story does not work—for the same reasons positive affirmations and positive thoughts do not work long-term to manifest your desires (especially the big ones). Because telling a good-feeling story all the time is too positive, it doesn't acknowledge how you really feel, and your subconscious will not allow such stories to influence or change your beliefs. Besides, there are lots of things that aren't "good" to you. Not everything your beliefs reflect back to you is pleasing, and you know why they're not supposed to be.

Of course, there will be lots of occasions when your best-feeling story will authentically be a great-feeling one, because there are desires you easily manifest in a pleasing manner or have had lots of success with, even if only intermittently. For these reflections, it's entirely natural that your best-feeling story really is a wonderful one. Just make sure you're only telling good-feeling or great-feeling stories when they are real, authentic, and natural.

How do you ensure you only tell good-feeling stories when they are real, natural, and authentic? Simply experiment and pay attention to the results. If you've been in the habit of always trying to tell yourself good-feeling stories all the time, like I did back when I was a positive-affirmation junkie, you'll undoubtedly try to tell some good-feeling stories when a less-than-good story is the authentic and appropriate one. When that happens, don't make a big deal out of it and don't beat yourself up. Just gently remind yourself about this instruction and re-tell your story to reflect your real, authentic feelings.

What, exactly, is a "best-feeling" story? I'll give you a real example regarding my ever-growing desires for financial abundance. I have grown financial abundance into a Home Run Desire, yet playing "Grow a Greater You" continues to bless me with even greater desires to grow into. My wife and I were recently discussing our plans to purchase a home in Charleston, SC, debating the merits of purchasing in the historic district versus one on the adjacent beaches.

During the discussion, I noticed some negative feelings coming up. I quickly surmised that my fear and worry was information alerting me that my current beliefs were not aligned with these desires. My beliefs that we would never be financially abundant enough to purchase our new home made me want to tell a bad-feeling story that might dampen my desires or personalize my feelings. I chose, instead, to tell myself the best-feeling story possible about my desires for a home in Charleston.

I told myself, "Although we don't currently have the money sitting in an account, waiting to be spent on this really cool, fun new adventure we're going to take, I don't need to try to figure out how all the necessary resources will come about to make this happen. While they're not pleasing in this moment, reservation and fear is a natural feedback loop from my currently out-of-alignment beliefs regarding our desires for a new level of financial abundance that will facilitate our Charleston home, so I'm not going to chastise myself or beat myself up for having them. However, I'm also not going to let this emotional feedback take control of who I am today. I have enough experience with growing my beliefs to match my desires to know with certainty that it's okay if I have no current idea how it will all come about. I know that if I continue to tell myself the best-feeling, believable story possible about this desire, the people, opportunities, and resources will appear effortlessly as my beliefs come into alignment with it. That will all occur when it's supposed to. For now I'm simply going to choose to trust that aligning my beliefs is all I need to do here, be okay with the quantum field's timeframe for connecting these dots, and acknowledge my current emotional feedback."

That story was not "good feeling"; it did not exclude any of my negative feelings or the doubt and fear they illustrated for me. Yet that story certainly felt better than telling myself "We'll never have that much money. I don't see how this can happen, and it probably never will. Why don't we have enough money to do this? Why haven't I experienced more financial abundance after all this time playing 'Grow a Greater You'? What's wrong with me?" At the same time my story was not a Pollyanna, too-good-to-be-true one like, "I'm going to ignore how I feel. I don't really have any doubts. I am Mr. Confident and actually know the money is so close to already being there, it's basically just around the corner."

But if I had found myself telling a bad-feeling story or a good-feeling one instead of merely a better-feeling one, all I needed to do was gently remind myself of the "Grow a Greater You" instructions for my stories. Yes, I do catch myself violating this instruction from time to time, and I'm sure you will too on occasion.

"Better-feeling" means you do not need to choose good-feeling stories for any your experiences, because not all of them will produce good feelings. Unless, of course, a good-feeling story is the natural and authentic one, stemming from your confidence in contextually creating pleasing manifestations. And it also means you should not choose bad-feeling stories for any of your experiences, because nothing is actually inherently bad. You can still acknowledge how you really feel about any "thing" without having to make your story a bad-feeling one.

The third portion of your instructions for playing "Grow a Greater You" with your Ground Rule Double and Home Run Desires will help you stay away from those two extremes of good-feeling and bad-feeling stories I just described. Making sure your best-feeling stories are "believable" is your key to avoiding both too-good-to-be-true and also bad-feeling stories.

The instruction to make your stories believable safeguards you from getting sucked into the easy appeal of being a positive-affirmation junkie. Your subconscious brain, after all, will not believe too-good-to-be-true stories; therefore, it will not allow you access to influence or change your beliefs so you can supersize your Home Run Desires and grow your Ground Rule Double Desires into Home Runs.

Conversely the instruction to make your better-feeling stories believable also helps prevent you from veering back into your old habit of telling bad-feeling ones. Follow the tips to keep your better-feeling stories believable and you'll find the side benefit is that you are much more effective at not going into the "this sucks" mode you may have in the past.

Making your better-feeling stories believable simply means you must acknowledge how you really feel about the thing you're assigning value to. Your feelings, remember, are a vitally important feedback loop, giving you information about the alignment between your beliefs and desires and alerting you about where you need to grow your beliefs. Your feelings are not "who you are," but honoring them in your stories keeps them where they need to be as an indispensable part of your "Grow a Greater You" toolbox. And acknowledging your true feelings also helps you retain your connection with them. The more you can recognize your feelings and honor them instead of responding with fear-based denial, the more influence you'll be exerting on all your beliefs and upon your growth while playing "Grow a Greater You."

How do you follow the important instruction to keep your better-feeling stories believable? Simply make sure your stories include a special suffix and prefix that honors how you really feel about the reflection you're experiencing. You'll find that your stories will be believable while still being the best-feeling ones possible. After all, making your stories believable doesn't mean making them bad feeling any more than it means you should make them good feeling.

Start your better-feeling story with some version of the following prefix: "Although I feel (insert your true feelings here) about (your desire)..." and end your story with the following suffix: "...even though, right now, I feel (insert your true feelings here) about (your desire)..." In between that prefix and suffix, tell the best-feeling story you can muster. And include additional references to your true feelings while not making them the primary component of your story.

For example, having a fulfilling, intimate relationship with my soul mate is a Home Run Desire of mine. Yet a couple weeks ago my wife and I had a big disagreement that caused each of us pain and displeasure. My painful feelings were important information alerting me that my beliefs were not currently aligned with my desires for a greater level of intimacy and vulnerability with my wife.

The better-feeling, believable story I told myself was, "Although I feel frustrated and angry with my wife right now, I'm pretty sure these feelings are simply a matter of fear and Neanderthal paradigms rising to the surface. I'm not going to deny how I am really feeling right now and, at the same time, I have enough experience with growing my beliefs to understand that I am simply being given an opportunity to grow my level of intimacy with her and release more of my guardedness in our relationship. I know, absolutely, that she is not responsible for my happiness or peace of mind, just as she is not responsible for it when I am unhappy. I am seeing a displeasing reflection of my own beliefs. Thus, while I am not glad it is happening, I do not have to blame her or hold her responsible for the displeasing universe I'm experiencing. I'm going to continue to tell myself the best-feeling, believable stories I can muster while I stay open to new perspectives about our relationship that will help me grow. Even though I currently don't see these new perspectives, I know they are there and I know I will see them as I raise my beliefs into alignment with my desires."

That story is definitely better feeling than, "I can't believe that she's so mean. Why is she choosing to make me unhappy? As usual, I can't stop from being reactive and defensive when these things come up. Why do I always want to keep people I love at arm's length?" The story I actually told myself was much better feeling than that. Yet, while it felt much better, the better-feeling story I actually told was also believable because

I acknowledged how I really felt and didn't sugarcoat or sublimate my true, negative feelings.

Because I included the suggested prefix and suffix in my better-feeling story, my subconscious brain heard it, felt it, and embraced it, which is exactly what needs to happen to utilize the symbiotic relationship between your stories and your beliefs. While telling yourself the best-feeling, believable stories alone will not be enough to transform your Strikeout Desires (you'll learn what else to do with those shortly), it is almost always enough to raise your Ground Rule and Home Run Desires, because it not only brings your beliefs back to alignment, it also nudges your beliefs upward into greater alignment.

Next let's focus on the fourth portion of your instruction: the use of the word "always," as in "always tell the best-feeling, believable story possible." Always is a very strong adverb. A directive to do something, without fail, every single time, might seem a tad intimidating. And, yes, I do mean every single time when I say "always."

But I want you to know that "always" is your goal. I have no doubt you'll reach that goal eventually because I mostly have, but I'm also not going to be surprised in the least if it takes you some time and practice to do so. "Always" is where you want to be, yet I know it's most likely not where you'll begin.

You've been telling the same old stories, based on "telling it like it is," your entire adult life, irrespective of whether or not those stories have felt good, whether or not they were aligned with your desires, and whether or not they improved the quality of your contextual creations in your own unique, individual universe. I'll bet you're like me in this respect: For most of your life the meaning and value you assigned to a good portion of your manifestations was hurtful, painful, and didn't serve you at all. And you had little encouragement from conventional wisdom to do otherwise.

In fact, for most people, the litmus tests used 99% of the time for what type of story they should tell themselves is "Is this the story I'm supposed to tell?" or "Is it the one everyone else would tell?" But starting today, you're no longer allowed to conform to the imaginary rules many people act as if they must follow. Your new litmus test for deciding what story to tell yourself about any "thing" is: "Does this story serve me by allowing my beliefs to be as aligned as possible with my desires?"

It will take time for this practice to become habitual and second nature.

In fact, using the prefix and suffix I recommend may feel stiff, awkward, and artificial at first. That's because it will be artificial at first; you will need to intentionally use it and it will be awkward until it becomes a habit. The idea of stopping yourself and intentionally choosing to craft a better-feeling, believable story about something, rather than just automatically telling the same old negative stories or too-good-to-be-true stories you've always told, will undoubtedly feel unnatural for a while. But, trust me, it will become easier and more habitual over the course of time.

It took me about a year before I was making almost every single one of my stories better feeling and believable without having to consciously think about it anymore. You will continue to tell yourself stories about everything. The only choice you have about that is whether you tell stories that serve you or you tell the same old limiting stories you always have.

Here's another important thing about the "always" portion: You are under strict orders not to beat yourself up when you catch yourself telling your old bad-feeling or too-good-to-be-true stories. You will absolutely catch yourself telling a negative or "that's just the way it is" story. And the same thing holds true for catching yourself telling a pie-in-the-sky, unbelievably positive story. Be gentle with yourself when that happens. Don't berate yourself for your mistake; it's nothing more than repeating ingrained, habitual behavior you haven't completely unlearned yet. Gently laugh with yourself. Say, "Oh yeah...I don't have to do that anymore."

Here are some examples of telling the best-feeling, believable story you can about some common displeasing experiences:

You just had a nasty fender bender.

Tell yourself: "Although I'm not happy about this, I can choose to withhold judgment about this event and just let it play out like it's supposed to."

As opposed to: "I really don't care about this at all because everything happens just like it's supposed to." Or "I can't believe this; my life sucks!"

You missed your flight.

Tell yourself: "This makes me stressed and I am not glad this happened, but I can also choose to believe that I can get where I'm going without derailing my trip."

As opposed to: "Awesome! I'll bet that flight was out of peanuts anyway." Or "Oh great! I knew I shouldn't have stopped at Starbucks. As usual, I'm such an idiot!"

A good friend hasn't returned your phone call.

Tell yourself: "Her non-response worries me, but I can decide to form no judgments about it, especially in regards to making it about me somehow. I'll reach out to her again tomorrow if I don't hear anything today."

As opposed to: "What's wrong with me? What did I do this time to drive a wedge between me and her?" Or "I love it when someone I care about doesn't call me back. It doesn't mean anything to me and I'm actually glad to have more free time today since I'm not tied up on the phone."

Lastly, let's discuss part five of your instructions for playing "Grow a Greater You" with your Ground Rule Double and Home Run Desires: "every person, place, thing, or event." For the sake of our discussion now, we'll use a term you're already familiar with to represent those things: a time-space event. A time-space event, you'll remember, is a portion of the quantum field that has collapsed, temporarily abandoning its state of potential and becoming a physical object in the material world.

A time-space event occurs when the quantum field forms coherence with your beliefs, via your true expectations. You, along with all the other consciousness-possessing time-space events are responsible for the ongoing collapse of the quantum field and continual, communal, contextual creation of the material world. And speaking for all of us, I'm glad you're here to help us all contextually create a much more pleasing universe.

A time-space event in your own unique, individual universe is always, literally, a reflection of your beliefs. Thus, when you choose to tell a bad-feeling story, when you choose to label a part of your life experience as "wrong" or "bad," you are actually labeling yourself "bad." Of course we are all going to do this from time to time, even after playing "Grow a Greater You" like an all-star. But the fact that we're all human and will naturally feel compelled to call things "bad" at times still doesn't negate the fact that it doesn't serve you to call your belief's reflections "bad."

As you learn to tell better-feeling, believable stories about the time-space events you experience, you're actually learning to tell better-feeling, believable stories about yourself. If you actively remember that you're really telling better-feeling, believable stories about yourself, you'll find it even easier to tell better-feeling, believable stories about the time-space events you experience. This is precisely why I have referenced the symbiotic relationship between your stories and your beliefs; this shows us how your stories not only reveal your beliefs to you but influence your beliefs as well.

Yes, your reactive stories are also useful, helpful information and feedback about your beliefs.

You manifest your life experiences by being them and you manifest new, more desirable ones by becoming those new, more desirable things. Once your energy, or your beliefs, is coherent with your desires for any "thing", you experience that "thing" because you <u>are</u> that "thing." The "people, places, things, and events" in your life experience are all you, as embodied by your beliefs, being reflected back to you.

Now, having covered those five components of your instructions for playing "Grow a Greater You" with your Ground Rule Double and Home Run Desires, let's look at them as a whole. And this section will also explain in greater detail how to use this instruction to tell yourself better-feeling, believable stories about your Strikeout Desires.

I will certainly allow that some events and circumstances present more difficult challenges to tell a better-feeling, believable story about, but that fact does not negate this idea. There is no rule that says you must tell any type of story about any event or circumstance. But have you ever noticed that people who frame things in a negative light, who tell "bad" stories regularly and who are pessimists, are often fondly referred to as people who aren't afraid to "tell it like it is"? I'm certainly not saying that someone isn't allowed to tell herself any story she wishes about anything she experiences, but I am telling you with 100% certainty that telling a pessimistic story is not "telling it like it is."

Not using this tool at all times is like choosing to not use your windshield wipers while you're driving in the rain. You've got them, they work properly, it causes no harm to use them, they allow you to see through your windshield when it rains, and you can actually drive much more safely if you use them. Who in their right mind would choose not to turn them on in the rain? You'd be nuts not to. And the same thing applies to telling the best-feeling, believable stories.

Telling the best-feeling, believable stories reinforces, grows, and strengthens any beliefs that are well aligned with your Home Run Desires. It also slowly but surely nudges into an ever-growing state of greater alignment any beliefs that are partially aligned with your Ground Rule Double Desires. And it bolsters, augments, and fortifies the process for raising beliefs that are way out of alignment with your Strikeout Desires. You'll learn to do this more completely with your Strikeout Desires in the next chapter, so don't concern yourself with that now.

In the past, when experiencing displeasing reflections from the quantum field, you've felt compelled to tell either bad-feeling stories or good-feeling stories about it. Those stories were either reinforcing your limiting beliefs or having no effect at all on raising them. Once a belief is established, your subconscious brain will not deviate from that belief, let alone change it, without being communicated with properly. Any hint of untruthfulness or unreliability will cause your subconscious brain to batten down its hatches and go into lockdown. Like a wild rabbit sensing movement around its perimeter, your subconscious brain is incredibly skittish about new information.

That's the problem with positive affirmations or positive thought. In most instances, and certainly in every instance with a Strikeout Desire, positive affirmations are simply too positive. Your subconscious brain's response to positive affirmations is to see right through them and identify them as not being aligned with your real beliefs. It will allow the positive affirmation to make you feel good in the moment, but it will not allow the affirmation access to your belief storehouse.

This is precisely why the law of attraction usually fails to allow for the manifestation of the "big stuff," the most important desires people have. Your subconscious brain is simply too vigilant and too good at what it does to fall for any positive affirmations. It sees them as too good to be true and, thus, potentially dangerous for you because it doesn't jibe with your true beliefs. To affect the kind of change needed to reinforce your Home Run Desires, nudge your Ground Rule Double Desires, and augment the intentional belief-raising you are doing with your Strikeout Desires, you need to be crafty, careful, and a little stealthy when communicating with your subconscious brain.

That is also precisely why these instructions are **not** titled "Telling Good-Feeling Stories About Everything." It is very important that your stories are believable; otherwise, you will be, at best, taking two steps back for every three steps forward. Never pretend that you feel differently than you do, especially when those feelings are ones of doubt, fear, worry, anger, distrust, shame, skepticism, discouragement, confusion or any other that are usually unwanted and don't feel good. Acknowledge and validate your previous failings, the rut you're in, or how improbable the manifestation of your desire feels in that moment.

Eventually you will be able to tell fairly positive stories about almost all your circumstances, but you should never concern yourself with making all your stories "good" ones. Including the aforementioned prefix and suffix in your stories gives your subconscious brain the requisite spoonful of sugar necessary for it to take the medicine. You're telling your subconscious brain that you're simply expecting reasonable growth and change from your efforts at improving the stories you choose to tell. And you are openly declaring your desires for greater alignment in a believable manner and helping your subconscious brain accept and embrace the greater you into which you're growing.

What you will find, with your continued practice, is that using the prefix and suffix combinations as prescribed will open you up to seeing new possibilities. You will notice a new freedom to tell yourself stories more aligned with your desires. You will find yourself authentically telling better-feeling, believable stories about your Strikeout Desires such as "Perhaps this is happening just like it's supposed to, although I may lack the perspective to understand why right now"; "Maybe this experience is just what I need, although it might not seem to be from my current perspective"; or "Although this is not what I desired, I can believe that this outcome is an improvement over my previous experiences, and I can believe that further improvements are possible if I keep playing 'Grow a Greater You.'"

With your Strikeout Desires, even your most miserable ones, you can always choose to tell the best-feeling, believable stories by simply choosing not to go full-out negative and beat yourself up. Even if the best-feeling, believable story you can tell is "This really sucks. I wish I weren't experiencing this and I don't currently see any way that this can be anything other than 'bad.' I do not feel inspired to tell myself a story other than 'I hate this and this is bad.' Yet, even from my current perspective, I can also acknowledge that I probably lack the metaview to see how this could be used by the quantum field to connect the dots for

Greg Kuhn

me in miraculous and unexpected ways as it's done before."

And, of course, when dealing with Home Run and Ground Rule Double Desires, you will often find that your prefix and suffix combination is infused with genuinely felt positive energy. Even when you need a nudge with your Ground Rule Double Desires, you'll probably find that your current feelings are often not off-the-charts negative or wholly undesirable. Staying vigilant and making sure you're telling stories of your choosing with your Home Run and Ground Rule Double Desires is an immediately rewarding exercise.

As you know, though, even with your Home Run and Ground Rule Double Desires, you will continually experience contrast, or pain, which tells you, "Time to nudge your beliefs back into alignment" or "Time to grow your beliefs to match your desires again." Now you'll know what to do when that happens with your Home Run and Ground Rule Double Desires. You might get caught off guard initially, surprised that an area of your life that is normally pretty effortlessly successful is throwing you a curve ball. Yet all you need is to utilize the prefix/suffix combination you just learned and start moving your beliefs back into alignment.

In fact, let's demonstrate how that can be done by using the tale of the man, his son, and the horses from earlier in this book. Except this time I'll use the prefix and suffix I taught you with the two "bad" twists this tale takes to illustrate how you can use them.

An old farmer had only one horse, and one day it ran away. When the neighbors came to console the farmer over his terrible loss, the farmer said, "Although I currently believe this might be terrible, I also believe that, with practiced effort, I can learn to tell better stories about my horse running away, over the course of time. And if I consciously choose to tell better stories about my horse running away, I believe that, over time, my beliefs will change about it and, thus, so will my material reality and experiences concerning it. "

A month later, the horse came home, bringing with her two beautiful wild horses. The neighbors became excited at the farmer's good fortune. "Congratulations!" they proclaimed. "Such lovely, strong horses!" The farmer said, "What makes you think this is good fortune?"

While training the wild horses, the farmer's son was thrown from one of them and broke his leg. All the neighbors were very distressed. "Such bad luck! We are so sorry for your misfortune," the neighbors wailed. The farmer said, "Although I currently believe this might be bad, I also believe that, with practiced effort, I can learn to tell better stories about my son breaking his leg, over the course of time. And if I consciously choose to tell better stories about my son breaking his leg, I believe that, over time, my beliefs will change about it and, thus, so will my material reality and experiences concerning it. "

A war came. Every able-bodied young man in the community was conscripted and sent into battle, where they ultimately died. Only the old farmer's son, because he had a broken leg, remained behind and lived.

I suggest that you make it your private "job" to frame all of your displeasing experiences this way. It'll be one of the most rewarding jobs you've ever performed.

Now let's address how to use better-feeling, believable words in the stories you choose to tell. I want you to follow the same guidelines for the words you use to tell your better-feeling, believable stories as the ones for telling the stories themselves. A large component of crafting better-feeling, believable stories you're telling should be your use of better-feeling words. Anytime you're using ugly words like "stupid," "failure," or "I can't," stop and gently rephrase your statements using uplifting, or at least neutral, word choices. Additionally, if you use words in your stories that are too-good-to-be-true, like "phenomenal," "unstoppable," or "I am the greatest," stop and gently lower the volume back to believability.

Don't berate yourself, either, when you catch yourself using ugly or too-positive words. You've been using these words for a long time, and getting out of this habit is a process just like telling new stories. Instead of saying, "I can't buy this because, as usual, I'm a failure with money," say, "I am choosing to not spend money on this right now." Instead of saying, "Why am I so unworthy of being loved?" say, "I haven't had a lot of previous success with relationships, but I'm open to raising my beliefs about it." Your words, after all, carry a lot of emotional weight. Choose them wisely and they will help your stories improve.

Keeping your better-feeling words believable is done the same way you keep your stories believable. Choose positive, uplifting words without going too far overboard into a vernacular your subconscious brain won't believe. There may be times when it's better to use "satisfactory" rather than "stupendous," for example. Let common sense and your feelings guide you here; you'll have a sense for what's too over-the-top.

The words you use to tell your stories are powerful and deliver a substantial measure of the meaning and value of your stories. And remember how vital it is to use your feelings properly as the feedback loop they were intended? Experiencing what you might call "failure" (or any other ugly word) is merely information like everything else; failure does not define you as a human being and is not what or who you are.

Let's do an ugliness experiment. Say the following aloud:

1. "I <u>am</u> a failure."

2. "I <u>have not yet experienced</u> the success I desire."

Can you recognize the difference between "I am a failure" and "I have not yet experienced the success I desire"? I've underlined the words that make those two statements as different as night and day.

The first statement says that "failure" is who you are; the second statement says that you are experiencing information that, while displeasing, is merely alerting you to a misalignment between your beliefs and desires. Using better-feeling, believable words will help ensure that your stories are enhancing your game of "Grow a Greater You."

Human history is replete with many examples of people who told stories of their choosing in almost unimaginable circumstances rather than succumb to conventional wisdom or "tell it like it is." The most noteworthy examples, however, should not make us feel that they are somehow more special than us or that we cannot follow their path—even while dealing with much less trying situations.

Louis Zamperini is one example who has come into the public eye through Laura Hillenbrand's wonderful novel *Unbroken*. Zamperini's B-52 was shot down over the Pacific Ocean during World War II. He and two fellow crew members survived the crash and climbed aboard a small survival raft. Despite having no food or water, Zamperini and another man survived for a record 47 days.

Zamperini vividly describes his choice to not accept the logical outcome of his predicament. Who among us can say with certainty that he would have the audacity to refuse to die if he were in Zamperini's circumstances: adrift under the brutal Pacific sun with no water or food for almost 50 days, when the United States Air Force had no idea where his plane had crashed? How difficult would it be not to resign ourselves to "the way it is" under those circumstances?

One of Zamperini's fellow surviving crew members joined him in his commitment to specifically carve out time each day to engage themselves in stories of their choosing that transcended "the way it is." For example, each day they took turns giving vivid, specific accounts of their life after the war—what jobs they would have, what their homes would look like, what hobbies they would have, and what their family life would be like. Part and parcel to this commitment was their decision to speak about such things in the present tense, as if they were all happening right now. Additionally, the two took turns each day pantomiming the preparation of sumptuous meals on their raft; they recited a menu, discussed the ingredients in minute detail, explained and pantomimed the preparation of their feast, and then pretended to eat it together.

Zamperini's third crew member, however, refused to join in. This fellow thought the other two were crazy and was adamant that their imminent death was "the way it is" and, thus, to suggest that their fate was not sealed was asinine. This third crew member removed himself emotionally and physically from their intentional better-feeling stories and became completely withdrawn. This fellow, of course, died, and Zamperini attributes the man's death to his adherence to "telling it like it is."

My favorite example of someone thriving under inhumane circumstances is Viktor Frankl. Dr. Frankl, a Jewish citizen of Germany, was a psychiatrist imprisoned by the Nazis during the 1940s. During his years in the Theresienstadt, Dachau, and Turkheim Nazi Concentration Camps, Dr. Frankl personally witnessed the death of his wife, parents, and many others at the hands of his captors.

What would the Neanderthal paradigms tell to expect regarding the perspectives of someone in Dr. Frankl's predicament? Who would blame anyone for "telling it like it is" under those unimaginable circumstances? Who would criticize Dr. Frankl for believing that the giver of gifts was a cruel tyrant who allowed undeserving innocents to suffer abject, unjustified, and unwarranted misery?

You already know that neither Dr. Frankl nor any of his fellow prisoners were to blame for their horrific experiences. But what other conclusion could someone laboring within Neanderthal paradigms come to in those circumstances except that they must be undeserving or unworthy of justice? Or that they were victims that life happened "to," compelled to imbue themselves and their experiences with horrifyingly painful meaning and value?

Who among us, our spouse and parents murdered in front of our eyes by the very people who continued to imprison us, could confidently claim that she could tell better-feeling, believable stories of her choosing—ones that aligned her with her desires rather than reinforce "the way it is" and multiply her suffering?

Dr. Frankl did what many would consider unbelievable. He chose to tell stories that served him rather than increase his suffering. Even amid the horrors, Dr. Frankl realized that he was the sole architect of the meaning and value he assigned to his life experiences and, as long as he exercised his choice to tell better-feeling, believable stories, he actually remained a free man in the truest sense. Dr. Frankl came to believe that his captors were the ones imprisoned—by their adherence to "the way it is."

As crazy as it might sound, Dr. Frankl actually began to pity his Nazi captors. This became his new universe. It became the material reality he experienced. No one but he could have done this for Dr. Frankl. He alone was responsible for the meaning and value of his circumstances. What an amazing example Dr. Frankl provides us that no one and nothing can ever force us to tell stories that don't serve us. As Eleanor Roosevelt said, "No one can hurt me without my permission."

It is not important, by the way, to try to recall all the bad-feeling or unbelievable stories you've told yourself and now "fix" them by going back and retelling those stories. All you need to do is stay aware and listen to the stories you're currently telling, amending them immediately the moment you recognize that the stories are not better-feeling, believable ones. Your old stories of "the way things are" will still sound like the truth for a while. Creating your new habit of telling better-feeling, believable stories is done by changing them in the present moment, not by focusing on rectifying previous ones.

With practice, your Ground Rule Double beliefs will grow more aligned with your desires. They will grow into Home Run Desires with time. You'll know when your Ground Rule Double Desires have grown into Home Run Desires when manifesting them becomes as effortless as your heart pumping blood for you. Not that you won't experience dips, potholes, and speed bumps. Those things will happen, but you'll know the solution is found not in fixing your "outside" material reality but in getting your beliefs back into alignment with your desires.

The same will happen with your Strikeout Desires. In the next chapter you will learn how to raise them from Strikeout Desires to Ground Rule Double ones. And, once they permanently become Ground Rule Double Desires, you'll turn those, too, into Home Run ones. Eventually, playing "Grow a Greater You" will continue to raise all your beliefs and, thus, your expectations, into alignment at the Home Run level.

And the magical nature of coherence, the manner in which your material reality is formed, ensures that you don't even need to concern yourself with how the manifestation of your desires will be accomplished. You can trust that not only will you have all the motivation and inspiration you'll need just when you need it, but so too will new, unexpected opportunities arise to ensure your success. You will experience a unique, individual universe with possibilities and opportunities that you literally couldn't see from the perspective of your previous beliefs. That is the magic of playing "Grow a Greater You"; you will continue to see a different universe for as long as you play.

Before we end this chapter, I want to share something with you about the phrase "see a different universe." This phrase is meant to be taken literally. But seeing a different universe doesn't mean that pigs will fly, leaves will be purple, and cats will start to act like they truly want you around. You will see physical, tangible changes to your material reality, such as a fit body, financial abundance, a loving soul mate, a satisfying career, a beautiful home. But your new universe is not limited merely to manifesting things you desire. Your new universe will also reveal possibilities and opportunities that always existed but that you were not able to see from the perspective of your lower, limiting beliefs.

A friend told me about a woman who moved from an island where there were no indigenous red-haired people. This woman lived in America for two months without "seeing" red hair on people until she had a discussion with a friend that involved red hair. After learning that some people had red hair, this recent arrival to America suddenly began to see red-haired people who had, of course, been there all along. She saw a different universe when her beliefs changed.

Seeing a different universe will often mean that you are experiencing the very same things you did before but now you see them differently. Remembering how your beliefs create your material reality, you will often experience a thing or event that is identical, in construct, with your previous experiences of it, but it will now be completely different to you in your more aligned, unique, individual universe. Your new beliefs have allowed you to contextually create that "thing" with an entirely new meaning and value for you.

This is exactly why successful people talk about seeing possibilities and potential where others see roadblocks and insurmountable obstacles. That is not simply a feel-good platitude, a worthwhile philosophy, or a beneficial frame of mind that a successful person chooses to share. That successful person literally sees possibilities and potential where many see roadblocks and obstacles because she lives in a universe where they are manifest, reflecting her true beliefs. She contextually creates that universe and it is a real, tangible thing for her.

For example, when someone cuts you off in traffic, you might have previously seen a jerk. There is no imperative not to call such a person a jerk. But when you have grown your beliefs to align with your desires, you may very well see and experience a different person in that situation. You may authentically say, "That person must feel like she has to get where she's going in a huge hurry. I feel sorry for her, since such actions almost always mean she's feeling stressed." Because that is the how your beliefs will authentically reflect that "driver" back to you.

As you play "Grow a Greater You" with your physical body, when you look in the mirror from the perspective of your new, more aligned beliefs, you will see a unique and beautiful person. Your universe will be different and you will see a different reflection, provided by your new beliefs about your body.

When you play "Grow a Greater You" with money, you will see a different paycheck. Even if the amount does not change, your new paycheck will be a reflection of your newly aligned beliefs about money. You will see a paycheck that authentically inspires you to say, "Thank you for this contribution to my financial health. I'm grateful that my services are so valued that someone pays me for them." Because that will be the new reflection of your paycheck as you contextually create it with your aligned beliefs about money.

When you play "Grow a Greater You" with your self-worth, you will see possibilities you were previously blind too. Your new universe, reflecting your raised beliefs back to you, will be brimming with exciting potential that was always there but couldn't be seen from the perspective of your more limiting beliefs. Upon awakening, you may be inspired to say, "Wow, a new day! I wonder what amazing adventures await me today."

That creative energy will be who you are and the universe you inhabit will inspire it. It will not be something you have to search for nor contrive.

When you play "Grow a Greater You" with your romantic relationship, you will see a new partner in your new universe. Your partner will still be the same person, physically, as the one in your old universe, which reflected your old beliefs back to you. But when your beliefs are aligned with your desires, you will see a new reflection when you look at your partner. You'll naturally tell yourself, "I am grateful to have a partner in whom I can invest my life. I'm going to treat him just as I'd like him to treat me today." You will naturally bestow the important people in your life with the qualities you desire most in them, because, as you create your individual version of them, that version will reflect your new beliefs back to you.

You will, literally, see these things and many others in your material reality and you won't have to force yourself to craft those types of stories. You won't experience nearly as much displeasure from reflections of beliefs like lack and scarcity because you will now truly see opportunities where once you saw absence and obstacles. You will also, of course, manifest many of your specific, long-held dreams and goals. Not only will you have the inspiration and the opportunities to achieve them, you will also have become these things. You will be the living embodiment of many of your most important desires as you discover that playing "Grow a Greater You" does, indeed, grow you into alignment with them.

Greg Kuhn

Chapter Sixteen

How to Play
"Grow a Greater You"
With Things Causing You Misery

You have areas of your life where you are not happy: things that are very important to you, things that you have long considered an important component of your fulfillment, things that have never manifested anywhere close to your desires. You have suffered off and on for a great portion of your adult life because of these unfulfilled desires.

Your Strikeout Desires are characterized by suffering, and they often make you very angry and sad. Yes, you feel the pain of sadness and longing for them, but you are also resentful about their absence. After all, you are a hardworking, kind, loving, nurturing, and good-hearted person who merely wants to be happy and fulfilled. What is so wrong with your getting to experience the manifestation of some of your most heartfelt longings? Not that you'd take them away or begrudge them, but why does everyone else get to experience these pleasures and not you—especially when it so often seems that you probably deserve them just as much.

You don't always suffer the absence of these most important desires. Unfortunately, however, the ups you experience, the times when you don't suffer as much, do not come from the true fulfillment of these desires. Those times of less suffering are more often related to distracting yourself from your desires, actively denying them, or somehow justifying their absence. You have often justified or rationalized the absence of that important desire—telling yourself some version of "I'm okay without that"; "People who achieve that are shallow or morally suspect"; "Having that thing I desire must be for other people but not for me"; or "I must not be worthy of having that." But, while those techniques provide you some temporary relief, they do not last and, eventually, your desires will catch up with you and the misery of their absence returns.

Strikeout Desires can seem very cruel. Why would God, or whatever name you give to the source of our universe, imbue you with the ability to desire things so strongly that you cannot have? Strikeout Desires can feel like a set-up or a twisted practical joke—like a book-loving, far-sighted man being stuck in a library without his glasses or a woman trapped in a fallout shelter stocked with canned goods without a can opener. Those Twilight Zone plots are so scary precisely because they mirror our own personal frustrations with our Strikeout Desires so well.

Yet you have had periods of high hopes for your Strikeout Desires. One of them may have been when you first encountered positive affirmations or positive thinking. Another may have been when you learned about the law of attraction. Both of these self-empowerment genres offer the promise of your dreams being realized, yet that didn't really happen. I'm not knocking self-help literature, but I know that most books and guides about positive affirmations and the law of attraction haven't helped you manifest some of your most important dreams. And now you know why: Until your beliefs are raised into alignment with those Strikeout Desires, no amount of positive thought will truly penetrate the guardian walls of your subconscious brain.

So, despite you best efforts, your kind heart, your earnest desires, your most noble intentions, and your good works, here you sit, still longing for that fulfilling career. Or your soul mate. Or financial abundance. Or a nice home. Or a healthy, fit body. Or any other of the myriad "big stuff" you desire so strongly. You already know that you desire those specific things for a reason. You also know that it is okay for you to desire anything and everything you do. And you don't need to be reminded that your happiness and fulfillment as a human being is, and will continue to be, compromised by your inability to fulfill your desires.

These Strikeout Desires you hold will never disappear, no matter how hard you try to forget about them, tell yourself you don't need them, or pretend that it's okay not to have them. They will never abate, in fact, until you do one thing: manifest them. And, while you won't be done growing, you will love how wonderful it feels to finally and completely manifest these big, important Strikeout Desires by playing "Grow a Greater You."

I imagine you can surmise how to play "Grow a Greater You" with your Strikeout Desires by connecting the dots.

- Dot one: Your expectations are forming coherence with the quantum field to contextually create your own unique, individual universe.

- Dot two: Your expectations are unconsciously created by your beliefs; hence, you are not consciously choosing your expectations.

- Dot three: Your beliefs are stored in your subconscious brain; hence, you are not consciously aware of them most of the time.

Those three dots probably lead you to an inescapable conclusion—and a wonderful conclusion at that. If you feel miserable on a regular and sustained basis by some aspect of your life experience, you must go to the source of that displeasure for the solution. You must change your beliefs if you wish to end your suffering.

The fantasies we have created for the fulfillment of our desires usually involve someone or some outside authority "giving" them to us. Yes, it would be nice if there really were a "man in the sky" or a genie in a bottle who wriggled his nose and, presto, we had those things we desired so greatly. It can be disillusioning to learn that there actually is no giver of gifts. That is an illusion, like many others, that we have cultivated from Neanderthal paradigms and it is sometimes a cherished one. How else can we explain that the term "disillusioned" has a negative connotation in our culture?

If you are ready to stop suffering, if you are sick and tired of being sick and tired, the good news is that changing your beliefs is not rocket science. It merely takes patience, practice, and persistence. But I'm quite sure you can muster those things knowing that the reward will be immense. Besides, time will pass either way; you can spend it trying the same old methods that will never work or you can have a little patience and persistence with raising your beliefs into alignment.

The easiest way to explain how to change your beliefs, how to transform your Strikeout Desires into Ground Rule Double ones (and, eventually, into Home Runs), is to start by telling you what it doesn't involve. It is not done merely through telling the best-feeling, believable stories you can muster about all your life experiences and it is not done through positive affirmations. Those are wonderful, useful tools that have many beneficial and appropriate uses. Even if those things won't change your beliefs in a way that will align them with your Strikeout Desires, they almost always make you feel better in the moment, and that, in and of itself, is valuable.

All a good-feeling story or a positive affirmation will do is make you feel good in the moment, which is precisely why positive affirmations can feel like they're working. They are working, just not at changing your beliefs about your Strikeout Desires. Now that you understand that you must change your beliefs to address your Strikeout Desires, you should relegate positive affirmations to what they are designed to do: make you feel good in the moment or get you back on track if you experience a hiccup or pothole with a Home Run or Ground Rule Double Desire.

Using good-feeling stories and positive affirmations on a Strikeout Desire is like continually rotating new buckets under a leaking faucet to collect the dripping water. That technique will never resolve the problem. Likewise, you can apply positive affirmations to your suffering like a salve and there is not necessarily anything wrong with doing that. But that is not how you play "Grow a Greater You" with your Strikeout Desires; it's a temporary solution that briefly alleviates the undesirable symptoms without fixing the cause of them.

Now that you know what not to do with your Strikeout Desires, you'll undoubtedly be pleased to know that what you do with them is actually very simple. The technique you're about to learn is incredibly powerful and will, almost without fail, transform your Strikeout Desires into Ground Rule Double ones. In fact, I hear from therapists, counselors, and life coaches regularly that they are using this technique with their patients and clients because of how effective it is.

As long as you follow the technique, be persistent, and have patience, you will not fail. Because you will be following a formula 100% guaranteed to allow you full access to your subconscious brain's belief warehouse. And with that unfettered access you will transform your beliefs so that they become aligned with your conscious and most important desires.

I recommend that you keep it simple by "simply" following the directions and leaving it at that. In other words, don't overthink this and don't complicate it by trying to unravel all the unknowns before using it on your

Strikeout Desires. I think you'll agree that sometimes "figuring it all out" beforehand is not only unnecessary, it's often impossible. Trying to get all the possible issues figured out before starting something is usually just a cleverly disguised form of procrastination.

Think of it this way: If you were teaching someone to jog, you'd probably give her a set of basic but important instructions.

1. Choose a route that will allow you to jog your desired distance.

2. Stretch your legs.

3. Lift your knees and look straight ahead as you run.

4. Keep a steady pace that matches your speed goals.

5. Walk to cool down after your jog and then stretch.

If you've ever jogged you know that those instructions are pretty much all your friend needs, right? But what if your friend responds by asking, "But what if it rains...what if there's a dog...what if there's construction...what if I get tired...what if...?" You would understand those questions and your friend's nervous curiosity, but you'd also know that if your friend simply goes out there and follows your instructions, she'll figure almost all of that out for herself experientially. And I heartily encourage you to approach working this process on your Strikeout Desires from the same mindset.

The way you play "Grow a Greater You" with your Strikeout Desires is you follow a protocol to gradually, purposefully, and intentionally raise your beliefs to align with your Strikeout Desires. Doing this is not rocket science; you'll find the protocol intuitive and straightforward. As you reach the end of this formal protocol, your Strikeout Desires will have become at least Ground Rule Double Desires—at which point you will treat them as such according to the rules of "Grow a Greater You." And your Strikeout Desires will eventually morph into Home Run Desires by practicing the tools of "Grow a Greater You."

I hope I've convinced you of the importance of aligning your beliefs with your desires. By now you're probably wondering how to go into your internal "rulebook," find beliefs that are keeping your Strikeout Desires from manifesting, and change them. It's actually a lot simpler than that. Best of all, your life experiences will become more pleasing, in small ways at first, almost immediately. You may even be pleasantly surprised with how quickly some of your Strikeout Desires begin to show characteristics of Ground Rule Double Desires.

To play "Grow a Greater You" with your Strikeout Desires, you'll need the Emotional Reference Chart that follows shortly. This chart allows you to work the protocol and will guide you as you improve your beliefs as thoroughly as necessary to manifest your longest held, most important desires. The terms I selected to label emotions on this chart are not necessarily important and do not need to be "written in stone" for you. Don't necessarily go looking for substitutes for the terms I've selected, but feel free to use other terms and other labels for the emotions if that helps your journey.

One additional and important rule is to work this process on only one Strikeout Desire at a time. You want your entire, undiluted and uncut focus on the Strikeout Desire you choose. Besides, you'll almost always find that you address other issues along the way. Like a rising tide lifting every boat, you'll experience improvements in your beliefs about ancillary issues when you work this process on your one chosen Strikeout Desire.

You'll get to all your Strikeout Desires eventually—the only limit would come from you. But what desire should you choose to work this process on first? Because you can use this process repeatedly, you needn't place any pressure on yourself when choosing. I recommend you start with your most painful, most pressing Strikeout Desire.

You may benefit from having a copy of this chart at your fingertips. If so, please feel free to visit the Resources page on my website to find a copy you can print for yourself. The chart will guide you up a range of emotional perspectives, so you have concrete direction as you build the new beliefs that will, eventually, turn all your desires into Home Run ones. You'll notice that it is written in ascending order, with the most negative emotions on the bottom. The emotions on the chart become gradually more positive and more empowering. The improvement of the emotional perspectives on this chart is purposefully gradual so that your subconscious brain will easily accept the new perspectives you adopt. The new perspectives won't seem unbelievable because they won't be too dramatic of an improvement or uptick over the previous perspective.

The idea of an Emotional Reference Chart, by the way, is inspired by the writings of Jerry and Esther Hicks. I first encountered such a guide in their wonderful book, *Ask and It is Given: Learning to Manifest Your Desires*, and they are responsible for inspiring me to create the following chart. If you haven't read the Hicks' work, I recommend you do.

The Emotional Reference Chart

1. Love/Ecstasy
2. Joy/Elation
3. Ease/Power
4. Confidence/Inspiration
5. Excitement/Passion
6. Anticipation/Eagerness
7. Enthusiasm/Ambition
8. Hopefulness/Optimism
9. Interest/Inquisitiveness
10. Acceptance/Peace
11. Introspection/Contemplation
12. Pensiveness/Melancholy
13. Indifference/Apathy
14. Unease/Discontent
15. Frustration/Aggravation
16. Worry/Nervousness
17. Doubt/Pessimism
18. Anger/Blame
19. Anxiety/Fear
20. Grief/Desolation
21. Despair/Worthlessness
22. Powerlessness/Dejection
23. Depression/Hopelessness

Now you are ready to begin playing "Grow a Greater You" with your Strikeout Desires. The process you're about to learn is not complicated, yet I caution you to adhere to the instructions exactly as written. Bear in mind that you will be changing beliefs that are as familiar to you as your favorite pair of blue jeans—and just as easy to slip into. Even though the beliefs you will be leaving behind are undoubtedly painful, do not underestimate how important predictability is to your subconscious brain.

We all share a compulsion from our subconscious brain to stick with what we've previously experienced, because that is the "safest" option. How often have you heard someone worry about whether something new might end up being even worse that what it's replacing? And we've certainly all experienced that it often takes a considerable amount of pain before we'll change.

In fact, neurologists will tell you that you are primarily creating what you are familiar with. Your conscious, neomammalian brain processes around 40 bits of information per second, while your subconscious brain processes about 40 *million* bits of information per second. In fact, estimates are that your subconscious brain is responsible for anywhere from 90% to 95% of all your information processing. Your subconscious brain truly is running the show.

You are only "seeing," or experiencing, a fraction of the information available to you at any time. Your subconscious brain is sifting through an almost infinite array of information and energy coursing toward and through you every second, using your beliefs to assemble a material reality for you. Your subconscious brain wants to create familiar, reliable, and predictable things. Thus, by playing "Grow a Greater You," seeing a different universe is actually a simple physical process.

Doing something new, even with the promise of freedom behind it, is unfamiliar and unknown; hence, your subconscious brain will not jump on board and happily spur you forward until it is helped to do so by following this intentional and gradual protocol. Knowing this, it is important to not only follow the instructions for how to raise your emotions connected to your Strikeout Desires, but also to stick to the timeframe you're provided.

You'll be "tricking" your subconscious brain into holding the new beliefs. But like you've tricked your children into eating broccoli or going to bed on time, it's a process that your subconscious brain will eventually thank you for. Your subconscious brain will enjoy the new beliefs as much as you and, like an adult who was forced to take piano lessons as a child often does, will look back from the perspective of new beliefs aligned with Home Run Desires, and say, "At the time, I didn't really want to do that, but I am so glad you subtly tricked me."

Another thing before you begin. You'll find me using the terms "beliefs," "emotional perspectives," and "feelings" interchangeably. In almost every instance in this protocol for growing your beliefs into alignment, those words mean pretty much the same thing. Since your subconscious brain speaks the language of feelings, deliberately and believably creating authentic new feelings about something creates new beliefs.

Here is the process. Please don't be fooled by how simple it might sound to you at first.

1. Using the Emotional Reference Chart, identify how you currently feel about your Strikeout Desire.

2. Select the next highest emotion up the chart and write about your absent desire from that perspective.

3. Live your way into that next highest emotion over the course of one to three days (or longer if you feel it necessary).

4. Select the next highest emotion up the chart from the one you just wrote about/lived your way into and write about it/live your way into it in the same manner you did with the previous one.

5. Never moving more than one emotion up at a time and never more than one emotion up per day, repeat steps 2 through 4 until you have moved yourself all the way up to the top of the Emotional Reference Chart.

Step One: Identify How You Currently Feel About Your Chosen Absent Desire

You begin this process by choosing one of your Strikeout Desires. Remember, you should only work on one Strikeout Desire at a time. Doing this with more than one Strikeout Desire at a time dilutes the effectiveness of the protocol and will not give you the results you seek. Remember that almost all emotional pain is the result of the distance between your beliefs and your desires. The greater the distance, the greater the pain. Thus, your Strikeout Desires are ones that cause you misery and suffering.

The first desire I ever used this process to raise my beliefs on was "being in debt" (or "having more money"), so I'll use that (former) Strikeout Desire to illustrate these steps for you. Of course, you should follow the same steps I'm outlining here for any Strikeout Desire you choose, such as self-worth, having a soul mate, career, weight, health, parenting, relationships, etc.

Simply take out a piece of paper and a pen (I like to use a journal since that keeps a record of all my writing in one place) and write about your true feelings regarding the absence of the desire you have chosen to raise your beliefs on. Let yourself freely write anything that wants to come out. Nothing is out-of-bounds or off-limits; however, stick to how you really currently feel about it—not how you *want* to feel about it or how you think you *ought* to feel about it.

It is very important to avoid anything that smacks of "ought to" feelings, intentionally positive thoughts, or ways that you've justified this desire's absence in your life. You really want to let it all hang out right now; open up your closet and shine a floodlight in there. If you've never done writing like this before, it might feel rather uncomfortable and you might catch yourself wondering if you're "allowed" to think about and write the things you're putting on paper.

Give yourself an honest assessment regarding how you truly feel about your absent desire. In my example, I first asked myself, "What are my real, gut-level feelings about debt?" Not, "Where would I like them to be?" but "What are they, really?" Another effective way to get at your real feelings is to state your desire aloud, as if you possess it in the full abundance you dream of, and pay close attention to the feelings you experience in response. I said, "I have more than enough money, I have no money worries, I am wealthy by anyone's standards, and I have no debt." Paying attention to my visceral and negative emotional reaction to such a statement, I felt sick upon hearing that—as well as sad, angry, depressed, resentful, and ashamed.

Why did I feel that way? Because those statements were unflinchingly accurate descriptions of my conscious, top-of-mind desires concerning debt and money. Thus, stating them in a positive way forced me to envision and imagine their tangible manifestation. Yet, rather than focus on the positive nature of my imagination, I made sure to pay attention to how I really felt about **not** having them in my life.

You want to be reflective and soul searching; your first responses to these questions may not be as honest as you can be, so keep digging. After all, you're not used to truly being honest about a Strikeout Desire because, of course, it's painful to do so. And, up until now, what reason did you ever have to be completely honest with yourself about such painful things anyway?

The feelings you will be journaling here are not going to be positive and they will not feel good either. Get past your wishful thinking. It takes courage to write honestly here, because these feelings are no fun to deal with, let alone even contemplate. You've undoubtedly been conditioned to worry about "negative feelings," since a lot of people teach that you must feel positive about something to manifest it. But remember: If your real feelings—and, thus, your actual beliefs—about your absent desire truly were positive, you'd already be manifesting it.

Besides, how could you really feel positive about it when your desire has been absent in your material experiences despite how badly you want that desire?

You need to write and write and write until you feel like you've emptied your gut of all the negative, scary, bad-feeling stuff in there. In my example of money and debt, I wrote things like:

"I hate that I never have enough money."

"Money is scarce and there's never enough."

"I'll never be able to pay off my debt."

"I never get ahead. When I do catch a break and get more money (an income tax refund, for example), it always disappears quickly and I never get to use it like I really want to."

"People who have lots of money are greedy."

"Money is the root of all evil."

"It's shallow and wrong to want more money than I need."

"Financial abundance is something that happens for other people, lucky people, but not for me."

"I deserve my debt."

"People do bad things to get more money than they need."

"I am a loser and a failure."

You'll know you're "done" when you feel an emptiness. That won't

Greg Kuhn

necessarily be unpleasant by the way. You'll feel something akin to a wrung-out sponge, on an emotional level. You'll get better at intuitively knowing when you're "done" with such writing the more practice you have. Playing "Grow a Greater You" will continue to give you lots of practice, so don't fret or obsess over doing this perfectly or exactly correct. You can't do it wrong unless you don't do it at all, and you'll get even better at being in touch with such self-reflection over the course of time.

Don't think of this as a homework assignment. You're not simply going through the motions and you're receiving no grade for this. The universe will not hand your writing back to you with red pen marks all over it like your English teacher did.

Here's something important that might help you have the courage to write honestly about a Strikeout Desire. I promise you will never write anything, no matter how negative or unpleasant it is, that you're not already dealing with every day, at least on an unconscious level. In other words, writing about these bad feelings doesn't "make them real" or bring them to life. They are already real. The only thing you're doing right now is openly and honestly admitting them and looking at them through your writing. It's only scary because you're undoubtedly not in the habit of honestly looking them squarely in the face every day.

You will never create a "boogeyman" during this process. You will only ever write about feelings that have always been there. You aren't creating, or solidifying, your beliefs by writing about your true feelings; you are merely acknowledging what's already there. Nothing is created or unleashed while playing "Grow a Greater You" that wasn't already present and hasn't been forming coherence with the quantum field for a long time. The feelings and beliefs you're showing the light of day have been creating a material reality of displeasing reflections.

Let's get honest here. When it comes to your most difficult-to-manifest, deeply-yearned-for-yet-absent Strikeout Desires, it's always been much more comfortable to ignore them, distract yourself from them, or pretend you're okay without them. The metaphor of putting a smiley face sticker over an empty gas gauge on your car's dashboard instead of stopping to fill the gas tank is an apt one. The empty gas gauge is your Strikeout Desire, which is just as painful to look at honestly as it is to experience. And the smiley face sticker is your natural human tendency to tell yourself that you don't really want your Strikeout Desire—to

160

rationalize or deny the pain of its absence.

Of course, you would never do this with your actual car in real life because you're sane. You know that, while you'd have a few moments of blissful ignorance, you'd eventually run out of gas and be stranded. And, since I'm quite sure you've slapped a few smiley face stickers over your feelings about the Strikeout Desire you're playing "Grow a Greater You" with, it's going to feel natural to encounter inertia. In fact, don't be surprised if television suddenly seems too interesting to pass up, you find it difficult not to watch a string of YouTube videos about cute talking pets, or you are suddenly filled with motivation to clean your house—all to avoid the writing.

I encourage you to officially declare, "No more smiley face stickers on my Strikeout Desire." In my example, I certainly didn't have any good feelings about money and debt. I hated that I didn't have the amount of money I desired. It sucked to want more money and not have it. And I was scared out of my mind about my debt. I was also very used to distracting myself from feeling like such a loser and a failure; I didn't enjoy confronting those feelings head on. But, as I promised, nothing came out in my writing that I wasn't familiar with—no matter how hard I had previously worked at not feeling it. Nothing ever has while playing "Grow a Greater You."

After you finish the emotional "vomit" of your real, honest, painful, current feelings about your Strikeout Desire, look on the Emotional Reference Chart and identify where you currently are. In my case I saw that my writing aligned me most closely with Powerlessness/Dejection because I was consumed with the belief that I was never going to have the amount of money I really wanted despite all my deep desires and hard work to attain it. I was dejected because all my previous efforts had been fruitless, I was a failure, and I felt like I must not deserve more money—no matter how much I wanted it.

By this time, it should come as no surprise that I was very low on the Emotional Reference Chart regarding "debt and money." After all, if I were high up the chart, my beliefs would be unconsciously producing expectations that would naturally and effortlessly create coherence with the quantum field in the form of financial abundance. All things manifest in accordance with your beliefs via the coherence formed between them and the quantum field. And since you are addressing a Strikeout Desire, you're obviously going to find yourself low on the emotional chart just as

I did.

At this point, at the bottom of your page, write the name of the next highest emotion from the one at which you identified yourself. I wrote "Next Time—Despair/Worthlessness" at the bottom because "Despair/Worthlessness" is the next highest emotion on the Emotional Reference Chart from the initial emotion I identified with.

Step Two: Select the Next Highest Emotion Up the Chart and Write About Your Absent Desire from that Perspective

When you're ready to begin moving up the chart (if you're motivated, the very next day), get out your journal and write about your Strikeout Desire from the perspective of the next highest emotion on the reference chart (the emotion you wrote, the day before, after "Next Time"). Look up the dictionary definition of that emotion because that helps clarify the emotion you'll be writing about.

Once you know the definition of that next highest emotion, sit down and write about your Strikeout Desire from the perspective of that emotion. The way you move into a new emotional perspective of your desire is to write in freeform how that desire will look/feel/sound/taste/smell/etc. from that new, slightly improved emotional perspective. Write in the present tense; instead of writing about how it *would* feel, write about how it *does* feel. While you write, once again give yourself permission to really feel that new emotion regarding your Strikeout Desire. Contemplate your Strikeout Desire from the perspective of this new emotion. Mentally roll around in this new emotion, set up camp in it, and write about it until you've, once again, emptied yourself out.

In my example, I learned that "Despair" meant "to lose all hope or confidence" and "Worthlessness" means "useless and contemptible."

So my next writing contained new thoughts and feelings like:

"I have no hope that I'll ever have more money."

"It's hopeless for me to think that I'll ever achieve my desires for being out of debt. Just look at my track record."

"My confidence level is near zero regarding my ability to have the money that I really desire."

"I have no confidence in the universe. I've been denied my desire for more money my entire life."

"I feel useless because I'm always one step behind, always in debt, and can't provide myself or my family with the life I want because I never have the money I want and need."

"It's useless to try. I'm obviously not worthy of the money I truly desire."

"People experiencing financial abundance are contemptible because it's not fair that they get to have something I want so badly but can never attain."

"I feel contempt for the universe because I work and try hard and desire money greatly but never have what I want."

Notice that I took great care to write about financial abundance, in the present tense, from this new emotional perspective—and that perspective is not radically improved from the previous one. Remember: You will take small steps to build new beliefs because your subconscious brain will not believe or accept anything except small, positive increments in your beliefs.

Pretend you're an actor and the script calls for your character to have the next highest emotional perspective when she's contemplating and contextually creating her Strikeout Desire. What will that feel like? What will that be like and what will it look like? Your character needs motivation to play her role, so write about that and give yourself the perspective from which to play the part.

When you've written everything you can, when your emotional sponge is wrung out and your gut feels empty, write the name of the next highest emotion on the reference chart at the bottom of the writing you just completed. I wrote "Next Time—Grief/Desolation" at the bottom because "Grief/Desolation" was the next highest emotion on the Emotional Reference Chart from the emotion I just wrote about.

Remember, these new perspectives won't feel incredibly more positive than the previous ones, and that is intentional. Yet each emotion is, indeed, a bit more positive, and you'll see that small improvement reflected in your writing—even though the uptick of positivity is usually very minor. This minor uptick will hold true each time you move one tick up the emotional perspective chart, yet you will probably also be surprised at the positive things you can find in what seem to be completely negative emotional perspectives.

Again, don't fret about doing this. By invoking a minor improvement of emotional perspective you are actually creating and bringing to life a new slightly higher belief. This slightly higher belief is a bit more positive and, thus, a little more aligned with your desire than your previous perspective. You didn't just create a monster; you're not Dr. Frankenstein. You actually created a new universe that, while not anywhere close to being aligned with your conscious dreams regarding this Strikeout Desire, is a little bit more aligned than your previous one.

Step Three: Live Your Way into that Next Highest Emotion Over the Course of One to Three Days (or Longer if You Feel it Necessary)

Next, make it your job to see your Strikeout Desire from the perspective of the emotion you just wrote about. Let the new emotional perspective be your filter through which you see the universe, through which you create your material reality regarding your Strikeout Desire. Think about your Strikeout Desire from that perspective, meditate about it, and let it ruminate in your mind. Throughout your normal daily affairs, roll around in the perspective of that new emotional perspective like a dog in newly mown grass. Embrace that new emotional perspective, pain and all, with full-on honesty regarding your Strikeout Desire. No justification. No rationalization. No wishful thinking.

Remember that actor analogy I just used? You're still an actor here, and the play calls for you to experience your Strikeout Desire from the perspective of a character who has those new feelings about it. What would your character do? How would she feel? How would she see the universe from that perspective and how would it reflect back to her upon forming coherence with it?

Another way you might do this is to treat that new emotional perspective like a pair of tinted sunglasses and the new perspective is the tint. Every aspect of your material reality, regarding this Strikeout Desire, will be filtered through those sunglasses. How does that look, how do you experience that desire, and how does that feel?

Also, make sure the better-feeling, believable stories you tell yourself about your Strikeout Desire are formed from this new emotional perspective. You will be tempted, as always, to tell yourself stories from higher or lower perspectives and, when that happens, gently remind yourself to go back to your current one and reframe it from that emotion. This will take intentional effort on your part but will be immensely helpful for living your way into this new perspective.

In reasonably short order, you'll truly see a different, slightly more aligned universe from that new emotional perspective. That is because the new emotion is really not that much more positive than the previous one. Your subconscious brain will allow you to see that slightly more positive and aligned universe. And it will also allow that new emotional perspective to take root and make changes to your existing beliefs about that Strikeout Desire. By anywhere from one to four days you'll feel like you've gotten a handle on your absent desire from the perspective of the new emotion.

I took care to keep the focus on Despair/Worthlessness and not on the feelings I wrote about previously. When I found myself drifting back to filtering my material reality about my Strikeout Desire through the feelings I had previously written about, I simply gently reminded myself to focus, instead, on Despair/Worthlessness. These were believable reminders since I wasn't asking myself to adopt new feelings that were way up the chart. I truly wasn't giving myself too-good-to-be-true affirmations, after all. The perspective of Despair/Worthlessness is, after all, only slightly more positive than my previous emotional perspective. My subconscious brain said, "Oh yeah, Greg, you want to use that perspective. I forgot. No problem. I'll allow that; here you go."

You're now tricking your subconscious brain into allowing you access to your previously sacrosanct beliefs. It's like putting a vitamin in a doughnut; your subconscious brain doesn't even realize it's allowing your beliefs to be subtly upgraded. And the changes will be so natural and gradual, it will actually never catch on to what you're doing.

And don't worry, by the way, about how openly and brazenly we're discussing how you're fooling and tricking your subconscious brain. You might, after all, worry that your subconscious brain will hear all this, be tipped off, and prepare to defend its storehouse of beliefs against playing "Grow a Greater You." This is, however, one time where it's to your great advantage that your subconscious brain doesn't understand or communicate with logic and language. It actually has no idea what you're reading, learning, and doing because it cannot understand the language-based modes of communication we're using.

The trickery can be illustrated with a metaphor about boiling frogs. I've never actually boiled frogs, by the way, but I believe you'll see the point of this. If you put a few frogs in a pot of water, put the pot over a burner on your stove, and turn on the burner, the frogs will never notice that the water is getting too hot until it's too late. Yet, conversely, if you boil the water first, then throw the frogs in, they will experience a huge jolt of pain because the sudden shock of the super-heated water will be drastically different than the temperature outside the pot. And they will jump out. That is because, of course, in the first example the frogs got used to the water temperature in real time as it slowly heated up; the change was too gradual for the frogs to notice.

Your subconscious brain is the frogs. Your beliefs are the water. And this belief-raising protocol is the stovetop burner. You must heat the water slowly and gradually if you want the frogs to hang around—except, of course, you're helping your subconscious brain (and, thus, yourself), not making frog soup.

Do not fall for the trap of jumping to a perspective way up the chart. The idea may be alluring and you'll feel capable of it sometimes because you're familiar with trying to adopt those feelings from your previous use of positive affirmations; they've been what you were taught you "should" feel about your Strikeout Desire in order to manifest it. You may say, "But, Greg, I really can feel those very positive feelings about this desire." And you're right; you can feel them and you could go there. But, if you go there, you will only be making yourself feel good in that moment; you will not be changing your beliefs about that desire.

I found that, with a reasonable amount of effort and attention, I was able to really make an actual transition from Powerlessness/Dejection to Despair/Worthlessness regarding debt and money. The transition started when I first looked up the definitions, catapulted forward when I wrote about debt and money from the perspective of Despair/Worthlessness, and solidified as I began to focus on my desire from the perspective of Despair/Worthlessness during my normal, daily affairs. I was really there; the new perspective was truly mine. I was then feeling completely desperate and worthless about financial abundance.

And, once again, here's how an authentic transition to the new emotional perspective (not just a fanciful "what if") is possible. It's not that big of a leap. It's a realistic uptick of emotional perspective. It feels real and genuine because it's only a slight improvement—not a smiley face slapped over an empty gas gauge. It's believable, and my subconscious brain will accept it because it's not some grandiose "quantum leap" way up the chart like positive affirmations attempt to do for you. Additionally, I was quite familiar with seeing money and debt from the perspective of Despair/Worthlessness anyway.

Your litmus test for knowing whether you have truly lived your way into your new emotional perspective is two-fold:

1. You find that is no longer so challenging to bring yourself back into your new emotional perspective. You don't find it as necessary to pull yourself up from lower perspectives, nor talk yourself down from higher ones. You find yourself more naturally telling yourself better-feeling, believable stories about your Strikeout Desire from your new emotional perspective.

2. You see a universe which reflects your new emotional perspective. Your material experiences regarding your Strikeout Desire are reflective of your new perspective, which give you the helpful feedback you need to know that you have adopted a new, slightly more aligned belief regarding your Strikeout Desire.

It is not necessary to do this perfectly before you move on to write about the next highest emotional perspective on the Emotional Reference Chart. While your ability to self-diagnose in this area will strengthen with practice, you can be assured that your feelings and your material experiences will provide you with the accurate and reliable feedback you need to direct your efforts.

Sometimes it takes a couple of days to really embrace the next highest emotion and live it. That's fine. It takes as long as it takes. But don't intentionally procrastinate on the process of living your way into it. Think about it, meditate about it, and write more about it (if necessary) until you have become that emotional perspective.

Greg Kuhn

Step Four: Select the Next Highest Emotion Up the Chart From the One You Just Wrote About/Lived Your Way Into and Write About It/Live Your Way Into It in the Same Manner You Did with the Previous One

You've lived your way, in slow, realistic, believable fashion, into a slightly higher emotional perspective than the one you held previously. You wrote, "Next Time" and included the next highest emotion from the emotional perspective chart at the end of your previous writing. Now it's simply time to get your journal back out and repeat the process with the next, slightly higher emotional perspective from the chart. Do the same things you did previously: Write about your absent desire from the new emotional perspective and then spend a day or two (or three—however long it takes) living your way into that new perspective from that new emotion.

In my example, I next wrote about debt and money from the perspective of Grief/Desolation, and my writing was aimed purely at seeing financial abundance from that emotion. As I had found previously, Grief/Desolation was a relatively easy perspective to attain as it was not that much more positive than Despair/Worthlessness and, as before, these were feelings I had some familiarity with. And, once again, I found that the new feelings and perspectives were only slightly more positive than the previous ones, not radically so.

Once again, dispel the notion that you are creating or empowering more displeasing manifestations by holding this slightly improved perspective. You are not creating displeasing reflections by living your way into it. Your material reality, after all, has always been a reflection of your true beliefs, so you haven't had genuine access to the real reflection you desired. No matter how good you can make yourself feel about your Strikeout Desire in any given moment, those high-end feelings never reflected your true beliefs about it. You won't be creating anything worse than you did previously and, actually, your reflections will be slightly improved. This new perspective is good news for your alignment and for your own unique, individual universe you are contextually creating.

168

Step Five: Never Moving More than One Emotion Up at a Time and Never Moving More than One Emotion Up Per Day, Repeat Steps 2 through 4 Until You Have Moved Yourself All the Way Up to the Top of the Emotional Reference Chart

Each new emotional perspective builds new neural pathways in your brain; thus, it builds new beliefs. And the new pathways are only slightly more positive at each turn, so it really works on your subconscious brain. In following this process as instructed, you are retraining your subconscious brain, replacing the limiting beliefs from your childhood rulebook with new ones that serve you because they are more aligned with your desires. And you're using new emotional perspectives to build these new neural pathways because emotions are the language spoken by your subconscious brain.

It is very important to move only one emotion at a time. And move, at most, only one emotion per day (no matter how "on fire" you are to live your way into the new emotional perspective and how completely and authentically you do that). Moving at a pace any faster is like slapping a smiley face on an empty gas gauge. Always remember: No matter how greatly you wish to finally manifest your long absent desire, you are coaxing a scared little bunny out of the bushes, asking her to take a carrot from your hand. That bunny (your subconscious brain) will only move toward you in small, safe, believable increments.

But don't fret about the seemingly slow pace of this process. As you move up the chart, you'll notice that what you're manifesting regarding your desire improves almost immediately. Sure, the improvements are not dramatic at first. In the beginning, you're still at emotional perspectives that are usually far from being aligned with your desires. But, even in the beginning, you will be improving your beliefs slightly, and that will send new commands to the quantum field even though your commands will, obviously, not manifest your desire in the grand manner they eventually will. That's because your beliefs (and, thus, your unconscious expectations, which send commands to the quantum field) are different with even a single tick up the chart. You'll see grander ones later, though, I assure you.

Even while you're still on emotional perspectives that are not truly positive in nature, even the negative ones become progressively more direct as you move up the scale. It's like the difference between direct aggression and passive; anger is a more forward and active negative emotion, for example, than depression. The forward, more direct characteristics of even the negative emotions will be empowering.

While living your way into each new emotion, remember to continue telling better-feeling, believable stories about your desire from that emotional perspective.

It's fool's gold, by the way, to spend any energy fantasizing about "how" your Strikeout Desire could be manifest. First, you may psych yourself out by doing that because it will all seem like just too big a task for the quantum field to accomplish. Second, you are not yet capable of seeing a universe from those higher perspectives you'll eventually reach. You've never truly held beliefs that form coherence with the quantum field from those perspectives. You'll find opportunities and possibilities from that higher perspective, when you get there, that you cannot see right now. For these reasons, trying to figure out "how" the quantum field will deliver your desires to you is like wondering what route the Domino's delivery driver will take. Don't fret; he'll make it to your house just fine; you don't need to worry about which streets he'll take. You simply order the pizza and let him do what he does best—get it to you.

What you might have thought you would be "doing" to manifest your desire often turns out very differently in real practice by the time you get to that emotional perspective. For example, I would have assumed the universe would reflect more money back to me by motivating people to buy lots of the books I had written with my Dad. That seemed like the most logical way for financial abundance to manifest.

As I worked my way up the Emotional Reference Chart, however, that's not how it happened at all. The quantum field connected the dots for me and reflected my new beliefs back to me in the form of incredible bank cooperation and manifesting buyers who were willing to purchase the properties I owned within generous guidelines allowed by the banks. Furthermore, my beliefs were also reflected back to me in the form of generous, sometimes miraculous, and incredibly helpful debt forgiveness by the lending institutions. It's wasted energy to try to imagine how it will happen; do not focus nor fixate on "how" the quantum field will work out reflecting your new beliefs back to you.

As I've continued to play "Grow a Greater You" with money, I do sell a lot of books and do a lot of speaking. Yet those actions are still not "how" the quantum field reflects what have now become my Home Run Desires about money back to me. Instead, my entire focus is on imbuing great value into my writing and speaking. That is because from the perspective of my joyful beliefs about financial abundance, I now understand that providing great value to the world is what abundance in any form is all about. My new beliefs are: If I'm delivering great value, the universe will reflect that back to me. I simply give what I desire.

I'm not sharing this to tell you to do likewise. You'll find your own inspirations and opportunities naturally arising for you from your new beliefs as you work your way up the chart. You won't need to settle for my results; you can surpass mine, and I hope you do.

It might be disappointing to hear that it may take weeks or months to get there, but I can't say this strongly enough: Do not get in a rush and try to shortcut this process. Remember that your subconscious brain needs to be coaxed toward the new beliefs on the higher end of the Emotional Reference Chart just like coaxing that timid rabbit to your back porch. This is how your subconscious brain works and, like training your dog, you cannot truly create new beliefs any other way.

Let's now discuss the discomfort of "where you are" regarding your desire during this process—especially when you begin, but also while you're at any of the emotional perspectives lower than where you want to be. Those lower perspectives are very uncomfortable, and it's natural to feel discomfort during this process. Any time there is a gap between your emotional perspective (your beliefs) and your desire, there will be discomfort and pain. The level of suffering you feel when you begin this process is why you only use it on Strikeout Desires.

If your perspective on your desire is uncomfortable, it follows that there **must** be a gap between your emotional perspective (your beliefs) and your desire. If there is a painful gap between your beliefs and your desires, the only way to remedy that is to move your beliefs higher to align with your desires. And if you don't get honest about where you really are, you cannot move up the Emotional Reference Chart because it is necessary, after all, for you to begin somewhere if you wish to arrive at a different location. You cannot move up to better feelings if you continue to pretend you feel better and have better beliefs about your absent desires.

No matter what discomfort you feel from any perspective during this process, weren't you were already uncomfortable every day anyway, at least on a subconscious level? And, unless you keep moving forward and change your beliefs in a substantive, lasting way, won't you always feel uncomfortable? Won't you always be suffering the pain of an absence of that thing you desire greatly? Once again, the old saying "Until we agree to suffer, there will be no end to the suffering" comes into play.

Being honest about your painfully out-of-alignment beliefs about a long-held Strikeout Desire can sound like you'll be paddling upstream. But remember: You will only be using this portion of "Grow a Greater You" on desires about which you've been feeling misery and not manifesting like you want for quite a while. So, every time you use this process, there is obviously already a significant gap between your beliefs and your desire. And don't feel ashamed about that gap; you didn't select those out-of-alignment beliefs, you shouldn't have "known better" than to have them because they were given to you.

Next let's address feeling snippets of higher emotions while you're writing/living your way into perspectives lower than those snippets. When you are writing from the perspective of lower emotions, you will often feel flashes of hope and other better feelings. That is natural, because you not only greatly wish to manifest your desire, you've also probably been in the habit of periodically giving yourself positive affirmations and thinking positive thoughts about it—not to mention that you do have authentic positive beliefs mixed in with the limiting ones you're replacing.

Once again, bear in mind that you are only using this process on Strikeout Desires that have been causing you misery and where you have been experiencing absence in your life. Obviously, your real beliefs on this topic are not illustrated by those better-feeling emotional snippets (even though you may be fully able to access the better-feeling thoughts at any time) or you wouldn't need to use this process on this topic in the first place.

Don't discount the better-feeling thoughts; it's fine to feel good about your desire, even if only briefly. Just make sure you re-focus on the current emotional perspective you're writing about and living your way into, which is lower than the snippet of higher feelings you might be enjoying.

Focusing on the current emotional perspective you've been writing about doesn't mean you must go around all day dwelling on "Worry" (or whatever the not-so-good-feeling emotional perspective is) either. Be cognizant of the perspective of "Worry" and frame your absent Strikeout Desire in those terms while living your way into that perspective, but don't make "Worry" your dominant focus for everything you experience during those days. But if "Worry" is truly where you are with the Strikeout Desire for which you're using this process (and if you're feeling discomfort then there **must** be a gap between your beliefs and your desire, right?) then you were already carrying "Worry" around with you all day anyway. So keep your stories about that desire focused on "Worry" while you're on that perspective.

Let's also address feeling snippets of *lower* emotional perspectives during your writing/living your way into higher ones. I call that "backsliding" and, yes, I backslide too. Sometimes backsliding comes from a case of the HALTS (getting too Hungry, Angry, Lonely, Tired, or Serious). If that's the case, continue your commitment to seeing your Strikeout Desire from the emotional perspective you're on, but take care of yourself. Get something to eat, blow off some steam, talk with a friend, get some rest, or find a moment to laugh gently with yourself.

Sometimes you'll simply be resisting the improvement of the new emotional perspective, or belief. When that happens, step back and gently reassure your subconscious brain: "I understand any hesitancy to be in this emotional perspective, because our old ones are much more familiar. Yet this new perspective is truly only slightly more positive than the previous one; there really is no reason for us to be scared of it or run away from it. It's believable and okay to adopt." Telling yourself that story immediately puts you back into an allowing and accepting mode.

Those old emotional perspectives, which you previously wrote about and lived your way into, are very familiar to your subconscious brain. Remember that old beliefs, even painful and limiting ones, are like your favorite pair of jeans—natural and easy to slip into. They do become much less powerful as you form new ones and, thus, use the old pathways less and less. But they stick around awhile, so don't feel disappointed or surprised when you find yourself using them again. When that happens, gently redirect your subconscious brain by saying, "That's an old belief and I understand why you went there—it's a familiar pathway. But we have authentically moved ourselves up the Emotional Reference Chart and have new beliefs now. Although I understand why you'd want to think that way, I want to focus on our new beliefs—which we have already embraced and accepted."

And while this might sound harsh, our backsliding is representative of our old beliefs and paradigms being an easier, softer way. I include myself as being susceptible to the easier, softer way of blaming an outside source for my misery. That's a defense mechanism created out of necessity when the only other alternative was to blame myself and call myself a failure. Thus backsliding into old beliefs of victimization at the hands of the giver of gifts or other people is easy to fall prey to. When that is happening, simply remember that your beliefs are the culprit, not you. And, additionally, recall that you are merely changing beliefs which were conferred upon you, not intentionally chosen by you.

I have also found that sometimes when those less positive emotional perspectives creep in, I might have moved up to the next highest emotion too fast. That's called, of course, "slapping a smiley face on it." When I slap on smiley faces, things almost always get at least a little bit scary. The new emotional perspective, or belief, can feel fake. I can feel out of control or even sense impending doom ahead. In that case, I slow down, backtrack, and spend a little more time with the previous emotional perspective I've just moved on from.

When I relax, get into allowing mode, and put my attention and focus back on the previous emotional perspective (or belief) the scary, fake, out-of-control, and impending-doom feelings disappear almost immediately and I'm back on track.

I've found that I start feeling better the moment I move just one tick up the Emotional Reference Chart. For example, Frustration really does feel better than Worry. Regarding my desire, is Frustration where I want to be in the long run? No way. But I notice immediate improvements in the reflections from the quantum field with just one tick up the chart.

And because those reflections improve, I also notice that I start to see new, more aligned manifestations as I move one tick up the chart. With each movement in a better-feeling direction, even moving just one emotion up, I begin to contextually create manifestations that are a little more aligned with my desires. In this manner, using this process feels a bit like slowly pulling back the curtain on a room full of treasure. For example, of course Worry/Nervousness doesn't allow as much of my desire to manifest as Joy/Elation will, but Worry/Nervousness does manifest a material reality more aligned with my desire than Anxiety/Fear did, because it is a slightly more positive belief than Anxiety/Fear and, thus, creates slightly more positive expectations, which are then conveyed, unconsciously, to the quantum field.

Based on my experience, your manifestations will start to feel like a steady, powerful flow, strongly aligned with your desires, somewhere around Hopefulness/Optimism. And you won't just experience manifestations more aligned with your desires; you'll reflect and see new, improved inspiration and opportunities. So, depending on where you start on the Emotional Reference Chart, a steady flow of aligned manifestations may be only weeks away. Just keep being honest and keep writing; the universe takes care of everything else for you.

The universe isn't a tease. No matter how much you align your beliefs with your current desires, you will always experience the awakening of still greater desires from their manifestation. And you will always have the tools in hand to continue to grow and align your beliefs with your new, greater desires, because all you'll need to do is continue to use this process and tell yourself the best-feeling, believable stories about them.

For example, am I "done" with financial abundance? Heck no. As I've continued to manifest my desires regarding financial abundance, I've always found that still greater desires awaken. And they can all be allowed to manifest by continuing to play this amazing game. Even though I am world's wealthier than I dared desire back in 2006, I am still actively raising my beliefs around financial abundance. I continue to see a new universe as I continue to raise my beliefs. I continue to receive new inspirations for joyous action and expansion from the quantum field as I continue to raise my beliefs. And I continue to see new opportunities manifest right in front of my eyes as I continue to raise my beliefs.

The same is true for my desires about my body, my health, my family, my relationships, my self-worth, my career, etc. In all those areas, I am growing my beliefs into alignment with greater desires than I ever would have dared dream prior to creating "Grow a Greater You" and learning this new way of life. Case in point: my greatest desire now is to make suffering optional. Wouldn't you agree that this is a big desire? Even one some might find too grand? But I know that all I need to do is continue to raise my beliefs into alignment with that desire. I no longer put handcuffs on the universe by setting limits of any kind on my expansion.

Today, I dare to expand into the limitless creativity and abundance of the quantum field. There is truly no end to this game, and I'm so glad that you, too, have decided to join me and thousands of others who dare to expand in this wonderful manner. Through this process, you now have the opportunity to expand into your greatest version of yourself and put an end to your suffering.

Chapter Seventeen

Your Path to the "Grow a Greater You" Hall of Fame

This chapter will teach you six amazing tools you can use to put yourself in the best position possible to play "Grow a Greater You" each day, telling better-feeling, believable stories and growing your beliefs in the most wonderful ways.

You've undoubtedly already started seeing a more desirable universe and begun feeling differently about yourself and your life experiences by playing this game. You're following through on your commitment to depersonalize your feelings, your pain, your reactive stories, and your material experiences by seeing them as helpful, useful feedback. You're telling yourself better-feeling, believable stories about all your life experiences. And you're growing your beliefs into alignment with your Strikeout Desires. Congratulations! As you now know, the results of these changes are real.

These tools, like all the instructions for playing "Grow a Greater You," will become second nature and habitual with practice. Some may feel like a radical departure from the way you've conducted yourself, but, even if they feel strange, they will be of great help to you, so apply yourself to them as thoroughly as you're able. I suggest you take each one of these six tools and focus on that tool for a week. Every month and a half you'll have cycled through all of them and, after a year, you'll have spent eight weeks focused on each tool. If you commit yourself to that schedule while you play "Grow a Greater You," you won't even recognize your life after the year is over.

Your goal with these six tools is to practice them every day, as often as possible. Do not beat up on yourself if you forget to practice them or if you feel like you're not getting as much from them as you should. And remember to use better-feeling, believable words when you have to remind yourself to employ them. There is no expectation of mastery for these six tools. There is no time you'll be able to say, "I'm finished; I now practice them perfectly."

Tell No Stories at All

Playing "Grow a Greater You" isn't that challenging when your circumstances are desirable and it's easy for you to authentically label them "good." But what if I told you that there is a technique available to you that allows you to play "Grow a Greater You" with the same ease even when your circumstances are undesirable? Even when they're horrible?

The first technique for enabling your "Grow a Greater You" Hall of Fame induction is to tell no stories at all. Does that even sound possible? After all, we seem born to define the value of each and every experience we have. We categorize everything.

Learning to tell better-feeling, believable stories is a way to train ourselves to not be so quick to label everything "bad" as most of us have been so apt to do. In fact, if you haven't already discovered it, you will soon realize that with practice you can definitely turn almost any experience you have into at least a partially "good" thing.

And when you can leave the potential for an experience to be "good," no matter how small that window might be with some of your more challenging experiences, you allow the quantum field its full potential to do what it does best: connect the dots and reflect your beliefs back to you in ways that manifest your desires in a sometimes unbelievable and miraculous manner. Refraining from calling your experiences "bad," in believable ways as you've learned to do, releases the quantum field from the tethers you've habitually placed on it.

After all, when you are steadfastly or definitively referring to something as "bad," the quantum field has no other alternative but to oblige you. And, thus, something that the quantum field was probably using to get all the "ducks in a row" (behind the scenes, if you will) so that your desires could manifest in spectacular and surprising ways, must now become "bad" and work against the manifestation of your desires.

Allowing the potential to remain alive for the quantum field to turn any experience into a "good" one, by using it to help manifest your desires, sets it free. Refusing to tell "bad" stories about something, no matter how displeasing it is in the moment, turns the quantum field into a pleasing-reflection machine equivalent to one of those robot vacuum cleaners— the kind that vacuums your house for you, 24 hours a day, even when you're not there.

And, yes, I have learned to tell authentically "good" stories about almost anything because I've practiced doing it for so long. As you know from the "Grow a Greater You" instructions, my "good" stories do not deny my negative feelings or the displeasure any life event causes me. I acknowledge those negative reactions, yet I also am able to tell good-feeling, believable stories while doing it—even with very painful and unwanted circumstances.

But what about your most challenging experiences? How are you expected not to tell a "bad" story about your father's passing? How would you avoid telling yourself a bad-feeling story about your son's automobile accident? Perhaps it makes you angry to imagine you must find a way to avoid making your spouse's recent cancer diagnosis "bad." What can you do with these types of experiences when you simply cannot authentically find any "good" in them?

I echo your sentiments. I do not want you to figure out a way to tell a good-feeling story about anything unless that story is natural and easy to craft. There may be some things you'll never be able to find "good" in, and for good reason. With this tool, you can still reach the "Grow a Greater You" Hall of Fame even if an experience is incredibly displeasing.

Even with your most challenging experiences, telling no stories at all is a way to use the positive energy of intentional storytelling in your favor. And you can actually use this technique on all your experiences, but it is golden with your worst ones because it will keep alive the quantum field's ability to use every facet of your material reality in your favor. Will it feel strange not to call something "bad" that you normally would? Or to refrain from calling something "bad" when anyone else "in her right mind" would do so? At first, yes, but you'll soon see how incredibly powerful this technique is.

How many times have you had something happen and thought it was absolutely terrible? Then, from the perspective of time, you came to discover that it wasn't as bad as you initially thought? In fact, that happens all the time, correct? And, if you're like me, haven't you even come to think of some of those initially "terrible" events as blessings? I can think of plenty; deaths, divorce, financial disaster, etc., have all facilitated remarkable personal growth. I can name at least four incidents that, although they caused me misery that I wouldn't wish on my worst enemy, led me to some of my greatest growth. With the passage of time, I have even found profound, authentic gratitude for some of my greatest suffering.

Jerry Lewis once told me that comedy is just tragedy plus time. Desires becoming manifest often follows that same equation. And with this technique, you are effectively reducing, or even removing "time" from that equation.

You know why this is? Because everything is information, even suffering. When the unresolved pain of my beliefs' being out of alignment with my desires eventually became suffering, via the reflections of it from the quantum field, that information finally got my attention. I was obviously in some combination of denial and ignorance about my misalignment and therefore never sought the true resolution of it until my suffering became great enough. This is why I can honestly feel gratitude for that information; as miserable as the information caused me to feel, the feedback was not the culprit. Instead the feedback finally got me willing to address the true culprit, my misaligned beliefs.

In this way, we've all experienced, time and again, that almost anything can become a blessing, a "good" thing. So, knowing that, why would you ever choose to definitively label something as "bad"? Seeing as you've plenty of experience discovering that which you initially called "bad" turn out to be good in the long run, why not give the quantum field the greatest opportunities to work things out according to your desires—no matter the circumstances?

And you can do just that by deciding to tell no story at all. It's relatively simple to accomplish; all you need do is tell yourself some version of: "Although I am not happy that this is happening, I also know that I don't have to label it at all. I know that, with perspective, even the seemingly worst circumstances can work out for the best. I'm certainly not going to call this 'good,' because it is highly undesirable. But I'm also not going to call it 'bad'—because I don't have to. I can call it, simply, 'information that I'm choosing not to label as 'good' or 'bad.' That doesn't mean I have to pretend I'm happy about the information, because I'm not—but it does mean that I'm giving the quantum field all the leeway it needs to somehow make these circumstances fit into the larger picture and help me manifest that which I truly desire. Even if I won't be able to see it for a while, I know that is what the quantum field does best. And I know that by refusing to label this 'bad,' while also not pretending I'm happy about it, I am giving myself the greatest opportunity to use this information to play 'Grow a Greater You'."

That story is believable. You are acknowledging your true feelings about the unwanted circumstances and, at the same time, you are also giving yourself the proper perspective to truly avoid labeling them "bad." It really works.

Recently, a friend of mine's teenage son was caught with marijuana in their house. Unwanted circumstances, for sure, and a situation where most people would virtually urge you to go deep into labeling it "bad." And, if nothing else, most people would certainly validate your calling it "bad."

Yet my friend is committed to this technique. So his first internal response was to acknowledge that he didn't like these circumstances at all. They made him angry, worried, and afraid. Then he immediately framed the story to himself this way: "I do not like this; my son's actions make me feel angry and disrespected. And, even more so, they make me feel worried and scared for him because I know that continuing down this path usually does not have a happy ending for teenagers or their parents. I refuse to call this 'good.' I also refuse, however, to call this 'bad.' Regardless of how tempting it is for me to label this 'bad,' I refuse to tie the hands of the quantum field by limiting its options for working things out according to my desires. I, therefore, choose to let these circumstances simply be information for me and I will not call them 'bad.'"

My friend most certainly laid down the law with his son. Choosing to not call something "bad" doesn't mean we can take no actions. Yet, alongside the circumstances his son was given, my friend also was able to have some open and honest dialogue with the boy.

A month later, over coffee, my friend told me that his son had learned a lot from the experience and had shown significant personal growth and maturation stemming from it. Even more exciting to my friend, however, was how walking through the situation together had taken their relationship to another level of trust and intimacy. As much as he was initially tempted to call it "bad," he now actually feels authentic and heartfelt gratitude for the opportunity his son's transgression has given them to grow their relationship.

Due to the relational outcomes, my friend was actually grateful it all happened. Would those outcomes still been possible if my friend had immediately labeled it "bad"? Maybe. Yet there is no doubt that his choice to tell no story about it was a fulcrum for a more rapid connecting of the dots by the quantum field—and quicker alignment with one of my friend's great desires: a significant and meaningful relationship with his son. Perhaps even more importantly, telling no stories allowed my friend to remain open to the potential inherent in using his material reality as information, even when it's very painful.

The way this technique allows you to remain open to using information as feedback reminds me of a study. A group of researchers followed two groups around for a year: one a group of self-professed optimists and the other a collection of self-identified pessimists. At the end of the year, the researchers determined that the pessimists had a more accurate track record of predicting outcomes in their lives. Yet the researchers determined that, although the optimists where not "right" as often as their pessimistic counterparts, they were found to be much more resilient and capable of responding well to their circumstances. In other words, the study found that the pessimists got to be "right" more often, but the optimists got to be more successful and resourceful.

The technique of telling no story at all gives you the opportunity to be the "Grow a Greater You" version of an optimist—an authentic optimist who acknowledges her negative responses to displeasing life experiences while remaining open to the possibility that the quantum field will use them in unexpected ways to reflect her desires. That kind of optimism is authentic even under the worst circumstances.

Be in the Present Moment

Being in the present is a wonderful technique for playing "Grow a Greater You" at your optimal level anywhere. It has to do with your focus and dispelling two of the greatest illusions you, and every human, is confronted with. These two illusions, the past and the future, act like anchors chained to your legs. So casting these anchors off as often as possible is of premium value for a Hall of Famer like you.

For a model of how being in the present moment works, watch a child play. See how utterly transfixed she becomes with her game. It's pure immersion; she has lost herself in the world of play. You used to do that too when you were a kid and you may think you can't follow that modality anymore. But you were born with the ability to be fully alive and to lose yourself in the present moment, and you still have it. It's one of your greatest gifts. Whenever you allow yourself to be in the present moment, you are fully present in the only time that really exists—right now.

The present moment is also the only time that your desires are manifest. Have you ever experienced the manifestation of a desire yesterday? How about tomorrow? Your joy is found right now, right here.

Legendary comedian Chris Rush once told me there are three things that root you in the moment, as an adult: "great sex, gunfire, and laughter." I'll add one more to his list: your conscious decision to go there. I know you occasionally find yourself lost in an activity; you occasionally lose track of time and lose your sense of "self" because you're completely immersed in what you're doing. But you can also learn to intentionally and purposefully lose yourself whenever you decide. And when you consciously invest yourself in the present moment, your desires more spontaneously manifest, which pours rocket fuel onto your game of "Grow a Greater You."

Have you ever been held spellbound by a gorgeous sunset, for example? How about being stopped in your tracks by a beautiful painting? Or what about the first time you laid eyes on your newborn child? These are all examples of times you were fully alive in the present moment.

When you're in the present moment you temporarily lose the illusion that you are separate from that which you are observing. And make no mistake: quantum physics tells us that, at our core, separateness is an illusion. In fact, since all material objects are made from the same stuff (a unique combination of mostly carbon, hydrogen, oxygen, and nitrogen) and are all manifest from the quantum field, it is correct for us to say that when we interact with the material world, we are interacting with ourselves.

Thinking that we are not interacting with ourselves, that we are separate from all we observe, is a very effective illusion and reinforces Neanderthal paradigms. If you ever doubt that separateness is an illusion, recall the last time you lost yourself in a moment. Didn't time cease to exist for you and weren't you truly in union with that thing? You became one with what you were observing.

When you are fully invested in the present moment, you are experiencing what Deepak Chopra is fond of calling "timeless awareness." Timeless awareness occurs when the observer, the observed, and the act of observing become one. During timeless awareness, all possibilities are present and alive—because the quantum field, with which you are in direct conscious contact during timeless awareness, is the living embodiment of limitless possibilities.

Why don't people normally spend the majority of their time in the moment? Because, if you're like so many others, your life is often dominated by two pressing illusions, the past and the future, that weigh you down like anvils tied to your feet. And you're in the deep end of a pool. If you're anything like most people, you've become so accustomed to these illusions that you have lost touch with just how much time you spend "living" in them, by fixating on your past and future.

You have tended to obsess over your illusions of your future by adding energy to your fears, hopes, guesses, dreams, etc. But the future is a lie, a time-waster at best and frighteningly immobilizing at worst. The future never arrives because, when it does, it will be the present moment. Thus, wasting time thinking about what might happen is not even a logical thing to do. When you really break it down, all you're doing is projecting your present self into a hypothetical future. You know from past experience that as your future present moments arrive, you are not the same person you were back when you were imagining them—especially when you are playing "Grow a Greater You."

You have undoubtedly also ruminated on the illusion of the past with harsh judgments, resentments, anger, and regrets. You've labeled all your past events and experiences as failures, successes, mistakes, triumphs, etc. But the past is a lie too; the past is no more and doesn't exist. At best, the past is a distraction, but most of the time it can be a paralyzing guilt producer. The past was once the present moment, but it is gone and isn't real anymore.

I'm no different than you. I'm not perfect and I waste plenty of precious present moments trying to be alive within those two illusions. Yet who could refute that the present moment is where all your fun is, all your success is found, and where your desires are manifest? In fact, who would argue that the present moment isn't actually the only time in your life that ever truly exists?

Theoretical quantum physicist Dr. Amit Goswami, one of my favorite authors, certainly wouldn't. Dr. Goswami refers to the present moment as the pre-cognitive moment. And he says that you can easily tell when you are fully alive in the present moment, or the pre-cognitive moment. The litmus test? You will feel joy.

Technically, in quantum physics, the pre-cognitive moment is a measurable fraction of a second that occurs between the time your awareness is put upon the quantum field and the time the quantum field collapses from its status as pure potential to form a unique individual universe for you. The pre-cognitive moment, for a quantum physicist, is the almost immeasurably fast instant when your expectations form coherence with the quantum field.

Seen through the filter of quantum physics, the present moment is a time of your greatest, most pure and unbridled creativity—and of possibility too. Science tells us that the present moment is the place where every deliberate creator finds her greatest power and influence over her material reality. So, obviously, the present moment is where you want to be as often as possible.

Conversely, how can you know if you are not fully present, fully alive, in the present, or pre-cognitive, moment? You will feel anger. Your litmus test, your thermometer, for this includes symptoms such as telling yourself stories like these about your life circumstances:

"This isn't supposed to be happening."

"Why is this happening to me?"

"Things never work out for me."

"As usual, I get the short end of the stick."

"Why can't things ever work out the way I want them to?"

"Why does this always happen to me?"

"I'm so sick and tired of falling short or failing."

Those feelings are important information for us to pay attention to because they tell us that we're probably not in the present moment. When I find myself telling those kinds of stories, a big, red light goes off and an alarm sounds. And I know it's time to tell myself a better-feeling, believable story that puts me back in the present moment.

Remember—the better-feeling, believable stories that you tell aren't supposed to be some pie-in-the-sky ones that ignore your true feelings. The new story should acknowledge, or validate, that you don't like your current circumstances. But it should also recognize the inherent, unlimited possibilities always present in every moment and infuse you with hope that finding them is always possible (both in the short and long run).

As in:

"I really am not happy, in this moment, that this is happening. But I can also believe that, in this moment, I lack the long-term perspective to definitively call this 'bad.' In fact, I don't have to call this anything; I can choose to place no value (good or bad) upon this circumstance. In doing so, I leave myself open to the possibility that this circumstance might prove to be a blessing in the long run (or, at least, not as 'bad' as it seems right now)."

Given that all possibilities are fully present and alive during timeless awareness, isn't it easy to see that being in the present moment is where a conscious creator should invest her energy? Doesn't being in the present moment allow you your greatest opportunities to manifest a life more closely aligned with your desires? And the good news for you is that you can be in the present moment any time you choose.

You can focus on things that will allow you to be in the present moment more naturally and more often. Be there any time you wish by choosing to focus on love, gratitude, and appreciation as often as possible. Deep feelings of love, appreciation, and gratitude have always been the vehicles that took you to timeless awareness. Knowing that, why wouldn't you choose to feel them as often as possible and be in the present moment? Where is there a rule that states that you must wait until a "big" event (like a sunset or the birth of a child) to feel love, gratitude, and appreciation to such a great extent?

You are already doing work that will allow you to be in the present moment more naturally and more often by working your way up the Emotional Reference Chart with your Strikeout Desires. You'll also be more in the present moment as you tell yourself ever-improving versions of the best-feeling, believable stories possible about your life circumstances. No matter how good you get at it, though, you will not stay in the present moment. You are a human being, after all, and humans are not made to constantly be fully alive in the moment except in extraordinary cases.

You will return to your illusions of the past and the future regularly. Yet, thanks to your opportunities to practice the technique of being in the present moment, you can continually return to it with more ease and regularity—and enjoy more spontaneous fulfillment of your desires. And the more fully alive you are in the present moment, the more vibrant, pleasing, and aligned your reflections from the quantum field will be.

Depersonalize Your Feelings

The third technique for reaching the "Grow a Greater You" Hall of Fame, depersonalizing your feelings, works in tandem with the previous one. Although it's been discussed at length previously, take time here to see how it works perfectly with being in the present moment. And also how this technique continues to work beautifully even after we've grown many of our beliefs into powerful alignment with important desires.

If you're like most people, you have spent most of your life identifying with your feelings. In other words, rather than using your feelings as the information they were intended, you have allowed them to dictate your state of being—to shape your self-image, to mold your idea of who you are. In this manner, as discussed earlier in this book, your feelings have often usurped the real you and have wielded an incredible amount of power. Power that your feelings have as much business wielding as a four-year-old has brandishing a loaded gun. And, just like the four-year-old with the handgun, your feelings can be just as dangerous when personalized.

Thus, your third technique to play "Grow a Greater You" like a Hall-of-Famer focuses squarely on reminding you to keep your feelings in the role they were designed for. Your feelings are the most accurate and reliable thermometer you could ever imagine for letting you know whether or not your beliefs are aligned with your desires. Your feelings are gloriously beneficial and should be showered with praise and gratitude for the invaluable information they provide. And with this technique you can freely do just that because they will no longer rule you

Greg Kuhn

like a tyrant.

Depersonalize your feelings. Stop identifying with them. Learning to see and understand that your feelings are not "who you are" but merely information being shared with you strips them of a role they should never have had. And, believe me, your feelings will be glad you're doing this because your relationship with them will improve by leaps and bounds.

In fact, you couldn't play "Grow a Greater You" at all without your feelings. Without your feelings you'd have no idea whether your beliefs were in or out of alignment with your desires. Most of us have had a bit of a love/hate relationship with our feelings. For example, haven't you had days when you've been feeling down or bad for seemingly no real reason at all?

Getting dressed a couple weeks ago, I felt like a sham. For no discernable reason, I had the following thoughts:

"You're a fraud, Greg."

"People will stop buying your books."

"Who do you think you are, conducting speaking engagements? You're a nobody."

Those were my feelings that morning. Those thoughts also happen to represent and illustrate some beliefs I used to have—so I'm well acquainted with those feelings. I told myself those kinds of stories repeatedly, for years, because they were some of my beliefs, my truths. And any writer or speaker who tells you she doesn't experience those feelings from time to time is probably not being very honest in that moment.

Until, of course, I learned how and why to use new paradigms from quantum physics to build new beliefs by playing "Grow a Greater You." And I've been playing "Grow a Greater You," telling myself better-feeling, believable stories and working my way up the Emotional Reference Chart, for many years now. Hence, my beliefs have changed. Converse to my feelings the other week, which I still feel from time to time, I now believe:

"I am immensely worthwhile."

"People love my books. A big part of that comes from my intentionally imbuing them with love and value."

"I am an amazing and valuable person—with much wisdom and value to offer."

So when I have unwanted feelings like I did that morning, I simply acknowledge and validate them. Doing so depersonalizes them. They are temporary after all; they are not my state of being and do not reflect my true beliefs about myself. And when depersonalized, my feelings no longer frighten me because I know they do not define me unless I choose to make them so by personalizing them and allowing them to dictate who I am.

Feelings aren't meant to be stuffed or denied; they are meant to be felt. Depersonalizing feelings takes away their power. They are no longer links in an unbreakable chain. My feelings are simply my feelings. They are not in charge of my state of being. I am in charge of what my beliefs are. And I take charge of my beliefs by playing "Grow a Greater You" today.

So a couple of weeks ago, although they weren't enjoyable, I simply felt those feelings and acknowledged them. I didn't deny them or actively try to chase them away as if they weren't really there. And I also felt a warm glow of confidence that who I am and what my true beliefs are will always be my choice. I choose to have beliefs today that align me with my desires. And I choose to be in charge of those beliefs through the stories I tell myself each day.

Depersonalizing our feelings, by the way, does not mean we're in denial. One of the worst myths about the law of attraction is that you should always have positive thoughts and feelings. Before I learned to play "Grow a Greater You," I learned the hard way that positive thinking is not a cure-all, nor is it always valid. Positive thinking does not take the place of telling better-feeling, believable stories that guide your beliefs into coherence with your desires. And the latter is how to truly use the law of attraction.

Everyone deals with unwanted and uncomfortable feelings. Whether they be fear, anger, worry, stress, or a myriad of others that cause you pain on any given day, you're going to experience feedback in the form of undesirable feelings. And one of the worst ways of dealing with unwanted and uncomfortable feelings is to pretend they aren't bothering you.

There are many ways you can avoid feeling unwanted feelings, and most of them will quickly cause you even more pain. People avoiding their feelings are prone to overindulge in things as a way to distract themselves. And, yes, positive thinking can be misused in this way too. Positive thinking, when done to avoid feeling your feelings, becomes unhealthy. Using positive thinking in this way is not how to depersonalize your feelings.

As opposed to the unhealthy variety, healthy positive thinking acknowledges how you really feel about something at the same time you're accessing its authentic silver lining. It does not mean that you must pretend you're happy about something unwanted. Healthy positive thinking is about enjoying the never-ending flow of opportunity the universe provides you, even during your frustrations and trials.

And, used properly, healthy positive thinking is your greatest ally when depersonalizing your feelings, because healthy positive thinking is one of the three most effective ways to root yourself in the moment. And, when it comes to depersonalizing your feelings, your relief will always be found in this moment.

When you are out of this moment and focused on the past or the future, that is when your feelings have their greatest opportunity to become your state of being. During these times your feelings can easily become who you are. But when you are in the present moment, your feelings are simply some valuable and useful information you're experiencing in this moment as opposed to being who you are.

This technique can be illustrated through the difference between saying, "I am angry" and "I feel angry." Try saying those two things out loud right now and feel the difference. Pretty dramatic, huh?

In fact, it would surprise me if you didn't have something pressing on your mind right now. You probably have an uncomfortable feeling providing you feedback about having a belief (or two) out of alignment with a desire. So try this technique right now: Say to yourself, "I feel (insert your unwanted feeling here) in this moment, but this feeling is not who I am. Additionally, I also know that I lack the perspective to know, definitely, whether what I'm unhappy about will truly prove to be 'bad' in the long run. And I also know that by playing 'Grow a Greater You,' I will be addressing these beliefs in a substantive and substantial manner—

looking at it that way, I am actually grateful for this feedback."

That is not just a depersonalization of your feelings; it is also healthy positive thinking.

All of a sudden, you are now merely experiencing a feeling instead of being a feeling. The feeling doesn't go away immediately. It's not supposed to because your issue didn't get "solved" right now and it wasn't supposed to get resolved simply through acknowledging how you felt. But it sure gives you some invaluable information about your beliefs and desires not being aligned—not to mention allowing you to be more resilient while playing "Grow a Greater You" and aligning them.

By the way, the new beliefs you're gaining from playing "Grow a Greater You" are real. Yet those new beliefs are also no more permanent then your old ones—which is great news. After all, the general impermanence of your beliefs is what allows you to change the old ones in the first place. Each day, you now awaken with a choice regarding your beliefs: Which beliefs do you want to focus on, hold, and grow?

Playing "Grow a Greater You" really works, as you know, and it has given you many more positive choices. Yet, each day, they're all still choices. So do not be discouraged by backslides into old negative beliefs as revealed to you via your feelings. Instead, simply remind yourself that old habits die hard. Until now, you'd spent your lifetime reinforcing those old beliefs, those old neural pathways in your brain. And, while they weaken with continued disuse, they do not go away overnight.

Your new beliefs are still unfamiliar when compared with the old. And, as surprising as it may sound, the familiar pain of your old beliefs is preferable to your subconscious brain, because your subconscious brain prefers the known and predictable—even when it is painful. So, when you do backslide, a great way to depersonalize your feelings is to tell yourself a story like:

"I'm feeling low right now; I'm feeling things associated with my old, out-of-alignment beliefs. That's curious. I wonder why. It's not enjoyable and I don't really prefer it, yet I also know that my feelings are not 'who I am.' My feelings are simply a feedback loop letting me know how in or out of alignment my beliefs are with my desires—in this moment. How nice to also know that my beliefs are arbitrary and personal; I can decided right now to begin the process of believing just about anything I choose."

That self-affirming story not only depersonalizes your feelings, it also halts any resistance and puts you back on the path of acceptance. This leads you back toward your new beliefs, which are more aligned with your desires.

Take a feeling most of us find undesirable, such as fear. Fear is pretty cool. Not only is it a handy tool, it's supposed to be there. Fear is actually your friend most of the time; there's no doubt we're supposed to have fear. Let's spend a moment illustrating how we can depersonalize fear through finding a better-feeling, believable story to tell ourselves about it—a story that might even allow you to find authentic gratitude for your fear.

Fear is the byproduct of an illusion of separateness. To be a human, we must have an illusion that we are separate from everything else. Without that illusion, we'd simply be what we really are: energy that is connected at all times with all the other energy of the universe. And if we humans knew only that we were interconnected with everything else in the universe, if we always knew we could never be separated from anything or anyone else, we couldn't experience being a human being on Earth—at least not in the manner we currently enjoy.

I'm grateful I have this illusion so I can temporarily enjoy a physical existence that seems, to my senses, that I'm separate from everything else. Being a human being on Earth is a very fun adventure, wouldn't you agree? And fear is a normal, natural human response to that illusion of separateness. We're afraid because it seems like we're separated and finite. Even though none of those things are true, they very naturally appear to the Neanderthal to be so.

Remembering this can lead you to actually feel grateful for fear. You can tell yourself a new story like:

"I'm grateful for my fear today. It is a natural and necessary byproduct of being human. And I most certainly wouldn't want to miss out on this incredible adventure I'm having called 'being alive.'"

And your new story can go even further. You can also tell yourself:

"I am also grateful that I can choose not to give fear so much power. Knowing the important reason that I was born to experience fear, I can choose to embrace its presence today, while also choosing to limit its power over me and my decision making today."

Because they're believable, telling stories like those eventually creates a new neural pathway and a belief that reinforces that you are just like you're supposed to be, that you don't need to be "fixed," and that you get to decide how much influence fear has in your life. So now, when you make decisions, you can objectively decide how much you're going to let fear dictate them. You have de-personalized fear and taken away its mysterious power over you. You're using healthy and authentic positive thought. Your fear is no longer you—it is merely information being shared with you that you are still holding onto some of the illusions of the Neanderthal paradigm.

There is no instance where you should deny or ignore your feelings. That would be like ignoring the pain of a splinter in your toe. Feelings are valuable and useful information. Yet there is also no instance where you cannot employ this technique, and doing so reserves your place in the "Grow a Greater You" Hall of Fame.

Still Your Mind with Active Meditation

Meditation is a phenomenal technique to center you, calm you, and put you in touch with the wisdom that is your birthright—the prescience of a conscious connection with the quantum field. In fact, meditating each day will make your game of "Grow a Greater You" much more powerfully played. Because of the powerful connection meditation facilitates between you and the quantum field, it instills inner knowing and confidence.

I highly recommend fifteen minutes of quiet, resting meditation each day. But there is another way to gain the benefits of meditation without sitting quietly for fifteen minutes each day: active meditation. And I want you to add active meditation to your toolbox of techniques for playing "Grow a Greater You" at a Hall-of-Fame level.

Meditation's greatest gift is clarity, the ability to make decisions without the emotional burden of fear and uncertainty. Clarity is the ability to know, with certainty, what you should do—what the "next right thing" is. Clarity is one of a "Grow a Greater You" player's most valuable assets, and its worth couldn't be equated in dollars.

In case meditation ever turned you off or sounded too complicated, let's call it by another name: listening. You see, you are already connected to the greatest intelligence and wisdom there is: the quantum field. When you meditate, all you're doing is listening to that connection instead of listening to your brain's endless stream of stories about everything. Some people have stated that, while praying is talking at God, meditation is listening to God.

Your essence, your true form, is this quantum field. It is from whence you were formed and it is to where you will eventually return. You are a part of it now and forever; you couldn't separate yourself from it if you tried. And it is only because of your brain that you hold the illusion that you are separate from that limitless, eternal, unbound field of potential, creativity, and intelligence. To reacquaint yourself with the quantum field's intelligence and wisdom, thus gaining astounding clarity and conscious connection, all you need to do is listen. And to listen, all you need to do is turn off your brain for a while, which is really all you're doing when you meditate.

Here's a simple sitting meditation technique that will put you in contact with your true form and shower you with clarity:

- Find a quiet space.

- Sit in a comfortable position.

- Imagine yourself gently scooping your brain out of your skull and lovingly placing it beside you.

- Kindly tell your brain, "My friend, I don't need you for the next fifteen minutes."

- Visualize a warm, orange flame emanating from the top of your "open" skull.

- Listen for fifteen minutes.

- When thoughts arise, simply let a light breeze blow them away.

What will you hear? I predict the communication you'll have with the quantum field will come primarily in the form of feelings and, sometimes, images (such as colors). You will feel calm and centered afterward. You will feel an ease of being based on your remembering who and what you really are. You will feel a confidence based upon communion with your true nature: eternal energy. Things will make more sense. You will feel clarity. How much depends only upon how much meditation you do.

As promised, there is another way to stoke your game of "Grow a Greater You" by listening called active meditation. As a "Grow a Greater You" practitioner, why should you need to subscribe to anyone else's ideas of what information the quantum field has for you? Why, indeed, when you can commune directly with the quantum field yourself.

When you actively meditate, you are also listening to, instead of talking at, the source of all life. You can certainly meditate by finding a quiet space and actively stilling all your conscious thought for fifteen minutes or more. Yet you can also actively meditate during your regular daily affairs, as often as you like, without disrupting your normal activities.

Active meditation is actually relatively simple to perform. All you do is stop your narration, your inner dialogue. To actively meditate, you simply observe and do—without your constant internal narration. Have no thoughts, except those related to, and necessary to perform, the task at hand.

Active meditation will take practice because your brain simply loves to talk and narrate. Your constant running commentary is actually how your neomammalian brain reinforces the illusion that it is "you." I suggest, therefore, being gentle with your brain during active meditation. Don't berate it. Simply tell your brain, "I won't be needing you right now, my friend. You're important to me, but I don't need the running commentary right now."

What will you find when you really listen in this manner? Just as with sitting meditation, you'll discover the unbound wisdom and creativity of the quantum field. You'll find a visceral and active communion with the energy from which your body emerged and you will always be a part of. You'll be in direct communion with the ultimate intelligence and source of all wisdom and life. And, with practice, you'll find answers to any question through feelings, solutions, inspiration, and motivation.

You see, the quantum field is imbued with all knowledge, infinite potential, and unbound creativity. It is omnipresent and omniscient. And all information contained in the quantum field is shared by every single portion of it, at all times, with instantaneous speed. Access to the omnipresent, omniscient source of all things is something a "Grow a Greater You" player cannot afford to cheat herself out of.

Practice Gratitude

Gratitude is the most transformational power in the universe—more powerful, even, than love. Gratitude tells the quantum field what you like and what is desirable, rather than what you don't want. And, since your brain's natural tendency is to focus on what you don't want, the technique of practicing gratitude is an invaluable tool for countermanding a somewhat debilitating inherent quirk of your brain's physical protocol and methodology.

By incorporating this technique into your playing "Grow a Greater You," you will not only overcome your brain's natural physical inclination to find and focus upon what you don't want, but you'll also transform your energy. Practicing gratitude transforms your perspective, which transforms your energy, which helps transform your individual universe.

As you're well aware, the meaning and value you assign to things in your life experience are subjective and changeable. Thus, a commitment to practicing gratitude brings about sometimes incredible changes because you are always finding the very real silver lining in every experience. Rather than focusing upon, and growing, the things that are displeasing, when you seek authentic gratitude in the correct manner you are practicing authentic, believable positive thinking.

You might say that practicing gratitude allows you to play "Grow a Greater You" instead of "Grow a Negative You." You can be grateful for, literally, anything as long as you're willing to be. Don't believe me? Let's take as an example something you might think I'm crazy for being grateful for: pain.

Be grateful for your pain? Am I nuts to suggest that? Who wants pain, after all? Here are two better-feeling, believable stories about pain that will allow you to have authentic gratitude for it if you choose:

1. Pain is nothing more than the gap between your desires and your current material reality. It's nothing mysterious or esoteric. Pain is actually a natural consequence and, thus, is neither inherently good nor bad. Although it may not ever be desirable, it is most certainly never a "punishment."

2. Pain alerts you that your beliefs about something are out of alignment with your desires for it. Your pain is nothing more than a red alert telling you: "Your Beliefs Are Not In Alignment With Your Desires!" Hence, your current material reality is producing pain as feedback; pain is actually useful information.

Isn't pain, seen these ways, actually your friend? After all, how else would you know that your beliefs are not aligned with your desires if it weren't for pain telling you so? You want to manifest your desires, do you not? So isn't anything alerting you to why you're not manifesting your desires really your ally? Pain is your guardian angel, tapping you on your shoulder and getting your full attention to say, "Pardon me; you're pretending you're not worthy of having your desire. You don't have to do that any more."

Additionally, who would argue that it's not wonderful to improve your material reality? Fulfilling your desires is awesome. And aligning your beliefs with your desires is all you now need do to experience those more pleasing circumstances you so desire. Well, what motivated you to do that? Your pain, of course. Without your pain to motivate you, wouldn't you still be "stuck" in your old, less pleasing material reality?

Now you have two better-feeling, believable stories you can tell yourself when you experience pain—two stories that actually make you authentically grateful for your pain because they don't ask you to pretend you're enjoying it. You'll probably never be whooping and shouting for joy as you experience pain—displaying the type of gratitude you would for a Publisher's Clearing House check. But you now have the option of feeling some genuine, believable gratitude for pain.

So don't tell me you can't find something to be grateful for in almost anything you experience. In fact, here is an example where I found gratitude in something incredibly painful. This was possible for me all because I practice this technique; I make it my business to find gratitude, somewhere and somehow, in anything and everything I experience.

I was going through my divorce in the summer of 2008. If you've been divorced, you know that it usually causes grief akin to a death. I certainly felt that way; I often found myself sad, depressed, and hopeless.

One particular afternoon, I was grocery shopping and stopped in the produce section. I noticed that the store's music system was playing Dionne Warwick's song "I Know I'll Never Love This Way Again." It's a classic tear-jerker about a woman mourning the loss of her one true love. I drew a deep breath and, in that moment, internalized the somber lyrics and music of Ms. Warwick's most famous composition.

"Yep", I thought, "I will <u>never</u> love this way again." Tears of sadness came to my eyes, and I actually fought the urge to run out of the grocery and go cry in my car.

Then I had a flash of inspiration. "Wait a minute!" I thought, "There is another way to process this song! There is a different perspective available to me in this song. There is a better-feeling, believable story I can tell about it."

And here's where I found my gratitude, even in that moment of abject sadness:

"You're damn right I'll never love <u>this</u> way again! I'll never again:

So completely invest my self-worth in someone else.

Depend upon another person as my sole source of happiness.

Define myself through someone else's love and acceptance of me.

Put myself in a position of such inappropriate vulnerability by not taking responsibility for my own happiness.

Make it someone else's 'job' to love me; I've learned the importance of being my own source of love.

Hell no, I'll never love <u>this</u> way again. And thank God for that! I've learned a lot about myself; I've grown tremendously. I'll never love this way again because it's my choice to never love this way again. Thank you, pain, for giving me an opportunity to tell this better-feeling, believable story!"

And, suddenly, that sad, depressing song became an authentic declaration of my new freedom. Dionne Warwick's biggest hit was no longer making me think about throwing in the towel; it was now an amazingly inspiring anthem celebrating my new beliefs about personal responsibility and growth. And I felt profoundly grateful.

I did the rest of my shopping with a palpable and noticeable vigor to my step. I was authentically on top of the world. In fact, I was almost giddy. See what a difference choosing to look for gratitude anywhere can make? With practice, such gratitude becomes genuine and it can change your perspective instantly. It can allow you to, literally, change your universe right in front of your eyes.

Here's a funny story about the potential for finding gratitude under any circumstance:

A monk is sitting on the toilet, enjoying his morning constitutional.

He reaches for the toilet paper and tears off a few sheets.

Before he wipes himself, however, he notices an ant on the sheets.

He then flicks the ant off the toilet paper with his index finger.

Later, he thinks about the ant. From the ant's perspective, the monk figures, getting flicked across the bathroom was the greatest tragedy that had ever befallen it.

Unless, he muses, the ant could know what the alternative would have been!

Who would blame the ant for feeling angry and completely victimized? Yet, with a different perspective, you know that the ant would have been profoundly grateful for her "greatest tragedy." In fact, the ant could have correctly chosen to tell herself, "I lack the global perspective to know how this falls into the grand spectrum of life's unfolding. Today I will choose to make no judgment about this and trust that no matter how things seem from my perspective, the quantum field can connect the dots for me in the most miraculous ways.

That story takes the handcuffs off the universe because it clearly sends the expectation to the quantum field that you are okay and that you expect things to continue to unfold in a beneficial way in the long run—despite what might look like a tragedy in the near term. It allows you to find gratitude in the most unlikely circumstances.

In fact, gratitude is so powerful, choosing to find it anywhere is like possessing a real-life superpower. Choosing to find gratitude anywhere gives you the superpower of consistently getting more of what you want out of life, not because of "luck," but on purpose and intentionally.

As a matter of fact, here's a way to start having intentional fun with gratitude. Ever find a penny on the ground? Of course, they're everywhere. But have you ever picked up one of those pennies and celebrated it? Probably not, if you're like most people. Oh sure, you might've thought, "Hey, it's good luck," but have you truly, intentionally felt extreme gratitude about that penny?

It's pretty natural to not celebrate pennies. Pennies are the fruitcake of the currency world; no one wants them. Heck, some people just throw them away because they consider them worthless. And, if you want to value them solely based on their purchasing power, pennies *are* basically worthless. But try this: After finding a penny, privately celebrate it like you just won the lottery. Go way overboard. Way over-the-top. Get silly with it. Privately shout hosannas to the universe!

Don't think that sounds like something you can authentically do? Doesn't sound realistic to celebrate a dumb little old penny? After all, a penny certainly does not represent the abundance you truly desire, does it? But here's where the power of choosing to be grateful kicks in. What you are choosing to celebrate is not the amount the penny represents; you are celebrating the reminder that it represents. You are celebrating the reminder that the universe is infinitely abundant and that manifesting anything is child's play for the quantum field.

You are celebrating the universe reminding you of its eternal abundance with this penny—getting your attention and saying, "Hey my wonderful, most special child! I am at your service and I can and will create anything your heart desires. I can create your heart's desire just as easily as I just created this penny. Isn't that awesome? Here, take this penny and allow it to remind you of my abundance. And celebrate the heck out of that reminder!"

And the trick is, the quantum field doesn't know the difference between your celebrating the amount versus celebrating the reminder. The quantum field simply forms coherence with your gratitude and readily lines up to bring you more of what you're grateful for.

Try it today. Find reasons to be truly grateful for as many things as you can—even the things you usually take for granted, like breathing, your ability to drive a car, your sense of humor, your wonderful mind, etc. Especially the things you commonly label "unwanted" experiences. Look for the hidden gifts and opportunities inherent in them. You will be unleashing your own, personal superpower capable of securing your place in the "Grow a Greater You" Hall of Fame in record time.

Give What You Want to Receive

Playing the game "Grow a Greater You" is, technically, always about aligning your beliefs with abundance. Your desires are always related to some aspect of abundance. And, in fact, not only is abundance at the root of all your desires, there is no end to how great your desires for abundance can grow. Our next-to-last technique for playing "Grow a Greater You" is tailor-made for manifesting abundance.

This technique, giving what you want to receive, is one you can use to send a clear message to the quantum field that you are already abundant. And it also sends a clear and believable version of that message to your subconscious brain. By giving what you desire, in believable and authentic ways, you teach and reinforce growing beliefs about abundance and your worthiness of it.

Quantum physics clearly tells us that our actions are not as important as our intentions, or expectations, behind them. Thus, as you've learned in this book, action is not the most important agent for changing something about yourself as you once may have thought. Yet action is always going to be important in the current time-space we occupy and you should be taking action to manifest your dreams and desires. You simply want to make sure, however, that it is inspired action you're taking.

What's the difference between uninspired action and inspired action? Uninspired action is action you "need" to take to "make" a certain result occur. Action taken from this perspective tells the quantum field that your action must bring about a certain result—that it is needed to make a desire manifest. Thus, from what you've learned about how you contextually create your unique, individual universe, you're actually telling the quantum field that you do not possess what you desire.

When you take uninspired action, you are sending at least three limiting expectations to the quantum field:

1. You are telling the quantum field that you "need" the desired outcome and the quantum field's response is often, "Okay, I'll form coherence with 'need'."

2. By "needing" certain outcomes, in a certain time frame, you are handcuffing the quantum field and keeping it from doing what it specializes in—connecting the dots for you in amazing and often unexpected ways.

3. By telling the quantum field you "need" something, you are actually reinforcing your beliefs that you are lacking abundance and that scarcity is real.

Inspired action, however, is action you take motivated by your raised beliefs. When you take inspired action you are doing so from the perspective of joy. And you are also doing so without expectation of a certain result; you take inspired action simply because you "are," and desire to "become" even more of, that which you desire.

When you take inspired action, you are sending at least three wonderful expectations to the quantum field:

1. You are telling the quantum field that you don't "need" that which you desire. Instead you are telling the quantum field that you "are" that which you desire, and the quantum field's response is almost always, "Okay, I'll form coherence with what you 'are'."

2. You are allowing the quantum field free reign to connect the dots for you in whatever ways it sees fit for you. You might not be able to clearly see those dots connecting from your current perspective, but, since you've taken action from a joyful perspective and without the expectation of a specific outcome, you can accept any outcomes without feeling that things didn't turn out like they were "supposed" to.

3. By telling the quantum field you don't "need" something, you are actually teaching your subconscious brain new beliefs that you are already abundant and that scarcity is truly a subjective belief that you are replacing.

Inspired action gives what you wish to receive. In other words, you are not giving in order to receive something you need; you are sharing what you already possess. Even if you don't possess it in the full amount you truly desire yet, you obviously, and literally, must already possess it if you're sharing it. In fact, try this: Any time you feel like you "must" take an action to "make" a desire manifest, stop for a moment and try to reframe your action. See if you can, instead, take that action from an inspired, joyful perspective. If you can't do that, hold off on taking that action.

Here is another way to utilize the technique of giving what you wish to receive. Do you ever catch yourself thinking, "(Fill-in-the-blank) *has* to happen."

As in: "To be happy or successful, I *have* to or need to:

win the lottery."

drop these ten pounds."

get an 'A' in my class."

have him say 'yes; to my proposal."

get her to accept me."

This is normal, and we all do it from time to time. We all sometimes tell ourselves stories like these, daydreaming about how we might have our greatest desires for success and happiness fulfilled. But have you ever considered that telling yourself stories like these might be a less than optimal way to contextually create your material reality and manifest your desires because it tells the quantum field, and your subconscious brain, that you do not truly believe in abundance?

You might ask, "Aren't these types of stories positive in nature? Aren't they focused upon successful outcomes? And wouldn't those outcomes actually fulfill my desires and make me happy?" And I counter by saying that our universe is, literally, one of infinite possibilities. Subatomic particles are not particles at all, after all. They are merely the *potential to become particles* until we observe them.

We repeatedly form the same material reality from the field of unformed particles simply out of habit. And our habit of forming the same things again and again can actually negate our universe's infinite potential—a potential that always exists in each new moment. And, when we tell these types of stories about how we will experience the fulfillment of our desires, we are actually putting handcuffs on our universe's creativity. We are not giving that which we wish to receive. We are, instead, conveying a powerful expectation to the field of unformed particles that there is only one way to see our desires fulfilled.

Given all this, I highly recommend that you practice giving what you wish to receive on the deepest of levels by telling a story like the following:

"Although I would love to (win the lottery, drop these ten pounds, get an 'A' in my class, have him say 'yes' to my proposal, etc.) and I hope that happens, I can also believe that the fulfillment of my desires is not dependent on this outcome. And I can also believe that I lack the current perspective to know what 'needs' to happen to see my desires fulfilled.

Given this, I can believe that however my desires are manifest, the universe knows what it is doing and things will happen like they're supposed to. All I need to do is continue playing 'Grow a Greater You.'"

In fact, there is even a very tangible way to give what you wish to receive. Physically give away what you want more of in believable ways. Remember the trick of choosing gratitude by celebrating each penny? Intentionally turn that trick around by keeping pennies in your pocket and throwing them on the ground for others to find.

When you toss a penny on the ground, tell yourself, "With this gift, I intend that the recipient is filled with gratitude for the abundance of the universe. I intend that the person who finds this penny feels blessed beyond measure. And I also proclaim my incredible gratitude for being so abundant that I can give away money to unknown recipients, simply for the purpose of helping them feel wonderful. Isn't it amazing that I am so blessed with abundance that I can do this with a joyous heart?"

That act sends a very clear message to the quantum field. That act builds, and reinforces, in a very believable way, the belief that you are abundant. How else could you afford to "throw away" money? And the belief that you are abundant, blessed with more than enough money, tells the quantum field to form coherence with you when you've authentically formed the following expectation: "I have lots of money. I am abundant. I have so much financial abundance that I can give money away."

And, as with finding pennies, you can make giving pennies away a believable act of sharing abundance by not focusing on the monetary value of the coin. Instead, acknowledge and celebrate the energy of abundance the penny represents. Sharing your intention for and beliefs in abundance with someone else, through the penny, is truly the most generous gift you can give. And you will be contextually creating a penny imbued with all the empowering and uplifting energy of those beliefs.

Start giving away what you wish to receive today. Do it believably by tangibly giving away small amounts of the material things you wish to grow your beliefs into further alignment with. And do it in spirit by sharing the energy of what you wish to receive, like sharing your love, attention, energy, kindness, assistance, and help. You'll be authentically building and reinforcing beliefs about having the things that you wish to manifest more abundantly because you already possess them enough to share.

Forgive Yourself Radically

Forgiving yourself radically, the final technique that will put you in the "Grow a Greater You" Hall-of-Fame, paves the way for all your inevitable mistakes. It provides you an avenue for believable relief amid the continuing contrast you're going to experience. And it allows you to stop limiting your growth by retraining you from the limiting and unnecessary habit of beating yourself up that you've inevitably developed.

Forgiving yourself radically is meant to be taken literally. I'm asking you to forgive yourself completely, without reservation, and without ever looking back. Are you even allowed to do this, you might ask? After all, this technique most likely flies in the face of many things you were taught about judging yourself and others.

If you're like me, you were taught that mistakes are bad, shouldn't be made, and shouldn't be tolerated. You may have even learned to internally chastise yourself just as the adults in your life did to you in your childhood. You've been told, "You should have known better" so many times growing up that you now give yourself the same message. Yet, let me ask you if you have ever made a mistake without first thinking, "This is okay for me to do" or "This is going to work."

I truly thought that some of my biggest mistakes were some of my best ideas when I made them. That's why we call them "mistakes," after all. Do you really believe that you, or anyone else, would have actually made her latest mistake if she knew better? In fact, how do we eventually know better? The only way we ever know better is by making the mistake and learning from the consequences; it's after we make the mistake, that we thought was such a good idea, that we know better. If we actually knew better, we wouldn't have made the mistake in the first place!

In fact, beating ourselves up and chastising ourselves or others for mistakes actually reinforces beliefs that keep us separated from our desires. It reinforces a belief that there is a giver of gifts from whom we must please to earn the right to be given our desires. And it reinforces beliefs that possibilities and opportunities are limited and scarce. That's a scary prospect considering that you, like me, are guaranteed to keep making mistakes.

But it's an obstacle you no longer have to create. So I propose you develop and tell yourself a new, better-feeling, believable story about your mistakes that allows you to completely forgive yourself for them without reservation. Since future mistakes are inevitable, your responses to them should no longer impede the manifestation of your desires.

I invite you to see your mistakes like volcanoes. And, from this perspective, you can not only stop beating yourself and others up for them, you can actually start to feel grateful for them. What are volcanoes, after all? A volcano occurs because of one of three things:

1. Convergence of tectonic plates

2. Divergence of tectonic plates

3. Stretching or thinning of tectonic plates in their interiors

When one of these three things happens, pressure builds from the Earth's molten core and a volcano can form. And once a volcano forms, it is only a matter of time until it erupts. It is not improper, then, to say that a volcano *must* erupt once one or more of those conditions exist, since it has no choice but to relieve the pressure of super-heated gasses and release its molten lava.

While a volcanic eruption is almost never desirable, we don't chastise the volcano, or our planet that spawned it, for the eruption. We know that the eruption, while undesirable, was simply something that needed to happen. No matter how undesirable it might be, the eruption was going to happen at some point because the conditions of the Earth's plates in that area created a need for it.

Seeing a volcano this way, isn't it possible to actually be grateful for the eruption? Isn't it possible to say that we're grateful that the conditions that made the volcanic eruption inevitable have now been relieved? We're not happy that the volcano erupted but at least now it's happened and we can relax knowing it's over. Let's apply the same better-feeling, believable story to your mistakes.

A mistake occurs when you thought something was a good idea, yet it turns out that you were wrong. In other words, the conditions existed for a mistake to be made—you truly thought something was a good idea that wasn't. Your misperceptions, like tectonic plates, created a need for a mistake; your misperceptions were, literally, a mistake waiting to happen.

In fact, as long as your misperceptions existed, that mistake was simply waiting, in a dormant state, to happen. And since you had no reason to correct your misperception until you realized it was present, that dormant mistake was never going anywhere until you made it. So, like our better-feeling, believable volcano story, can you see how unnecessary it is to chastise yourself for making a mistake that, while undesirable, was eventually going to happen because of the conditions for it? The conditions for your mistake, your misperceptions, were not going to go away until you learned otherwise, and the mistake is actually what gives you the opportunity to correct them.

Like our volcano example, can't you also foster authentic gratitude for your mistake? Now that the inevitable mistake has occurred, can't you be grateful that it's finally over and now you don't have to make it again? Let's take forgiveness a step further by saying that your mistake is actually providing you with some incredibly valuable and useful information about some misperceptions you can now correct. Now we're adding gratitude to supercharge the technique of forgiving yourself radically.

So here is a new, better-feeling, believable story about mistakes:

"Although this mistake I just made is not desirable and I'm not 'happy' I made it, because it's causing problems for me and others, I can honestly believe that I don't have to beat myself up for it. I made this mistake, after all, with good intentions; I thought it was a good idea. I didn't know this wasn't a good idea until I learned otherwise. No matter how much I might be tempted to tell myself I 'should've known better', I simply didn't. And, since I didn't make this mistake on purpose but because I thought it was a good idea, I can choose to tell myself at least three better-feeling, believable stories about it:

1. I can choose not to beat myself up simply because I thought something was a good idea that wasn't. Now that I know better, I can learn and grow, and I never have to make this mistake again.

2. I can choose to feel grateful that I made this mistake. After all, this mistake was something 'waiting to happen' since I did think it was a good idea. I can choose to be grateful for the fact that I know better now and never have to make it again. This mistake is made; the 'volcano' has erupted and it's over.

3. I can choose to see my mistake as useful and valuable information—feedback that is alerting me to misperceptions I can now choose to correct.

In this manner, although I am not happy to have caused pain or difficulty for myself and others, I can let go of my self-chastising and use the

information as it is intended—to give me feedback for playing 'Grow a Greater You' at higher levels. Forgiving myself, and finding gratitude, after all, is much more aligned with my beliefs than beating myself up or listening to others who might want me to."

The better-feeling, believable story I just framed for you doesn't sugarcoat or deny real feelings of regret about a mistake. But doesn't the new story feel better than:

"You idiot! How could you be so stupid! You should've known better!"

If you're like me you've spent a great deal of your life around people who become angry or disappointed with you when you make mistakes. And you, too, have probably done the same with others—and yourself. Since you're going to continue making mistakes, forgiving yourself for them is an imperative. You can never control anyone else and make them forgive you. You're inevitably going to be an ass to someone, after all, because you're human and you can't avoid mistakes. It's like George Carlin's famous axiom: every other driver on the road is either a maniac going too fast or an idiot going too slow.

In that same vein, no matter how hard you try to be positive and nice, someone, somewhere, is always going to be put off by your mistakes. Perhaps it is actually impossible to avoid making other people angry in this way, since other people will invariably "need" me to behave in certain ways. While I rarely have a desire to intentionally make someone mad at me, I'll never be able to control his or her decision to label something I do as an unacceptable mistake. Nor will I ever be able to control their decision to chastise me for it.

Once again, here's where this technique becomes so important. What value is there in beating myself up in addition to the consequences I naturally experience from a mistake? Early in my life, I was taught by well-intentioned people that when someone is angry with me I should say, "They're right! I am an 'ass'. I should have known better. Why am I like this?" That, my friends, is no way to align one's beliefs with one's desires.

I'm certainly not saying that I don't care what other people think of me. But if you've made a mistake, and it's made people angry, let it go. Apologize for your mistake and do what you can to make amends. And know that your first and most important amend will always be letting go of the stick you're beating yourself up with.

I don't know about you, but it's been a long time since I willfully did things that I knew were wrong or harmful. Most of my mistakes that might put me into someone's "ass" category are one of two types:

1. I honestly had no idea I was negatively affecting someone else.

2. I actually thought that what I was doing was a good idea and the fact that it wasn't took me somewhat by surprise.

Either way, how will not forgiving myself immediately, completely, and radically help me align my beliefs and my desires? And how will not forgiving myself radically for my mistake put me in the best position to make amends and rectify any harm I've caused?

My desires for my own children are my litmus test for how radically to forgive myself for my mistakes. Sometimes my sons make me mad and I almost always let them know when that happens. Then, after I share my feelings, I let it go and it's over. If one of my sons were beating himself up after making me mad, however, I would hug him fiercely and command him to stop doing that. I would tell him that making mistakes is okay and that he is not responsible for me being angry, that my response is on me and he should never feel the need to act a certain way just so I'll be happy with him. At my very core, I want my sons to quickly and completely forgive themselves for being human and making mistakes—no matter how angry I might have been about it.

And if that's what I want for my sons, why wouldn't I want the same for myself? So if you have been in the habit of not letting go of your mistakes, or of beating yourself up for being human, go overboard in the other direction. Completely forgiving yourself might feel like something you're not "allowed" to do at first, but you'll love the freedom it brings you. Since freedom is rocket fuel for a deliberate contextual creator like you, employ this technique in every occasion where you make a mistake—and when others make them too. I've already got your spot in the "Grow a Greater You" Hall of Fame reserved.

Greg Kuhn

Chapter Eighteen

How I Manifested
"Grow a Greater You"

If you've read my other books in this series and spent time on my website, you are undoubtedly already familiar with my story. Yet my intention here is not only a recount of my life, but a comprehensive focus upon the experiences that led me to formulate "Grow a Greater You"—and how I was able to mold this game from its exciting and powerful origin into its present magical state.

I've heard many wonderful stories and read some amazing personal narratives from readers playing "Grow a Greater You." You are joining a vast group of powerful manifestors in your mastery of this amazing game. In fact, the legion of "Grow a Greater You" all-stars grows by the thousands each month. You've now claimed your spot on the all-star team, and I'm thrilled that you're joining us. If you feel inspired, send me your story as you play. Make it as detailed as you want and, with your permission, I may include it in a future book of inspirational "Grow a Greater You" success stories. Simply contact me via my website (http://whyquantumphysicists.com/) when you've got something to share. I can't wait to read about your success, be inspired by it, and live it, vicariously, with you.

How did I become "Greg Kuhn" as I know him today? My journey may be uniquely mine, yet I know you'll find much to relate with in it if you allow yourself to. I'm no more and no less special or blessed than you. And I may not have faced circumstances any more or less challenging than you. Those are relative perspectives. What I can say is that I was blessed with the gift of almost unbearable misery that motivated me to create "Grow a Greater You"—misery for which I am profoundly grateful, since, among other things, it gave me an opportunity to not only escape the Neanderthal paradigms I held but also to have the opportunity to be of value to you. Being of value is a gift only you can choose to bestow upon me, and I am humbled by it if you so choose.

I was born a blessed child. The oldest of two children, I have a beautiful sister almost two years younger but, throughout my life, almost always many years wiser. My parents are compassionate, open-minded, educated, fun-loving people who always made their family a top priority right from the start. No matter how successful my mother and father became, my sister and I always had lots of love, attention, support, motivation, and help. My mom and dad raised me to be that way too, and my commitment to becoming a better father, husband, friend, and human being shows me they succeeded.

My mother retired early from a career as an elementary school teacher to devote herself to raising my sister and me in a home full of activity and love. When my sister and I were teenagers, our family moved to a farm, where Mom was able to manifest her dream of being a steward of a 30-acre spread with horses, cows, sheep, chicken, dairy goats, pigs, guinea hens, rabbits, and too many cats and dogs to count. My mother instilled many wonderful lessons throughout my upbringing, primarily the value of family and the importance of time invested in each other.

My father was the Associate Chair of the Department of Psychiatry at the University of Louisville School of Medicine. He devoted the later half of his career to working with patients who had chronic pain and diseases such as cancer. His work inspired him to develop a second career as an author and speaker; calling himself "The Laugh Doctor," my father has worked with such luminaries as Jerry Lewis to spread the message of taking ourselves less seriously and how important that is to our health, success, and well-being. I have met many highly successful people and been given some amazing growth opportunities though working with my father, but, like my mother, his most important lesson to me was the importance of making family a priority.

Like any human being, however, I also learned and adopted many limiting beliefs. Prior to my early 30s, I simply viewed my Neanderthal-paradigm beliefs as "the way it is" and I did not even see such beliefs as limiting. My beliefs were simply the unchangeable rules of life and, like it or not, they were what they were. It wasn't until my early 30s that I discovered the need to change my beliefs. I'll discuss that in greater detail momentarily, but until that time I never even gave any thought to having beliefs at all.

The limiting beliefs I carried into adulthood were most certainly not the fault of my parents. Whatever limiting beliefs they transferred to me were not done so intentionally and were usually done for one of two reasons: either they were trying to protect and help me or they were merely unconsciously transferring the beliefs they had been taught. Like all of us, my parents were not perfect; they, like every other parent, inadvertently taught many limiting beliefs to their children. There is no reason for anger at my parents' human imperfections, for who but a child would expect their parents to be perfect?

Because every person, including me, is a work in progress, parents, too, are not immune to teaching children some limiting beliefs—even under the best circumstances and even if only unconsciously. In fact, perhaps that is exactly the way it is supposed to be—since it is the suffering our limiting beliefs causes us that motivates us to play "Grow a Greater You." By making the story of limiting beliefs better-feeling and believable in that manner, perhaps my children will one day thank me for the one's I've taught them—because I've most assuredly unintentionally done so.

The limiting beliefs I carried with me into adulthood and blindly accepted as the unyielding truth led me into a personal hell that manifested in my mid-30s. Don't get me wrong, I also had many wonderful beliefs that served me well and allowed me to enjoy a successful career and a good relationship with my family. And they also allowed me to be a relatively well-liked person, by all accounts, with a good sense of humor.

As I approached my 30s, I was experiencing a successful life of home ownership, a good income, family, and career, yet I was still not completely satisfied. I didn't feel fulfilled or happy on a deep, soul level. I enjoyed my life but always felt there was untapped potential within me that remained dormant. At around age 30, I began to seek solutions for my fulfillment by reading the books of personal development giants such as Napoleon Hill, Og Mandino, Zig Ziglar, Wayne Dyer, Brian Tracy, Frank Bettger, and Jim Rohn. I was also open to religious and philosophical sources, and I even studied quantum physics then.

My greatest desire was to be wealthy. Part of my desire for wealth stemmed from an inner gnawing to grow, expand, and be important and worthwhile—to take my place in my community as a leader and a contributor. There are five millionaires in my immediate family, which I allowed to make me feel like an underachiever if I "settled" for the merely "adequate" income I was making.

During my quest for self-improvement and fulfillment, I read voraciously. It was Napoleon Hill's classic book *Think and Grow Rich* that provided me with my final revelation. Building upon what I had learned from my previous searches, Hill revealed a great secret that I embraced: the power of your thoughts. I had read this secret in many iterations—from *The Bible* teaching that the simple faith of a mustard seed can move a mountain to Dr. Wayne Dyer telling us that we'll see it when we believe it.

But I made a classic yet understandable blunder after reading *Think and Grow Rich*. I had discovered that my thoughts were the most important energy to employ for making my dreams come true. I had also learned that my negative beliefs were holding me back and needed to be changed. And, therefore, I deduced that positive thoughts were the great secret to human fulfillment; positive thought was capable of changing my beliefs and making my dreams for wealth come to fruition.

I had not yet read much about the law of attraction. And, in fact, I didn't study the law of attraction specifically during this time of my life. It wasn't until later, during my most desperate hours, that I started reading about it—in conjunction with a much more in-depth study of quantum physics. But I'm pretty certain I'd have gleaned the same message about positive thought from law of attraction books if I had read them.

If you've read a lot of self-empowerment literature, you know that positive thought is a cornerstone of it. I am not demonizing nor demeaning the wonderful teachers and their wisdom I availed myself of. Anointing positive thought and employing it in the manner I did was my interpretation and conclusion. None of my sources of wisdom explicitly taught or commanded me to do the things you're about to read.

Furthermore, self-empowerment literature is 100% correct in touting positive thought. Positive thought is an amazingly important and powerful tool—and it works wonderfully with Home Run Desires. The limitations of positive thought, however, immediately appear when we use it on some of our Ground Rule Double Desires. And its inadequacies come fully into the light when we use it as our sole method for manifesting our Strikeout Desires. Your subconscious brain knows that positive thought is way too unbelievable to allow it access to your internal belief storehouse. Thus, in almost every case, positive thought can make no actual changes to your beliefs.

But I had no concept yet that my desire for wealth was a Strikeout Desire. I had no knowledge of how ineffective positive thought is on changing our beliefs about a Strikeout Desire. Worse still, I was completely ignorant about how our subconscious brain really works and, therefore, I had no clue regarding how to truly change a belief. Because I was certain that I had uncovered the secret to changing my beliefs and fulfilling my unrealized dreams for wealth, I was very excited to employ positive thought and simply knew it would facilitate my greatest desire.

My entire adult life, my greatest unfulfilled desire had been financial abundance. I had a Master's Degree, I made a good salary, I'd even been the grateful recipient of financial gifts from my family—yet I never had enough money. I was always in some sort of debt with credit cards and I could never get ahead. My income always disappeared quickly with little to nothing of substance remaining except more debt. I worked hard, I greatly desired more money, and I was a good person. My money failings were a source of misery.

Imagine my excitement, then, when I realized that, by employing positive thought to its greatest effect, I could finally escape the misery my lack of money had always caused me. I truly believed that God was smiling down on me, beaming like a proud father, saying, "All right, Greg! You finally learned the solution I've been waiting for you to discover. This is the great secret so many never fully embrace, let alone understand. Now I can help you live the life you've always wanted! This is awesome, I'm so proud of you, I'm so happy for you, and I can't wait to help you realize your dreams!"

I wanted to experience financial abundance for all the right reasons, too. I wanted my family to have nice things, I wanted to help people and give to charities, I wanted to provide for my sons' future, and I wanted to be an admirable, accomplished, successful man. So many people in my family had great wealth, and I was a smart, hard-working person just like them. The icing on the cake was that I had no inclination to take advantage of anyone or deprive anyone else of success or happiness in the process of accumulating wealth. In fact, helping others with my wealth was something I couldn't wait to do.

Given that my intention and my motivation were purely good and positive, it seemed to me a 100% no-brainer, can't-fail proposition to combine the secret of positive thought with some positive actions. Now that I knew this great secret, how in the world could I possibly fail? This was truly destiny unfolding before my very eyes; very soon my family would be so happy about all our new financial success. And relatives and neighbors would be tremendously proud of me too.

I began to research actions I could take to become wealthy—ones that I could take without going back to school, leaving my current career, or starting anew up a corporate ladder. After considering many possibilities, my research eventually led me to what seemed like the perfect business: real estate investment in partnership with an accomplished property manager. Given the time-constraints of my full-time job and that of my then-wife, this business seemed the perfect positive action to take. It combined our talents, great credit, and financial resources with my positive thought and positive intent, so reaping the rewards I had been waiting for suddenly seemed a forgone conclusion. What a blessed future awaited my family now that I had the courage to take action on my dreams. Now that I knew the secret to making that action successful, nothing could stop us.

My (then) wife took some time to thoughtfully arrive at a place of agreement with my plan for a real estate business. After checking around, I found the perfect property manager, and we interviewed her together. Both of us concluded that she was a good choice to oversee the day-to-day operations of our business. Additionally, I studied the business of being a landlord extensively, learning from books, videos, and acquiring a mentor. I already had the secret of positive thought in place; now the practical pieces were ready for us to finally achieve my dreams of financial abundance.

We went all in—with full faith and confidence in our endeavor. Using our resources, we acquired a small army of rental homes and our property manager began to supervise their operation. Armed with knowledge about the business, I simply monitored the income/expense data and met at least once a month with our property manager to go over the results of our business. And, because we were using a property manager, my wife and I were both able to keep our 9-to-5 jobs. It was the best of all possible worlds that, combined with my unsinkable commitment to positive thought, simply could not fail.

When I reference my commitment to positive thought, by the way, I mean a total, ironclad, non-negotiable, and complete one. I prayed and meditated with positive thoughts and energy every day about the business. I journaled regularly about the business from only the most positive perspectives. I refused to speak about the business except in positive terms. And I actually monitored my own thoughts about the business too—stopping myself anytime I found doubts, fears, or misgivings creeping in and correcting my thoughts back to positive ones. I made a 100% commitment to positive thought as if it were my full-time job because I considered it more important to the success of the business than anything else we were doing.

I truly felt that, as long as I stayed positive, God (or the Universe), would reward me with the wealth I desired. After all, God knew that I had the best of intentions and motivations. As I mentioned earlier, I felt that God must've been so excited that I'd figured out the secret of positive thought and was now only too happy to finally be able to bestow upon me those desires for wealth I ached for—desires that would be of great value to so many people. I imagined God saying, "You placed the last puzzle piece; you learned what your portion of our partnership entails. Now I'm finally able to do these things for you. And I've been wanted to do them for you for so long. Let's get started!"

So imagine my surprise when things didn't immediately go well. The business produced more months in the red than I expected. We had difficulties keeping sustained occupancy, and the costs of repairs mounted after tenants vacated. Normal expenses seemed to always eat up a good portion of our monthly net income, too. Yet, due to my commitment to total positive thought and my unwavering faith that all the pieces were in perfect order for our success, I redoubled my efforts in all areas of total positive thought at every turn.

Every time we encountered bumps in the road or needed to dip into our personal income or savings, I simply told myself, over and over, something like, "This is okay. This fear is an illusion. I am being tested, that is all. And this will all work out in the end. We cannot fail. If I stay the course with positive thought, the Universe will reward us." I played that loop on constant repeat every day. Even when the bumps in the road became potholes. Even when the potholes became chasms. I kept the faith, anticipating the day I could look back on these trials and tribulations, laughing at the fear that had once tempted me to pull the plug and run away. Laughing at the fear that I had walked through and actually destroyed, a day at a time, with my positive thought.

Until the day, however, that we ran out of money to pay the rental home mortgages or the repair bills and our property manager ran out of "duct tape" solutions. When there was no more money available for me to "rob Peter to pay Paul." Until the day I had to face my family and report we were past the point of no return, which seemed to come upon us so quickly. We appeared to be ruined; we now had almost $1 million in mortgage debt we could never repay, we owned fourteen properties mostly in unrentable disarray for which we could no longer make mortgage payments, and there was nothing left of our personal savings to float the business any longer. We were decimated—the future held foreclosures, bankruptcy, and a lifetime of litigation and unpayable debt. No college for the kids, no retirement for us, no living a lifestyle equitable with our 9-to-5 incomes.

We were able to continue paying our home mortgage and our personal bills, but after hiring an attorney we stopped paying any of the mortgages on the rentals. I began to personally manage the few properties that still had tenants and simply worked long hours to make sure their needs were taken care of in the fair and humane fashion they deserved. It didn't take long for the calls and letters from the banks to begin. We knew that was coming; the banks wanted their money, after all, but such contact was frightening. What I wasn't prepared for, however, were the unnerving and scary appearances of sheriff's deputies at my home and workplace delivering notices of court action by the banks. I forwarded those notices to our attorney, but they reinforced the terrible reality that this was really happening.

How could this be happening, I cried? How could my total commitment to positive thought not have turned the challenges our business faced into mere bumps in the road on the way to great success? So great was my faith in a successful outcome from my positivity that I still continued to think positively for months after initially sharing the bad news with my family—blindly assuming that, even amid the horrific state of our business, a "white knight" was surely on its way to save the day. The universe simply couldn't leave me high and dry, I thought, and wouldn't I look even more like the hero when we emerged victorious on the other side of these terrifying circumstances?

My family was devastated. Frightened and enraged. Livid that all my positive-thought-based plans, actions, and efforts had become, at best, nothing more than the rantings of a lunatic bent on causing us all harm. And an unmitigated pack of destructive lies at the worst. It only enraged them more that I still continued to practice positive thought and was encouraging them to do so. Yet I couldn't blame them for feeling that way. How could I adequately explain my unreserved faith in my plan? How could I justify the decimation and devastation my plan had wrought? What comfort could it give them to explain how completely I had believed that my positive-thought plan couldn't fail?

Before long, however, I could no longer manage to believe that positive thought was going to rescue us. As this stinging reality finally sunk in, I began to feel more alone and abandoned than I imagined possible. My pain and sorrow over the devastation I created for my family was titanic, and my personal humiliation was just as immense. I did not feel worthy of being alive, and I accepted all the anger, blame, and disappointment directed toward me from my family—because I deserved it. Despite this being our business, it had been my idea and my plan; I had been the one who convinced everyone to go along with it. I felt deserving of every bit of their anger and rage. I agreed with their blame because I had failed them and, ultimately, lied to them.

I, however, also had my own growing bonfire of personal rage. It wasn't toward anyone in my family—they did nothing wrong and had trusted me implicitly—and it wasn't even toward the people involved in our business, even though many of them did not fulfill their legal or fiduciary obligations to us. My cauldron of molten rage was directed at one thing: God, or the universe.

Not at first, mind you. Because, as I wrote, for months after the business was first exposed as a financial ruin and, in retrospect, a terrible idea, I kept the faith that the universe was still going to step in and manifest my desires—somehow saving the day in some unexpected and miraculous way. It wasn't until I finally realized that no salvation was coming, that our ship really was going to sink and take everyone in my immediate family down with it, that my rage was unleashed.

This failure was my complete, final, and penultimate "Up Yours!" from the universe. I had desired financial abundance my entire adult life. I had no inclination to harm anyone in acquiring and possessing more money. And, in fact, I wanted to do good, charitable things with the money—things that would benefit many deserving people. I had many immediate family members who were incredibly wealthy. There was not one single wrong nor inappropriate thing about my desires for money and nothing but good could have come from its realization.

Our business had followed a well-designed blueprint for success. We had a solid, logical plan and worked hard to make it successful. Additionally, and more importantly from my perspective, I had thoroughly researched my part in the creation of my desires. Not only had we created a logical protocol to run the business, from a practical perspective, but I had engaged the universe from a spiritual one as well. From many trustworthy sources, I had divined the supposedly heretofore hidden secret of using positive thought to change my beliefs and I had created it authentically, consistently, and powerfully, just as I felt I had been taught.

And, in the end, how did the universe respond to all those efforts? It said "No." It said, "Greg, I considered your desires and how much they mean to you, evaluated your good intentions and motivations, noted the many people in your family who have already achieved such success, and weighed your incredible commitment to positive thought, which you employed just as you were taught. And I've decided that my answer will be 'no'. Yes, all these other people, many without the incredible commitment to positive thought you fulfilled and without the good intentions and motivations you hold, do get to be financially abundant. But not you."

"Yet that's not the end of it, Greg. In fact, that's not even the half of it," I envisioned the universe continuing. "You aren't just being denied the realization of your financial dreams. Even though their manifestation wouldn't have harmed anyone, even though you are a good man with good intentions and motivations, and even though you maintained virtually nothing but positive thoughts to back up your positive actions, you aren't simply being denied the financial abundance you desire. No, you fool. Your outcome is more than a mere denial of your dreams; your outcome is getting crushed like a grape underneath an elephant's foot. You're about to find out what happens to someone like you when he dares to think he might be worthy of abundance. That's right, Greg, you're getting utterly destroyed—wiped out almost beyond all recognition. And, because I know how to make your misery life-threatening, your family will bear the brunt of this total humiliation—this total rejection of your value and worth. Your family will suffer in even greater fashion all because of you. How dare you imagine yourself worthy? I will now teach you what horrific things happen to someone who dares think himself worthy of more."

From my point of view, I couldn't imagine how a crueler, more sadistic joke could have been played on me. I hated the universe, positive thought, and self-help. I hated it with a passion that probably went far beyond the anger, fear, and disappointment my family was feeling. I imagined the universe laughing while watching "piranhas" eat me one painful little bite at a time. From now on, instead of focusing any more energy on positive-thoughts, I focused upon working with attorneys, banks, realtors, and on repairing houses in an effort to mitigate the impending doom and regain some trust and confidence from my family. I hated God and what the universe had done to me.

I want to take a time-out from my story for a moment to illustrate how profoundly I misunderstood the creative process (the very process that you've now learned to play with aplomb). You may be able to relate to my perspectives during that time and the incredible anger to which they gave birth, because they are those of Neanderthal paradigms. In my universe, I was being denied, by a gatekeeper, access to what I wanted. I directed my incredible anger toward an outside authority, completely separate from me, who possessed the power to deny my desires, revealing my Neanderthal paradigms and corresponding limiting beliefs. I was enraged at a giver of gifts who decided what I would receive in return for my efforts—a force separate from me with final authority, who arbitrarily told me "no."

Additionally, at that time, I thought that my positive thoughts should have corrected, overcome, and rebuilt any beliefs that needed to be changed. My misunderstanding of how our beliefs function in creating reflections from the quantum field, as well as my complete ignorance of how our subconscious brain works in regards to changing our beliefs, poured high octane fuel on the growing bonfire of rage I directed toward that mythical giver of gifts. After all, according to my understanding, I had done everything required to earn the favor of that gatekeeper. I had, in my view, changed my beliefs through my complete commitment to positive thinking, but the giver of gifts didn't do his part. He left me standing alone and humiliated at the altar and also destroyed my family as a cruel "added bonus."

For a little over a year, nothing happened. No one was interested in purchasing our dilapidated properties and, with my full-time job, I could spend only weekends getting them in a more sellable condition. Our attorney was able to hold off the banks from foreclosing, even though no payments were being made on any mortgage except our primary residence. The realtors we engaged to sell these properties, although working hard on our behalf, had nothing to report but bad news regarding potential buyers. No one in her right mind was going to pay what we owed on these properties. And our attorney had no legal solutions simply because there were none available. In short order, we retained a bankruptcy lawyer and made plans for the inevitable implosion.

As I've shared, the suffering and anger of my family was tremendous. My guilt, shame, and anger formed a toxic mix with my family's reactions and I truly began to wish for my own demise. Through my death, at least I could prove myself worthy and valuable to them with the life insurance payout necessary to rectify the debt. In fact, there were probably more than a few occasions when the only things that prevented me from assisting my own death were how much additional harm it would do to my sons, my belief that the giver of gifts would probably continue his cruelty by allowing me to live but be horribly disabled afterward, and the fact that it would be extremely difficult to fool my insurance company anyway. Other than those three notions, I had little reason to hold on. For months on end, I had absolutely no hope. In fact, at my bottom, I went to sleep each night demanding the giver of gifts kill me in my sleep if he wasn't planning to fix all this for us.

As you know, the universe never killed me in my sleep—unless I'm a ghost, which I'm pretty certain isn't true. And, in fact, the universe actually did fix everything for me—just not in the way I imagined it would, nor through any methodology I could have conceived from my Neanderthal paradigms. What actually happened is that I learned how the universe's creative process truly works, how we can greatly influence that creative process, and, therefore, harness the power of the universe. And this game you've learned, "Grow a Greater You," now allows you to do the same. You've now tamed, befriended, and saddled up the strongest, largest, fastest, most legendary wild thoroughbred that ever existed. And she is now yours to command as you wish.

Here's what happened. By the spring of 2007, I was working as hard as I could on all the homes, keeping in touch with our attorney, and meeting regularly with our realtors. But I was whistling past the graveyard. Nothing was happening except doomsday drawing closer one day at a time. Then, out of the blue, an old college friend with whom I hadn't spoken in a long time, Joe Chabot, contacted me to tell me he had recently moved to Lexington, Kentucky, with his wife. He was particularly excited to tell me about a book he'd read, *The Secret*, and how much the law of attraction was helping him.

Joe insisted that I allow him to send it to me, to which I acquiesced and thanked him. But in reality, he would have been better off throwing that book in a dumpster instead of giving it to me. I had forever sworn off self-help and positive thought as worthless garbage that had done nothing but set me up and hoodwink me with its cruel lies. Never again would I humiliate myself by subscribing to pure b.s. like that.

In early June of that same year, I got a fateful call from my attorney telling me that she could hold off the banks' litigation for only four or five more months. We had until late fall before a financial hell of unrepayable debt would rain down upon us, trapping us within its prison forever. The doomsday we knew was coming was now squarely in the rearview mirror and about to overtake us. And there was no indication of an 11th-hour pardon from the universe.

Then a funny thing happened. In the midst of making peace with what was surely our horrible future, I happened to have quite a bit of time on my hands one morning as my sons attended a summer day camp while we visited my (then) in-laws. Guess what I discovered buried in the driver-side door pocket, after dropping them off for their first morning of camp? That copy of *The Secret* that Joe had sent me. I had shoved it in that space after opening the mail the day that package arrived.

"What the heck do I have to lose?" I thought, since I had nothing but time on my hands that morning in a strange town. Out of boredom but without much optimism, I read *The Secret*. I had never really learned much about the law of attraction, at least not the way it was explained in that book, and, in my desperate state of circumstances, I was quickly hooked by its promise of the influence we could have over our life experiences. As I quickly finished that short book, my complete desperation, helplessness, and hopelessness actually overcame my resentment toward self-help and I found myself inspired, especially since nothing else had worked and our doomsday was just around the corner.

One of the most exciting things about the law of attraction, as *The Secret* explained it, was how much it reminded me of what I already knew from quantum physics. Prior to my ill-fated business venture, I had read about quantum physics as part of my studies for manifesting wealth, and I had become enthralled by the new paradigms it provided us. What I had learned by studying quantum physics had, in fact, been an important validation regarding my use of positive thought.

Quantum physics clearly indicates, after all, that the individual observer plays a very important role in the creation of our material world. That is a fact which strongly validated my use of positive thought as the seminal component of our business venture. And here was a book basically claiming the same thing. Because of that similarity, it occurred to me that I just might have stumbled upon some solutions to our financial doomsday dilemma.

Calling it the law of attraction was semantics to me; what did I have to lose by seeking such solutions? Nothing else had worked, and our canoe was swiftly approaching Niagara Falls, so who would care if I tried to use quantum physics' new paradigms and they didn't work? Yet as much as I could see that new paradigms available to us through quantum physics might actually provide me the solutions we sought, where were the instructions? Could *The Secret*, and the law of attraction, be giving me the clues I needed to put these new paradigms into action? And, if so, where could I find the blue print, the game plan, to do this?

An internet search on the law of attraction revealed that the most impactful law of attraction teachers were Jerry and Esther Hicks, to whom I owe an immense debt of gratitude. I immersed myself in their seminal book *Ask and It is Given* while also dusting off my collection of quantum physics tomes (some of which I've referenced for you in the Introduction). And it was through the melding of the Hicks' writings about the law of attraction and my renewed study of quantum physics that the initial version of "Grow a Greater You" was formed.

I didn't start playing "Grow a Greater You" using the fully fleshed-out, cannot-fail game plan that you now possess. Yet I applied myself so thoroughly, completely, and devotedly to the basic processes I was able to formulate that I overcame the initial inadequacies I would eventually iron out for you. Fortunately, you do not need to possess the almost insane level of motivation I did to play "Grow a Greater You" like a Hall-of-Famer; the instructions you've learned are streamlined, time-tested, honed to beautiful perfection, and ready to let you ride your dreams to reality.

Although my results may sound magical, even challenging to believe, everything you read really happened for me. It didn't happen because I was lucky; it happened as a direct result of playing "Grow a Greater You."

And I've found that it only gets easier and more exciting to play "Grow a Greater You" with practice. Since my initial foray, I've used it to manifest my desires concerning my health, weight, family, relationships, self-worth, and marriage, among many other areas of my life.

What I did (and continue to do) with this process is not an anomaly. You can do it too. In fact, I encourage you not to limit yourself to merely duplicating my successes; there is no reason you can't do even better than me.

In 2007, when I created the rudimentary version of this wonderful game, "Grow a Greater You," I didn't really know what I was doing. At that time, I would have called the game "Saving My Life." It wasn't until later that I realized I'd created something I could actually expand and use to manifest any desire under any circumstances. I had created a plan that, with a little fine-tuning, was fun, sustainable, and incredibly important to share with you.

As you know, in 2007, I was facing bankruptcy, a little over one million dollars in debt, a sputtering career that I did not find fulfilling, a marriage close to over, and I was (surprise, surprise) miserable. So low and unhappy was I that, outside of my three sons, there was often little motivation to get out of bed in the morning. With each passing day it became progressively more challenging to go on.

Today, however, all those pressing issues have been long resolved with not a single lingering effect. And I contextually create with ease desires I didn't even dare harbor in 2007. My life is richer and more rewarding than I ever imagined, and I mean that literally, since, at that time, I couldn't even foresee being *worthy* of creating the dreams and desires I have fulfilled today.

Today, you see, I truly understand that what I created within the seeming unlikely forge of my nearly unbearable desperation and suffering is a game that embodies everything we came to Earth to do. "Grow a Greater You" is our purpose for being here. It is our whole reason for choosing to inhabit these vessels we call "human bodies" and experience life on this planet.

Flash forward to May 2008. On a Monday afternoon, I got a phone call from my realtor, telling me that the very last of my properties was sold and that the bank was forgiving all of my remaining debt. After that phone call, I had finally gotten rid of every single rental property, never had any foreclosures, had no debt remaining from any of them, never had to declare bankruptcy, and actually had money in the bank. How did that happen?

Quite simply, it did not happen for me because of how badly I desired it. Make no mistake; I did desire it more than anything else in my life, but my desire wasn't the key. If the level of desire we held were of primary importance, I have no doubt you'd be manifesting almost everything you want. It happened for me because I played "Grow a Greater You."

This process took my family from sure bankruptcy to a release from all litigation, total debt forgiveness, and relaxing financial solvency in less than a year. As amazing as that might sound, it's not an overhyped version of what happened after I created and employed the first version of this game. What happened is actually so fantastic that I am sometimes hesitant to share all of it because of how incredible it sounds.

For example, when I started playing my infant version of "Grow a Greater You," during the time between June 2007 and May 2008, I had large checks arrive unexpectedly in the mail. I had bills mysteriously be far less than I expected for no reason at all. I had money appear in my checking account seemingly out of thin air. I had banks tell me they would accept far less than I owed on properties, so I could short sell them, and then tell me I didn't have to repay about $800,000 in loans. At one point, in fact, my attorney said to me, "Greg, I have no idea why (this bank) is being so good to you. I've never seen anything like this before!" But I knew why— because that's what my new beliefs about debt and money were commanding the quantum field to manifest in my own unique, individual universe.

I clearly remember another attorney who was involved with some of the various short sales and debt forgiveness almost falling out of his chair, saying, "Why in the hell would (the bank) do that for you?!" When he said that, I had an initial flash of fear, "Oh no! He's right! The bank won't really do this for me." Then I quickly relaxed, remembering that the quantum field will move mountains to connect the dots in the fulfillment of my desires when my beliefs are aligned with them.

While working this process for the first time on debt and money, I discovered that we are the ones who decide to dream small and play small. We are not compelled to do so by any conventional wisdom. The quantum field sure doesn't care whether we dream big or small; the quantum field doesn't know the difference between manifesting a penny on the sidewalk versus manifesting a bank saying, "Greg, we'll let you sell this property for far less than it's worth. You don't need to go bankrupt. And, I tell you what, instead of going bankrupt, why don't you just forget about this huge loan for which you are 100% liable? I know we could hold you liable for the remaining loan and easily force you to repay it, but for almost no reason at all we're simply just going to forgive it."

Here is a specific example of how the quantum field connects dots: At one point, I finally sold a huge albatross of a property when the bank agreed to a short sale (which means the buyer is paying far less than the remaining mortgage amount). The buyer planned to pay cash and rehab it. There were some unavoidable snags on my end, however, which delayed the sale for a couple of weeks. The buyer became increasing agitated and called my realtor on two occasions demanding reductions in his purchase price. Both times we gave him reductions amounting to a total discount of $3,500.

I chose not to label these price reductions "bad," even though they frightened me because they were adding to the amount we were still going to owe the bank after the sale. I simply told myself the best-feeling, believable story possible: "Thank you, God. Thank you, Universe, for lining up this buyer. I am not happy this is happening, but I trust that everything is happening in a way that will allow you to line up the dots for us. I'm not going to call this 'bad' because I not only lack the perspective to definitively do so, but labeling it so would also tie the hands of the quantum field's infinite potential to allow it to manifest my desires."

At the closing, the buyer showed up and paid us the full purchase price. There was no mention of any of the discounts he had demanded and no anger on his part. Believe me, this buyer was an experienced property owner, an old hand at the real estate business; he didn't just "forget" to give us $3,500 less for the property, he just chose not to. I had no explanation for this other than the explanation I had for every other way my desires were manifesting: my beliefs were aligned with my desires and the quantum field was connecting the dots for us.

I mentioned reading the Hicks' book, *Ask and It is Given*, which was a revelation to me, and using it as a form of instruction for how to employ what I knew about quantum physics. "Grow a Greater You," then, owes a great debt of gratitude to the Hicks. While I was crafting my own version of "the quantum law of attraction physics" by melding these two sources, I could see, very plainly, how I had gone so wrong with the business endeavors: I had focused completely upon positive thought without actually truly changing my limiting beliefs and I also took actions without first ensuring that my beliefs were congruent with my desired outcomes.

My failures were making a lot more sense to me. My dedication to raising my beliefs about debt, born from my unbelievable pain and total desperation, allowed me to move relatively quickly up the Emotional Perspective Chart. It usually took me only one day to truly live myself into the next highest emotional perspective, and, thus, I was able to keep moving up the chart at what I know now is a rather rapid pace. You may not find that you, too, can authentically live yourself into your new emotional perspective in a day, so don't be concerned if it takes you longer. In fact, I often find that it takes me a little longer to move up the chart today because I have nowhere near the pain and desperation I had when I played my first version of "Grow a Greater You."

I began my writing from the emotional perspective of Depression/Hopelessness regarding financial abundance and went from there. And I focused on the process for raising my Strikeout Desires (although I hadn't labeled them as such yet) with all of my energy each and every single day. Of course, my writings from the lower emotional perspectives were mostly full of negative things. Those were my true feelings and beliefs about debt and money at the time.

But by the time I was merely up to the perspective of Grief/Desolation, I could already see and feel the difference and improvement in not only my emotional perspective, but also in the reflections of my new beliefs being provided by the quantum field. At the lower perspectives, even though I knew my beliefs had not yet been raised to where I wanted them to be eventually, I could tell that this game was real and was making a noticeable difference in my own unique, individual universe. So, even from the lower emotional perspectives, I began to develop a strong sense of hope in the process I had created.

I was, literally, seeing a different universe even from one tick up the Emotional Perspective Chart. The quantum field was reflecting a different material reality back to me, forming coherence with my new, slightly more positive beliefs that accompanied the new, slightly more positive emotional perspective.

I knew, even from the lower emotional perspectives, that my beliefs about debt would eventually get where I wanted them to, and I also knew that my reflections would grow much more aligned with my conscious desires when that happened. And, throughout the process, in addition to the positive experiences with my emotional perspectives and my material reality, I was continually motivated by the thought, "This is really working."

By early August 2007, I began to experience some very encouraging reflections from the quantum field. By this time, I was writing from the perspective of Anticipation/Eagerness and higher. Bills were lower than expected for no reason. Money appeared in my bank ledger unexpectedly. Cash and funds manifested out of thin air. And, perhaps most importantly, I was gifted with new insights, I could see possibilities that weren't there previously, and I found inspiration for positive action that wasn't available to me from my previous, lower emotional perspectives about debt and money. Just as quantum physics tells us that each individual sees her own unique universe, I found that, with each movement up the Emotional Reference Chart, a whole new world became available to me. I saw new opportunities blossoming all around me with each step up the chart.

How did all that happen? There are many things I did every day—things that the Jerry and Esther Hicks and quantum physics taught me and inspired me to do. But there is one specific thing I did regarding money that poured rocket fuel into my manifestation of it: I decided to celebrate any money, no matter how small the amount, to the maximum extent possible. So I created the Penny Game I taught you in the Hall of Fame techniques chapter. The inspiration to do this came in early July 2007, when I recalled an instance of receiving money during the darkest days of our financial and personal turmoil.

In August 2006, I opened my mailbox to discover a royalty check from some of my writing. Being $1,000,000 in debt with no recourse in sight, I was eager to open the envelope. I rushed into my kitchen and opened the envelope to discover a check for $101.07. Luckily my children were not home at the time because I became enraged and screamed, angrily, "Are you freaking kidding me, God? I'm $1,000,000 in debt and this is what you send me? Take this check and stick it where the sun don't shine!"

Bear in mind I was expecting the universe to step in and save me from financial devastation. With that expectation, the check felt like an insult—a cruel joke from the universe. But remembering that reaction almost a year later was chilling for me. Knowing what I now did about how my beliefs are reflected back to me from the quantum field, my reaction to the check became the perfect illustration of why I had never manifested more money. After all, if that was my response to a small amount of money, what chance did I ever have of growing my beliefs about money?

I had no concept of celebrating that check. The amount of that check and my negative feelings about it could have been important, valuable, and useful information for me about how nonaligned my beliefs about money were with my desires for it. I didn't have any concept of that, though, because I was still laboring under Neanderthal paradigms.

What happened after my last property finally disappeared and my debt was completely gone? I wanted to scream for joy loudly enough to be heard on the moon. Wow, it was over after all, and this game really worked, reliably and predictably. The quantum field really does reflect my beliefs back to me and connects the dots in the most miraculous ways to make that happen. I was so happy, I wanted to explode like a firework.

My life was so different now. I was living in a different material reality, one where I was worthy of not being shackled with debt. My beliefs had truly been raised to the perspective of love regarding "debt." I had grown myself into worthiness regarding being out of debt. It really worked and, for a while, I floated on air in a state of bliss.

I witnessed opportunities appear where there had been none before. I knew now that those opportunities and options were always there waiting to be commanded into creation from the limitless potential of the quantum field. Just waiting there for me to see them. All the quantum field needed was my beliefs to be aligned with them.

After the dust settled, I took inventory and figured that smooth sailing was ahead. By this time my divorce was final, so my next biggest desire was to eventually manifest a true soul mate, although I wasn't in a hurry to even start dating until I had given myself a chance to grieve and heal. I was now a single dad because my boys' mother moved to another state. Additionally, I wanted to manifest a lot more money—enough so I didn't have to worry about taking care of my young sons, managing our now single-parent household, and my personal needs and desires.

Why wouldn't I have anticipated smooth sailing? I had just manifested the removal of almost one million dollars in debt, even though many people (including me) had once deemed that impossible. How difficult could it be now to command the quantum field in other ways?

Actually, believe it or not, I found manifesting some of those other desires very challenging at first. And that perplexed me greatly. How could I have done the impossible—manifest almost one million dollars in debt removal at the eleventh hour—yet now be struggling with manifesting these other desires that weren't nearly as "impossible" for me to imagine?

At first I tried to explain my struggles by attributing my debt relief manifestations to the incredible passion that fueled my efforts. I had been motivated by life or death circumstances, after all, and now my attempts to manifest love and money were merely spurred by more "everyday" desires. These more common desires and my garden-variety motivations must be the culprit, I reasoned; my passion for these new manifestations was simply not as great.

But this explanation didn't put things to rest for two primary reasons. First, although my desire for debt escape was white hot, my desires for love and money were ones I'd felt for much longer so it just didn't ring true for me to call them not as important. Second, although it's true that my desire for debt dissolution was spurred by a life or death energy, my desires for money and love had, in fact, been largely responsible for my actions that got me in to my debt in the first place.

I decided that my manifestation of debt relief had been like a war-time economy. It's often relatively easy for an entire country to galvanize around a war effort and get everyone's cooperation in the production of the things necessary to win. This phenomenon helped lift America out of the Great Depression when World War II struck. And that's a reasonably accurate description of the burning resolve I felt during my greatest hour of need, which kept me focused on manifesting debt resolution.

I resolved to amend my game so I could manifest my desires in "peace-time" too, because, after all, how often was I going to have (or, more accurately, be gifted with) that type of extreme motivation? I needed a thorough and comprehensive blueprint that would work on any type of desire and with any degree of motivation. A plan that would allow me to reliably duplicate and replicate the results of my debt relief manifestations even when I wasn't forced to play "save my life."

Thus "Grow a Greater You" was grown into a game that does just that. I actually started formalizing the current iteration of "Grow a Greater You" as I became open to dating again after my divorce. I had the meat of "Grow a Greater You" and many amazing tools with which to play it already in place from my debt relief manifestations. I knew these things worked, I simply needed to create a sequence and protocol that was easily followed and would reliably create a material reality much more closely aligned with my desires.

I was able to all but finalize this wonderful game as I manifested my soul mate, the beautiful wife who is a fulfilling reflection in my universe today. Additionally, I manifested other relationship desires with it as well, creating beautiful and fulfilling relationships with my sons, my parents, my extended family, and my co-workers. Even with my ex-wife.

The story of manifesting my soul mate is as cool as you might imagine. I hope you've never been divorced, but if you have you know how incredibly devastating the experience is. I don't want to slight the hardships divorce created for my sons and my family. There is much else to share about my divorce and the effects upon others, but this chapter is about my personal game of "Grow a Greater You." So as empathetic as I am toward my children, this description is not about their challenges.

Additionally, I don't want to demonize or blame my ex-wife in any manner. She was not the cause of our divorce. In fact, I now know that our divorce was the perfect reflection of my growing beliefs. It was a perfect reflection of the changes I was going through as I grew my beliefs into being worthy of debt relief. Just as our union had been the perfect reflection of my beliefs as a 20-something, my new beliefs of worthiness had been accurately mirrored back to me as my ex-wife and I realized we no longer had a desire to be married. And the always accurate mirror of material reality continues to reflect my ever-growing beliefs back to me today via my current relationship with my ex-wife, which is a cordial manifestation of our joint commitment to our sons.

I intentionally aligned my beliefs about being lovable, desirable, and worthy with my desires for a soul mate. In retrospect my experience with "Grow a Greater You" has shown me that, in my early 20s, I manifested my ex-wife, a woman who was willing to meet my needs for feeling loved and worthwhile. I made her responsible for those feelings because I did not have beliefs that were aligned with my desires. But as I grew my beliefs to manifest debt relief, I no longer desired a partner who wanted to play those roles. I had learned to do that for myself. There were other factors that greatly contributed to the end of our marriage, of course, and I'm certain my ex-wife had her own similar experiences.

Romantic relationships were a Strikeout Desire when I started playing "Grow a Greater You" with them. I followed the protocol I was perfecting for moving myself up the Emotional Perspective Chart, telling the best-feeling, believable stories about my relationships with women along the way. I clearly remember a conversation with a friend that encapsulated my beliefs at that time. In response to my sharing about my feelings of undesirability, my friend told me, "Greg, when you are ready, you are going to discover that there are tons of women out there who will want to be with you. In fact, they'll feel lucky to get to be with you. Look at who you are and what you have to offer. You may not believe all that now, but I promise you it's true."

I distinctly remember her words making logical sense to me then, but I truly did not believe them. Or, at least, I could not see that universe from the perspective of my beliefs at that time. Having had the experience of manifesting debt relief, however, I also knew that I would be seeing a new universe, perhaps the very one she was describing, in a matter of time. While I couldn't experience that universe then, I knew that the only thing preventing me was a journey up the Emotional Reference Chart.

The first really noticeable changes in my material reality were that I felt freely motivated to spark up conversations with highly desirable women. I remember that distinctly because I had previously often felt inhibited about talking with a desirable woman, sometimes telling myself, "Why would she want to talk with me?" It's funny—I'd always been told by the women in my life that I was a handsome, desirable guy. But those were not my true beliefs about myself and, thus, their compliments only served to make me feel good in that moment.

Of course, one of the problems this caused me, prior to playing "Grow a Greater You" with romantic relationships, was that I became virtually dependent on a woman's praise and compliments to feel desirable, loveable, and worthwhile. You know what a set-up that is; not only is that another living illustration of the Neanderthal paradigms, but it is also a terrible job to assign to another person. And, in fact, anyone willing to take that job has just as many issues as the person who asks her to do it.

Can you see why my divorce ended up being the perfect reflection for a person who got married within that Neanderthal paradigm? If even one of the people in that marriage changes those paradigms and begins to give him or herself those feelings of desirability, lovability, and worthiness through new beliefs aligned with their desires for such, the attraction born of the earlier "need" is likely to vanish like early morning fog in the sunshine.

And that's exactly what I was doing by playing "Grow a Greater You" with finding a soul mate. Rather than going to a gym, joining online singles sites, getting a new car, going out to singles events, or reading books about how to pick up a woman (which might all be great methods or actions to take to achieve a romantic relationship), I chose to focus on raising my beliefs into alignment with my desires for desirability, lovability, and worthiness.

Before I was to the top of the Emotional Reference Chart I was already believing myself desirable, loveable, and worthy in very satisfying and fulfilling ways. How did I evaluate that? The same way I always measure the alignment of my beliefs while playing "Grow a Greater You": by using my reflections as information.

As my beliefs aligned with my desires for a soul mate, the things in my material reality did not necessarily change radically. In other words, everything I was experiencing in my new universe, reflecting beliefs more aligned with my desires, had always been there before I started playing this game on the subject of my soul mate. But since, back then, I was experiencing my limiting beliefs being reflected back to me, I literally couldn't see them.

And just as with manifesting debt relief, there was almost no way I could have envisioned how the quantum field would connect the dots to manifest my soul mate. From the perspectives of the limiting beliefs I once held, it was not possible for me to project how my debt would disappear once my beliefs were aligned, and the same was true for manifesting a soul mate. I wasn't living in that more aligned universe so those manifestations weren't things accessible to my imagination.

My debt relief manifested in a series of incredible, almost unbelievable "coincidences" and miracles. The manifestations grew grander and more pleasing the farther up the Emotional Reference Chart I went. And all the actions I was inspired to take along the way to facilitate those manifestations could be called "a good, solid, logical step-by-step game plan to get out of debt." To a Neanderthal, it would have appeared that what happened was simply the logical outcome of some great actions combined with some fortunate circumstances. And the Neanderthal wouldn't be incorrect; she would merely not be privy to the true source of those manifestations—the beliefs that had become aligned with my desires.

In fact, I could have written a book called "Your Complete Step-by-Step

Guide to Getting Out of Debt." I could have explained every single action I took in a manner you could copy perfectly. And all the actions in that hypothetical book would indeed be worthwhile and valuable for anyone to perform. They really did work for me, after all.

Isn't that actually the way almost all self-help or how-to books are written? From a Neanderthal paradigm, what you do and how you do it are the most important components for any change. For the Neanderthal, the way to manifest your desires is to copy the recommended action steps created by an expert in that field.

But you now understand how irrelevant "what" I did, the actions I took, were. Yes, I was inspired to take a lot of actions, from each new, improved emotional perspective on my journey. Just as you, and anyone else, will be inspired as you play "Grow a Greater You." Whether or not you're inspired to take some of the same actions, when growing into any desire you choose, is unimportant. The only thing that mattered, in my manifestation of debt-dissolution, was that my beliefs were aligning with my desires. The actions took care of themselves.

My manifestation of a soul mate was also an amalgamation of inspired actions combined with incredible, almost unbelievable, "coincidences" and miracles. Not only could I not have predicted the ways in which the quantum field manifested my soul mate desire, but many of its methods were so out of the blue they played out like a Hollywood script.

After meeting women who grew progressively more desirable, I was finding myself not only seeing a new universe of romantic relationships but authentically believing myself a very lovable and desirable man. I effortlessly approached women I wouldn't have thought myself "worthy" of under my old, limiting beliefs. It was truly magical because I'd never really experienced that before. I created and experienced a universe where I was one of the hottest bachelors in town. Every woman that I dated was a wonderful person who I respected and treated with honesty and compassion to the best of my abilities, because I believed they were as worthy of that as me.

My present experiences with my wife, by the way, are even more magical than those bachelor days I just described. With each passing day of my marriage, as I continue to play "Grow a Greater You," what had been a Strikeout Desire becomes even more of a Home Run. My belief's reflections in my marriage couldn't be more pleasing, and it's difficult to imagine feeling more blessed. My relationship with my wife grows more pleasing and fulfilling all the time.

I also want to call your attention to the contextual creation of Greg as a desirable, lovable, and worthy partner via the stories women I dated chose to tell themselves about me. Their stories were just as important as my intentional belief raising. The women I dated were choosing to tell wonderful stories about me, imbuing me with loads of desirability, love, and worthiness. I was incredibly grateful for each of their decisions to do this for, and with, me. I did not arrive into their own unique, individual universes with pre-established meaning and value (except that which I assigned to myself). And, in gratitude I always did my best to return the favor to them.

I am grateful my wife continues to tell herself great stories about me that imbue me with a growing meaning and value for her. She decides, on a daily basis, that I am a masterpiece. Well, on most days anyway. That is a choice she makes that I do not take for granted. And I gladly do the same in return and, thus, our marriage stays vital, vibrant, and exciting.

When I met my wife I did not know that she would become my soul mate. She did not manifest in my own unique, individual universe with a pre-determined meaning and value, after all. But by this time in my journey, I knew without a doubt that I was manifesting and creating wonderful women in my universe that reflected my raised beliefs about my desirability. So it did not surprise me when our relationship blossomed into that of two soul mates.

And here is how magical the quantum field is. My wife and I dated and had been "in love" as teenage sweethearts back in the mid 1980s, but we hadn't seen nor spoken with each other for almost 23 years when we happened to reconnect. And our reconnection "coincidentally" occurred at a time when she had healed and grown after her own divorce. What were the odds of us meeting again, after not even speaking to each other for over 20 years, at just this perfect time? Who could, through his or her actions, manipulate circumstances to occur like that? Only the quantum field can do that, and it beats the pants off the most talented Hollywood screenwriter.

And as we both realized that our relationship was imbued with soul mate potential, I began to play "Grow a Greater You" with my desire to create a blended family. She has a son and I have three—and everyone knows the challenges a blended family presents and the relatively long odds against it working out. Logic dictates that blending two families like ours doesn't usually work. But, of course, by this time I was no longer taking marching orders from conventional wisdom or prevailing communal beliefs.

By the time I began to play "Grow a Greater You" with my desire to have a blended family, Shawn and I were already inspired to talk with a counselor and seek guidance and advice. In our first session, our counselor told us "Ideally, you want the boys to ask you to get married. You want them to be invested and part of the decision. Of course, in these situations, that rarely happens." And when he shared that with us, neither of us responded with optimism about that happening. To be honest, at that time such an outcome actually looked grim when viewed from the Neanderthal paradigm. The boys did not relish such an outcome, and we couldn't really blame them. Without going in to spurious details, all four boys had experienced more trauma and emotional challenges than even a "typical" divorce forces upon children.

But fortunately I was already well versed in "Grow a Greater You." And while I knew that there was no certainty for a specific outcome, I also knew that if I raised my beliefs to align with my desires, I didn't need to focus at all on "how" it could happen. And I certainly knew there was no value in fixating and focusing upon how impossible it all might seem.

What happened? The same thing that regularly happens as I continue to play "Grow a Greater You." I could write a book prescribing specific how-to instructions for what actions to take to successfully blend a family, even under very challenging circumstances like we faced. But you already know that the real power behind the blended family we contextually created came from aligning our beliefs with our desires.

Once again, the quantum field proved to be a miracle worker and reflected a universe that would make a movie so unbelievable you might roll your eyes at it. A year or so after that initial session with our counselor, our boys, unprompted, told my soul mate and me, "Why don't you two get married? We think you should." Of course, our blended family has not always been a cake-and-ice cream experience. What rewarding journey ever is? In fact, there have been moments when each of us has probably recalled the old adage "Be careful what you wish for because you just might get it."

But all kidding aside, without trivializing the challenges, our blended family has been a true source of joy and growth for all of us. Every member of our family has experienced a more desirable material reality, even with the expected (there's my unavoidable participation in communal beliefs again) ups and downs of having step-parents, step-brothers, and step-children. There is no doubt that each of us is blessed by our blended family, and we continue to grow closer and more grateful with each passing year.

I play "Grow a Greater You" each and every day in all areas of my life. Another example of a desire I've been able to grow from Strikeout to Ground Rule Double to Home Run is money, or financial abundance. You know my desperate financial situation that spurred my creation of this game, and you know that I was able to align my beliefs about debt with my desires for its disappearance. But you should also know that I have been able to align my beliefs with my desires for financial abundance. Money had become a Ground Rule Double Desire after growing myself into debt disappearance and it became a full-blown Home Run Desire for me a few years ago.

Extremely gratified by my success with my relationships, I next played "Grow a Greater You" with my desire for financial abundance. As in my experience with growing into my desires for relationships, my manifestation of money was predicated on raising my beliefs to align with those desires. Not on specific actions I should take. By this point, I had learned that if I got my beliefs aligned with my desires the necessary actions would appear before me, along with the inspiration to take them, with effortless ease.

In fact, I was sharing a very revealing memory with my wife a few weekends ago. Back in the very early stages of playing my initial version of "Grow a Greater You," on my debt, I used to listen to the Hicks' Abraham workshops while I made my many six-hour drives to facilitate my sons spending time with their mother who lived two states away. At that time, I did not yet fully understand that my feelings were an important feedback loop informing me of the alignment (or lack thereof) between my beliefs and desires.

I recalled often thinking, "Esther Hicks says she is channeling information from a non-physical energy calling itself Abraham. Writing her books and speaking at her workshops is effortless for her because of this. And she gets to be a millionaire because Abraham 'chose' her to channel through. How come she gets to be their mouthpiece? Why couldn't they have chosen me? I want to do that; how come she is so lucky and not me?" I was envious, and my feelings were providing me with useful, valuable information about how unaligned my beliefs were with my desires (even though I didn't realize it at the time).

Bear in mind that I had been writing self-help literature with my father for years. And, although I had seen some money through these efforts, it was never anywhere close to what I desired. I was not pleased by my manifestations back then because my beliefs were not aligned with my desires for success. Thus, no matter how hard I worked at writing great stuff, and I did invest loads of time, money, and energy into actions like those, my material reality could never be anything other than a reflection of my limiting beliefs.

On that weekend, I sat in my study taking a break from writing and realized that I was "here." I had become the very thing I desired all those years ago. I am now a best-selling author and sought-after speaker, just as I had sometimes enviously fantasized about during those long drives. And I got teary-eyed with gratitude at the immense blessings and opportunities afforded to me and to us all—even when we start our journey from a place of abject hopelessness like I did.

I do not claim to channel a specific entity or group, as Esther Hicks does, by the way. But, as I have grown my beliefs into alignment with my desires about financial abundance, I am definitely channeling non-physical energy. The way I explain it is (as I live my beliefs into alignment with my still growing desires in this area) I am able to allow a greater, freer, and more authentic expression of the quantum field (the non-collapsed true "me") to flow into my creations. This process is tangible and it is, actually, effortless now. I can write and teach how our universe works and how to play "Grow a Better You" with ease. It flows effortlessly from me now because of the immense connection between my beliefs and desires. And my creations resonate with people because of that alignment.

It might not surprise you, by the way, that as I played "Grow a Greater You" with my desires for financial abundance I actually changed the target desire in fairly short order. I realized that my focus should shift to growing my beliefs about money to growing my beliefs about the value of my creations. Instead of playing "Grow a Greater You" on my desire for more money, I started playing it on my desire to imbue my writing with immense value. And, as my beliefs grew into alignment with that desire, my writing began to take flight as never before.

I'm still playing this game on my writing, by the way, along with my desires to imbue my speaking and teaching with tremendous value. And I find that what I'm able to create, within the universe I now see from my ever-growing alignment, is magical and amazing. I'll bet, if you go back and read the first book in my *Why Quantum Physicists...* series, you can tangibly feel the growth of my message. Although I'm very proud of all my previous books, I expect that growth in my writing to continue as I keep playing this beautiful game.

Once my beliefs were in keen alignment with my desires for producing incredible value, the money became a natural and pleasing feedback loop. Manifesting more money now doesn't surprise me at all, nor does it make me wonder if I'm really worthy of it. The financial abundance I experience today is who I am; it is merely a reflection of my beliefs about the value of what I create. And I never have to expect a reflection different from my beliefs now.

Additionally, my sky-high beliefs about the value of what I share have resulted in wonderfully desirable feedback in other forms too. Hearing from grateful readers, meeting beautiful people at my speaking engagements, and being told about transformed lives are reflections of my beliefs that I cannot even place adequate value upon. Those manifestations are beautiful things that often eclipse the financial abundance my family now experiences. And as I have experienced more pleasing manifestations via my writing and speaking, which are incredibly fulfilling, I am excited to report that I've also been continually blessed with greater desires to grow into.

What were the odds regarding what I'd become from that universe of abject hopelessness I inhabited when I played my first rudimentary version of "Grow a Greater You"? Our old paradigms, conventional wisdom, and prevailing logic strongly indicate that I was destined to become a broken man, bankrupt in more ways than financial; that my children would be expected to have emotional problems and act out in self-destructive ways; that I might engage in a series of meaningless romantic relationships doomed to failure born of my desperate desires to continue experiencing the worthiness that I needed women to give me; and that I would grow continually resentful, blaming the giver of gifts and those who wronged me for the miserable reflections I was experiencing.

Odds are, with Neanderthal paradigms, the reflections of my beliefs would cause me misery that I could neither rationalize nor explain. I would become a perpetual victim and tell myself stories lamenting how unfair life was—stories about how I always got the short end of the stick while the chosen, lucky few got their desires fulfilled.

But, because of "Grow a Greater You," that is not my lot in life. I get to define the meaning and value of every "thing" in my life and every experience I have, on terms of my choosing—terms that serve me and align me with my desires. And, in fact, I have been able to grow a sincere gratitude for all my challenging circumstances because they have truly become tremendous blessings. My challenges have provided me with amazingly effective motivational fuel. And they have afforded me unique experiences that, having now grown my beliefs into alignment, allow me to share real solutions with you.

In addition to the other self-help books I mentioned, I could now also write a how-to book teaching you to become a best-selling, independently published, self-help author. And I could also write one about how to create a highly trafficked website and become an exhilarating and empowering professional speaker and teacher. And all my how-to instructions would be worth their weight in gold because they would contain specific instructions about actions that continue to work almost like magic.

Yet, if I did write all those how-to books I've mentioned in this chapter, from the Neanderthal paradigm of "copy my actions if you want what I have," I would be doing more than a disservice to you. I would be lying to you. Copy my actions all you like (and you're certainly welcome to), but my actions are absolutely not responsible for manifesting this dream life I am living. My actions are not even close to being the most important agent in creating this universe I now live in—a universe more fulfilling than I ever dared dream during my darkest days and one I know I will continue to expand as I grow my beliefs into alignment with the new, grander desires I'm continually gifted with.

When I reference my "darkest days," by the way, I'm not solely referring to when I faced our financial holocaust. From the empowered universe I now experience, from the top of the creative pyramid, my "darkest days" include most of my life prior to playing "Grow a Greater You." Not that I was never happy before, but living within the old Neanderthal paradigms was almost always frightening and maddeningly frustrating.

Playing "Grow a Greater You" is solely responsible for the miracle of my life. And to give credit to any actions I've taken, no matter how inspired and effective they have been, is to direct you back to those outdated, incredibly ineffective Neanderthal paradigms. The actions are unimportant, even potentially dangerous and harmful, unless done in conjunction with beliefs aligned with your desired outcomes.

And, no matter, how skilled I become at playing "Grow a Greater You," and no matter how many people I am blessed to have the opportunity to teach to play it, my family and friends don't need to worry. I will never get so full of myself that I'll become an egotistic jerk, nor ever get too big for my britches. Because I know how the universe works, just as you do too now. I do not await discovery by anyone in a pre-determined state of "good." It is your individual decision to tell yourself stories about "Grow a Greater You" that make it great, not any inherent value it has independent of you.

In response to anyone who holds religious beliefs, by the way, I do not believe that anything about playing "Grow a Greater You" supersedes a religion or a religious-based God. "Grow a Greater You" does not teach you to become "God." By playing this game, you are actually becoming more of what God, or whatever you choose to call the very real, non-physical, omnificent, omnipresent, omnipotent energy of the quantum field, intends and hopes you to be. By playing "Grow a Greater You," you are becoming the living expression of God, the quantum field, the universal mind, or whatever you wish to call the source of all life and the universe.

You are working, hand-in-hand, with the very source of our physical universe to contextually create your material world. There must be little doubt by now that this is your role; you are the contextual creator of all that you see and experience. Since this is how our universe truly works, how could this not be what you are here to do? And how could you truly be serving the source of life, if service is your desire, by playing small and abdicating your role?

Are my books works of genius? If they are, in your own unique, individual universe, you are the one who makes them so through the stories you decide to tell yourself about them and the meaning and value you choose to imbue them with. However "good" you choose to make my books in your universe, it is I who must thank you for that gift, so much more than you need to thank me. Let's end this chapter by discussing what I mean by that. And by talking about how genius gets created in the first place.

You know how your individual creation becomes a communal one. Through the process of other people experiencing an individual creation and imbuing it with meaning and value through the stories they choose to tell themselves about it, others collectively create it. No thing we create in our individual universe holds a pre-determined meaning and value, except that which we choose to bestow upon it.

So what makes a thing become a beloved, renowned creation? The things we call "masterpieces," or works of "genius," are truly not pre-imbued with inherent, pre-determined meaning and value either. Why do we label some things a masterpiece while others we don't? Why, for example, do we call Monet's paintings masterpieces, yet we tell stories about a local artist's paintings that make us yawn?

First, our discernment between "genius" and "ordinary" is a great example of the power of collective beliefs. Much of the meaning and value we bestow upon things is heavily influenced by the collective beliefs of all humans. The meaning and value conferred by authority figures and experts we trust such as parents, textbooks, museums, the media, analysts, and religions have a high level of influence on the stories you choose to tell yourself about those same things when you contextually create them.

Of equal weight is the influence exerted by public acceptance. If "everyone" tells the same story about a thing, or even if you are led to understand that everyone is telling the same story about anything, it is natural to tell similar stories about it. Here in Kentucky, for example, some people call the University of Kentucky's athletic teams "good" and the University of Louisville's "bad." (And vice-versa, of course.) But is either of those teams really "good" or "bad," except in the personal stories their fans have been influenced and taught to tell? Of course not.

How much chance is there that you won't call Claude Monet's paintings masterpieces? Since you've been taught that they are masterpieces by some very credible authorities, chances are slim that you won't. And, additionally, if you didn't, chances are that many people would say that you know nothing about art, have no cultural appreciation, and are unsophisticated. In fact, we have names for people who tell divergent stories about things: iconoclast, counterculturist, deviant, and heretic. Those are not usually desirable labels for a person to assume; it can sometimes even be dangerous to tell different stories than the rest of society.

Yet all those facts actually reinforce another idea that helps explain why some things are called genius while others are not. Despite being taught about what is genius, not everyone agrees with all the communal stories.

Illustrating the notion that nothing has a pre-determined meaning and value except that which you confer upon it, some people simply do not like Monet's paintings very much.

We might be able to explain some of these choices to deviate from our communal stories as someone choosing to be a maverick and go against the herd. We all know people who do not see "good" in things that almost everyone else does. Be they movies, political ideologies, or religions, we know that some people do not see genius in things that many others do. Calling something "genius" is truly a choice we make, individually, no matter how great the social customs and peer pressure may influence us.

So what, exactly, separates the genius from the ordinary? And how can you take advantage of this information to manifest more masterpieces as you contextually create your material world? The bulk of the first answer is found in the initial creation of a thing. You may have been thinking, earlier in this discussion, that I am crazy to suggest that some things aren't pre-ordained with "genius." "Monet's paintings are genius," you might say, "and they were already genius before I contextually created them in my universe."

It is true that "genius" in a thing is imbued in it during its initial creation. Yet there are some clarifications about the bestowing of genius, upon creation, that are valuable to understand. A thing is, indeed, imbued with the energy that allowed the creator to manifest it; a thing is a reflection of the creator's beliefs, after all. People who create things from beliefs that are strongly and delightfully aligned with their desires make it much easier for us to call their creations "good" as we contextually create them in our own unique, individual universe.

Initially, genius is created through channeling. For those unfamiliar with channeling, it is a term for serving as a conduit for information from the non-physical universe—the quantum field. Channeling is usually thought of as an esoteric practice and is something most people find far removed from the mainstream. The first time I encountered channeling was reading the Hicks' book *Ask and It is Given*. Esther Hicks maintains that she channels a non-physical group of entities calling themselves "Abraham" and, when I learned that, I almost put the book back down. In fact, only the forward written by Dr. Wayne Dyer reassured me enough to read it despite my reservations about channeling.

Yet, here I am, years later, telling you that genius is channeled? What prompted me to not only embrace a concept about which I was once very skeptical, but also led me to actually use the term in my own writing? The answer is simple: Channeling is not actually a mystical or esoteric act. In fact, channeling is as ordinary and pedestrian for a human as chewing gum, because channeling is simply a new-age term for what we're all doing each moment of our lives. Not only is genius channeled, so are all our "ordinary" creations.

Channeling a masterpiece is not commonplace, however, and is, in fact, very special. But anyone can do it, including you. In fact, I'll bet you've channeled genius a lot so far and never thought about it as such. We've established that the real you is a non-physical energy. Your consciousness is an uncollapsed portion of the quantum field. The real you is actually a part of the quantum field.

Any time you contextually, or literally, create a thing, you are doing so because the rest of the quantum field is becoming coherent with your beliefs. A thing is a physical manifestation that you have ushered into material existence via the coherence your beliefs have unconsciously formed with the rest of the quantum field. If that thing is pleasing to you, then your beliefs are aligned with your desires, which means the quantum field is also aligned with them.

A channeler brings forth information from a non-physical source into our material world. A channeler is a conduit for non-physical energy and information. How is that definition any different from what we are all doing every day? Every human being is a conduit allowing non-physical energy and information to manifest itself into the physical, material world.

While manifesting genius is not the exclusive domain of a chosen few selected to be special conduits, it is still not a common occurrence. The seeming rarity of manifesting genius leads us, naturally and logically, to conclude that it must be something you're born with the ability to do. But nothing could be further from the truth. Yes, people who create masterpieces should be revered and exalted. But not because those people have been touched by the "hand of God" any more than you have been. They are revered because they have created something uncommon that pleases us greatly to experience.

To explain how genius is manifested as distinct from "ordinary," ask yourself the question "What would make a thing the most pleasurable creation possible?" Since pleasing things are a result of having beliefs in alignment with your desires, doesn't it stand to reason that creating the most pleasing things involves having beliefs almost perfectly aligned with your desires? The closer your beliefs are aligned with your desires, the greater the degree of good your creation will be imbued with.

The truest, purest alignment between your beliefs and your desires creates the most perfect things through the coherence being formed between your beliefs and the quantum field. A masterpiece is simply the physical manifestation of pure alignment, pure joy. A masterpiece is a thing created without the inhibiting filters of any limiting beliefs held by the creator.

And the very reason so many of us are apt to identify the masterpieces of creation is the perfect alignment that allowed its creation. That energy of pure, unfiltered joy that became a tangible, physical object is still within that thing. Those untainted and unabashedly manifest beliefs of love, joy, and explosive excitement resonate with us as we contextually create that thing in our own unique, individual universe. You feel the connection; you know you are interacting with, contextually creating, something wholly real and perfect.

This is why we are so astounded by genius. We know we are experiencing and contextually creating something that is wholly original and perfectly aligned with the greatest beliefs its original creator could hold. This is why we are drawn to it and we exalt it; it resonates with us in ways we don't even need to put into words.

Isn't it nice to know that there really are no "anointed" people? I'll bet there are many areas of your life, perhaps some of them you're in the habit of overlooking, where you, too, are doing masterful work. And by playing "Grow a Greater You," you'll be putting yourself in a position to elevate all of your desires to the masterpiece level.

A life of your dreams is yours for the taking—yours for the growing in to. You never again need to suffer unless you choose to. And you never again need to play small to avoid suffering. I am beyond excited that you're joining our revolution—our celebration called "Grow a Greater You."

Chapter Nineteen

An Inside Look: Dwight's Journey with "Grow a Greater You"

I met Dwight Scoles via email in early October 2013. He read my book *How Quantum Physicists Build New Beliefs* and it resonated so clearly with him that he reached out to me through my website. He asked me if I would mind him sending me his writings as we worked his way up the Emotional Reference Chart regarding his Strikeout Desire for wealth. He assured me that he didn't expect any feedback or coaching, but would be interested in anything I was willing to share with him.

Would I mind? I was, in fact, honored that Dwight imbued me with enough value to share his journey with me, and I was grateful for the additional opportunities he was willing to give me to continue to be of value. Being of value is, after all, the number one priority of my writing and speaking, so I never take those opportunities—or the people willing to give them to me—for granted. I didn't arrive in Dwight's own unique, individual universe with a pre-determined meaning and value; Dwight is the one who chose to tell himself those stories about me. So, no matter how much he thanks me, it is truly me who must thank him.

Dwight's honesty and earnest work moved and inspired me, as I hope it does you. He has given me permission to share his journal with you, so here it is: uncut, personal, honest, and raw. You'll read his journal entries and also share cards he sometimes made himself, to help himself tell new, better-feeling, believable stories along the way.

The universe Dwight now inhabits, from his much more aligned beliefs about wealth, has inspired him to create a business focused on unleashing human potential: Quantum Inner Dialogue. I call him a friend today and he shares my greatest desire to make human suffering optional. In fact, I am creating content with him for his website, quantuminnerdialogue.com/welcome.

Dwight proudly shares that his business, Quantum Inner Dialogue, "taps into the quantum field of all love to rediscover and release your unlimited potential." If you are inspired by his journey up the Emotional Reference Chart and his reformation of wealth into a Home Run Desire, please visit his site and tell him "thank you."

Journal of Transition in Life for Dwight Scoles

Playing "Grow a Greater You" with Greg Kuhn's Emotional Reference Chart

October 17, 2013

Today starts a new chapter in my life.

I read Greg Kuhn's book, *How Physicists Build New Beliefs*. It is time.

It is now time to bring myself into the place in which I can accept wealth. Grateful for the wealth that I receive, looking forward to a life that is:

- Flowing with abundance of all types, friends, finances, freedom, soul work
- Debt free
- Finances overflowing into all areas of my life, serving as the foundation for a new way of being
- Easily asking for appropriate payment for my work
- Long Talks with the Avatar of my Ideal Client
- Clear and clean description of the Value that I bring to others
- Presentations that are clean, precise, compelling, inspirational, a motivation for right action
- Living at the top of the emotional scale regarding finances, self-worth, and others

- Raising the life of others, as a catalyst, for their own complete and compelling Life

My Relationship with Money—October 17, 2013

So, what do I think about material wealth?

What do I think about Money and the pursuit of Money?

Relationship with Money and Material Wealth

Depression / Hopelessness

I do not deserve any more than I am given

The Universe does not understand, or turns a deaf ear to my cries

I will never have any more than just enough

Lately, it appears that I will never even have enough ever again

I clearly cannot ask for money, as my life has shown that does no good at all

I am angry about being stuck without the inner and spiritual resources to break into financial freedom

Nothing ever comes of my efforts to make a clean break from my past patterns

No matter how much I make, there is never enough to cover all of the bills and all of the simple daily requirements

I am angry and feeling despondent that we have entered a phase in which every month seems to be worse than the month before.

I feel terrified with a tightness in my chest that at this rate the final gong will be struck

I am angry that we have been forced into untenable financial positions

I feel doomed to never escaping the dilemma of 'never enough'

If we do not get a different calculus in our financial affairs, we are done. And I am afraid.

I cannot peddle the bike any faster. There is nothing more I can do to escape. Hopelessness

Greg Kuhn

Giving in to the inevitable, our financial life ends soon. Despondent.

I'm not smart enough or cleaver enough to make it in life

The cars need work. The house needs WAY too much work. The yard needs work. We do not have the money to keep it all up. I feel poor, even making a lot of money.

I am to blame. If I had not made all of these bad decisions we would have money in the bank.

My life is a mess because I am running as hard as I can to make more money

It is bad to have a lot of money

I cannot charge what I am worth

I cannot even know what I am worth

I am afraid to ask for money for what I do

Money is the root of all evil

If I focus on money, I am selfish and un-spiritual

If I have material wealth, others will be jealous and angry and feel I am pompous

If I have money others will feel I am arrogant and uncaring

If I become wealthy, my family will think I think I am better than they are

If I become wealthy it will put a wedge between me/us and others

If I become wealthy it will cause us to grow apart over how to handle the money

Money is evil

People who have money took it from other people more deserving than they are

No matter how much I give to the world, I do not deserve to be wealthy

Wealthy people are mean and cruel—like the political power players

Wealthy people lose touch with reality and with regular people

Wealthy people think they are better than everyone else

Wealthy people look down on everyone else and blame the poor for their poverty

Wealthy people do not care about anybody but themselves

I will never be rich, and I hate it

I hate it that there is never enough money to go around

Money slips through my fingers like air

My parents were poor, and I will always be poor no matter how much I earn

I cannot escape the mental patterns that create poverty and lack in my life

No matter what I do with personal-growth techniques, I am up against a powerful barrier that I can never break through

Next Up: Powerlessness/Dejection

Card for Depressed/Hopeless:

October 17, 2013

Although I feel depressed and Hopeless about ever finding a path out of my financial mess, I sense there is some possibility that the quantum field can reflect a new reality of abundance and my beliefs can shift through this process, and I am grateful.

I can also believe, or begin to believe, that everything is exactly as it is supposed to be. And, that there is some possibility that I will get what I want, financial freedom and free-flowing abundance, and that what I want is perfectly aligned with Spirit and my true Happiness.

October 18, 2013

Relationship with Money—Day 2

Powerlessness/Dejection

Lacking strength or power; helpless and feeling totally ineffectual.

Lowness of spirits; depression; melancholy: heavy hearted

I feel so powerless to make any move to improve my financial lot in life. No matter what I do nothing seems to get me over the hump

I get angry about how powerless I feel to get more money flowing from the Universe

This game is not easy. It is disheartening and depressing because I do not see how it will change anything.

I'm already working as hard as I can. I do not have the strength to work any harder than I do now.

I see no possibility that what I could do beyond my current work will be effective. I feel powerless over the future of my finances.

I am so dejected because I've tried over and over to make a run at the entrepreneurial path. And, it looks like I'm just terrible at it based on the ineffective outcomes I've had up until now.

It does not seem to be a move up from depressed and hopeless to dejected and powerless. And, I feel dejected and heavy hearted about the possibility of any reasonable outcome.

I feel so out of strength and dis-spirited today. How can I have any hope that this path will help me get out from under the burden of my debt and break free of the financial malaise I am in?

I'm throwing myself at this with everything I have, and still I don't see how it will help. I feel so powerless to make a dent in the mountain of debit.

I'm going in so many directions at once that it may not be possible to even finish any of my projects. And, besides, I'm feeling dejected and powerless to get everything done in my to-do list. But, I have to make this work. I feel so dejected about it all.

October 18, 2013

Card for Powerlessness/Dejection:

Although I feel powerless and dejected as I work to find a path out of my financial mess, I sense there is some possibility that the quantum field can reflect a new reality of abundance as my beliefs shift through this process, and I am grateful.

I can also believe, or begin to believe, that everything is exactly as it is supposed to be. And, that there is some possibility that I will get what I want, financial freedom and free-flowing abundance, and that what I want is perfectly aligned with Spirit and my true Happiness.

October 21, 2013

Day 3—4

Despair/Worthlessness

I feel despair about the lack of ability to move my life forward along the path

I feel worthless because I'm still unable to move into my full mastery of life and generate the abundance around me in my life

Every day I wonder what I am doing trying to be 'something' in the world, and my failures fill me with despair

What if this process does not work? I never have been able to "pull it off" before. What makes me think I can this time?

I feel so bad that I would rather just lay down and not move again... never try again. But, I am desperate to make it work.

When will this heaviness be lifted? This cycle of feeling worthless is really a drag.

Next up: Grief/Sadness/Desolation

October 21, 2013

Daily Card Despair/Worthlessness

Although I feel despair and worthless about ever finding a path out of my financial mess, I sense there is some possibility that the quantum field can reflect a new reality of abundance and my beliefs shift through this process, and I am grateful.

I can also believe, or begin to believe, that everything is exactly as it is supposed to be. And, that there is some possibility that I will get what I want, financial freedom and free-flowing abundance, and that what I want is perfectly aligned with Spirit and my true Happiness.

October 22, 2013

How am I feeling today about Financial Abundance and this project?

Fear...

Sick to my stomach

Powerless and Dejected did not fit so well... Actually, 'dejected' did not, but powerless, now that is something I can relate to. Did that for two days.

Actually, I am afraid that this process will not work. A few other things 'work sort of' but don't get me across the finish line. Really, I'm not so confident today.

Today it is "Worthless and Despair"

These do not really agree with me. Well, I guess 'despair' does resonate when I am at my lowest point, but it is much more like 'terror' than despair.

I don't really feel in despair, but I can switch into terror pretty easily today. Not really sure what that means...

Sticking with "worthless and despair' even if that does not 'make sense'. I'm sure 'terror' will fit along the line some place.

Next up: Grief / Desolation / Sadness

October 23, 2013

Grief / Desolation / Sadness

Feeling Abandoned and in ruin (desolation)

I feel sad about the constant cycle that never seems to change, although there have been shifts in the way I feel with bits of hope from time to time.

Over the years, I have experienced so many losses when I have tried to create an entrepreneurial business and I have had to grieve those losses many times, like our attempt to do our health newsletter business.

Financially, my life has pretty constantly been in ruin, or nearly so. There is so little time that I have ever been more than a few months from financial ruin. And, this grief and sadness has been a life-long companion.

I have felt sadness as an underlying river and sometimes the grief is unbearable.

I often feel abandoned by life and by the forces of Spirit. There seems to be little that I can do to escape the feelings of impending ruin.

Next up: Anxiety/Fear/Worry

October 25, 2013

Anxiety/Fear/Worry

I feel worried. I am anxious most all of the time at my emotional level. It is a gnawing feeling in my chest below my heart.

I worry that we will not get our revenue stream flowing before the financial bell rings.

I feel afraid that even though we have assurances that all will be well, and that everything is exactly as it should be, that my 'faith' such as it is will be in vain

I feel afraid that whatever I do will not be enough.

I feel worried that my imagined process will lead to naught when applied in the real world

I worry that we will not have enough money to fix the car and anything else that might break down such as computers or printers or the dog needing help at the vet

I worry that we will have to pay someone to scrape off the roof during the winter and will not have enough money to hire someone

I am anxious that even though Greg says that this works every time, that I will be the first one because of all of the failed efforts in my past

I feel fearful that even if we figure out how to attract some customers to the business that there will still not be enough money to go around and get the debts paid off before we run out of our credit limits.

I feel fearful that this will be the spot in the ladder that stops my forward progress.

Next up: Anger/Blame

October 25, 2013

Card for Fear/Anxiety/Worry

Although I feel fear, anxiety and worry about whether I can ever find a path out of my financial mess, I sense there is some possibility that the quantum field can reflect a new reality of abundance and my beliefs may shift through this process, and I am grateful.

I can also believe, or begin to believe, that everything is exactly as it is supposed to be. And, that there is some possibility that I will get what I want, financial freedom and free-flowing abundance, and that what I want is perfectly aligned with Spirit and my true Happiness

October 27, 2013

Fear/Anxiety/Worry

Last week when I was out of town, the thought struck me, "If this works, it will mean that I am finally successful in my life."

If I am successful at this process, then the rest of my life process automatically falls in line. I have the sense that I know the rest of the steps... that I've been preparing this path and understand it so clearly that the end of the old struggle is on the way.

I mentioned to my spouse that this path and Wallace D. Wattles' book on money have brought me to realize that the emotions, the type and the intensity, are the fuel for the quantum field to bring our desires into reality. Yet, someone who is really on fire for a very positive "way out there" goal is considered a nut case even more than someone who is "out to shut down the government if it is the last thing that we do." The 'weirdo and the crackpot' is the one who wants to save all of the children in the world or wants to create a new form of corporation that is respectful and generous. But, our emotions are the very KEY to the process of becoming fully human and fully alive.

Yesterday was my day for 'fear and anxiety and worry.' I was looking forward to it because I've mostly felt worry and fear working on the more 'negative' emotions. Well, it turned into a day to remember.

Actually, writing up the 'fear experience' turned out to be more difficult than expected. Much of those feelings had simmered down by yesterday. It was actually sort of surprising. However, the day itself was all negative 'rock and roll' with reservations about my life, and facing one of the most significant decisions of my process over this past year. I figured that this particular topic might even require a week to resolve. However, we went to a light and sound and music healing concert last night. I did not think that much was going on. Half way through I had a 'talk' with the Universe about, "OK, Get me to the other side of the river. Let's get over the bridge and put this fear of failure and fear of outcomes behind me." That is sort of a typical conversation I have with the Universe.

When I woke up this morning, I felt so much lighter. I did my energizing meditation session like normal. And I have noticed all day that the fear/anxiety that has been a pretty much constant companion was gone. That is way cool. I keep sort of waiting for it to rear up again, but there just seems to be a new state of inner being/inner peacefulness. I am so thrilled, and grateful!

Next up: Anger & Blame

October 27, 2013

Anger & Blame

Tough topic... I did not think there would be anything to ruminate on as of yesterday (day 1 of anger/blame). Ha!

We had a pretty tough discussion about my behavior with other people. And, I feel angry about the implications.

I may yet again be on the verge of depression and giving it all up. Not a fun time.

I feel angry that the process of moving into abundance takes so long... sort of like watching paint dry. I guess that is the point, after all. Let's not spook the rabbit by leaping over the fence.

Right now, anything that would normally just be minor irritants instead become triggers that could easily lead me to all-out anger. However, I can still let those experiences pass. And, I am grateful for that better management of my reactions.

I feel angry because I feel there is so little I can do to move my life into a better state of experience and relationship with wealth.

Why am I feeling angry when my contract just increased the amount of time, therefore billable dollars, that I can work/earn?

I think I will sit on this one for a time. I did not do my Higher Brain Living energizing meditation today, so the energy levels were rather spotty. Even given that, though, I made it through today without any more episodes of recrimination. And, I am grateful for that.

So, I blame other people for bringing up things that I really do not agree with. Yet through that process, I realized three very fundamental shifts that are required for me to bring more value to the world. These would not have come to light without the messy process, or at least, the messy process allowed them to come to my attention (judging, reliving trauma, social balance of yin/yang).

Next up: Doubt/Pessimism

October 28, 2013

Significant quote that was helpful to me at this time

Significant Greg Kuhn quote

"I can guarantee that, if you have an unrealized desire, dream, or goal, your true beliefs about that material object or experience are negative and not aligned with that desire. How can I make such a bold and seemingly presumptuous claim? Because of the new architecture paradigm that clearly teaches us exactly how our material reality is created. You are the creator of your material reality, as the quantum field responds perfectly to your beliefs and expectations when creating your material reality, so it is a certainty that your material experiences are a perfect match with your true beliefs. In other words, it is impossible to experience the absence of something desired if your beliefs about that desired thing are truly positive. So, if you are experiencing an absence of a desired outcome, your true, underlying beliefs about that thing must be negative. If they were truly positive, you would already be experiencing that desired outcome right now. This is exactly why it is so important to inventory your true beliefs about your absent desires in order to change them.

Although it may be tempting to view this aspect of the architecture paradigm in a negative light, I encourage you to see the freedom found through it. Am I saying that you are responsible for all your troubles, your suffering, and the absence of your desires? I suppose that's one way someone could choose to view it , but I choose to say that you are not responsible for your previous "failings" and, instead, are now responsible for your future "successes." I am not claiming that people in horrific circumstances, like abused children, are responsible for their circumstances. I have no explanation for abusive situations like this, nor do I intend to minimize them here. I do know, however, that for the attainment of the overwhelming majority of personal dreams and goals, even for people currently suffering greatly, there is tremendous freedom in the architecture paradigm, because, through it, you are no longer an unconscious victim of your old beliefs."

Why Quantum Physicists Play "Grow a Greater You"

Kuhn, Greg (2013-01-05). Why Quantum Physicists Do Not Fail (p. 92).

October 30, 2013

Doubt/Pessimism

I have doubt about my ability to just go out and do it, like my two teachers are suggesting.

It takes a lot of guts, and I feel pessimistic that I can make that leap.

Regarding money flowing in, without me knowing how to create the waterwheel of wealth, I feel doubtful that it can happen.

Even me stating these doubts and this pessimism makes me feel like, hey, if I feel this way, how can it ever even happen?

I doubt that the money will just magically show up. And as I feel that doubt, it doubles the doubt because I see how little faith that I have. And, isn't faith and confidence required for the shift to happen and a new way of living to sprout and grow?

Everything is all shifting and changing and I do not see it shifting in the right direction. I feel very pessimistic about how the outcome can possibly turn out good.

Now that the business arrangements are shifted, I have more stress about extra expense. And I am pessimistic about how I can do my work and earn extra income without being ready to spend the proper time with people each week.

Next Up: Worry/Nervousness

November 3, 2013

Worry/Nervousness

I feel worried that things are not sifting fast enough.

When the bills keep showing up at a gallop, it makes me very nervous

I want to say "I am" on these, but I know that worry and nervousness are just thoughts and feelings and have no power unless I give them power. They are not me.

I am dreaming more about the project I see coming as my life ministry, acting as a catalyst for others to shift into their True Powerful Self. Yet, I worry that this is just a pipe dream.

I get nervous about whether the actual interactions with others can be as dynamic and impactful as what I imagine.

I worry about whether the financial shift can come in time for us to keep from total ruin.

I have this nervous feeling in the pit of my stomach that we went too far with our expenses for training and that the next thing will take us over the edge.

Hey, we already seem to be over the edge, and that is something that I really can worry about.

I worry about whether I am far enough along this path to be helping others get their own quantum results.

I worry about whether I can provide enough value to people that they will be willing to pay the costs of sessions with me to experience these shifts into their quantum true being.

Up next: Frustration/Aggravation

November 5, 2013

Frustration/Aggravation

I feel frustrated that the process seems to take so long, even though it is only a few days.

I have some level of aggravation that the experience can be so difficult on certain days. It means that I really start doubting myself.

I feel somewhat like a 5 year old... frustrated and aggravated: Daddy, are we there yet?

I feel frustrated that everything right now is preparation. How can the money flow if there is nothing really happening?

I feel VERY frustrated that the doom and gloom swirls around my head about feeling like we are going to end up in total ruin.

I woke up feeling agitated and aggravated and scared about the bills that I'm adding to our debt load by the training that I'm signed up for.

I feel aggravated that the whirling like the wind continues outside of the windows of my mind and that such strong feelings can still be here when I am moving up the emotional ladder with consistency.

Up next: Unease/Discontent

November 5, 2013

Card for frustration/aggravation

Even though I'm feeling frustrated that I don't see a clear path and I feel aggravated that things are moving so slowly, I acknowledge that it's possible for me to believe that someday I will experience release from debt that is the absence of abundance right now. So right now I am OK feeling frustrated, and it's okay for me to feel frustrated and feel the expectations that arise from this. It's okay to be right where I am. I am in the process and I'm willing to give it a chance and I believe what Greg is sharing with me and I believe it's possible but for right now it's okay for me to be right where I am.

Thank you Universe! Thank you for flowing love and acceptance and resources into my life. Thank you for people who believe in me and in the gifts that are flowing into their lives through working and being with me. Thank you for reminding me that although I'm not where I want to be with manifesting the resolution and release from debt, I will stay the course. Thank you for reminding me that you are infinite, abundant, creative, and anything is possible with you and it is easy for you to manifest the desires of my heart. We are all on the same page with that! And your gracious and generous gifts today remind me of your complete support of my path.

November 6, 2013

Unease/Discontent

I feel uneasy because as I get more engaged it seems there is more energy of unease around me.

I feel discontented about the methods that my teacher uses because they seem to have a foundation of blame

I am feeling uneasy about whether the changes in my financial status and income will happen in time to avert the disaster of total financial ruin.

I am feeling discontented about the dis-ease of not knowing how I am impacting the people that I work with... does she feel offended with my messages as though I am not honoring all that she already knows and has experienced?

I feel uneasy that there are not many feeling spaces to tap into as I do this topic Unease/Discontent

I feel discontented about the 'messages' that imply I should have no feelings of discomfort about my current life situation. I am certain that these ideas of 'no bad feelings' are off target.

Next up: Indifference/Apathy

November 7, 2013

Indifference/Apathy

I feel rather indifferent about whether this process goes forward because things are relatively fine right now in my life.

I feel fine about being in the state of the 'calm before the storm' and I'm happy to just sit for a while

Since my mind is rather split right now, I think I will just rest and not work so hard... feeling rather apathetic about moving into the more positive states.

A number of things have been going well, like sessions with two clients. So, maybe there is time to not work so hard. I am rather indifferent about moving into the 'real' work that is ahead.

Up next: Pensiveness/Melancholy

November 8, 2013

Pensiveness/Melancholy

I have been feeling very pensive and unsettled today.

Melancholy and feeling a bit lost are taking a hold at times as this process seems to drag on. Sometimes this feeling expands or has tinges of doubt about the grand process or plan that is under foot.

Some sadness is felt about how complicated all of the methods seem to be. Mostly I think the Melancholy is from being way low on inner energy and the need for sleep.

Feeling some melancholy now about what I am leaving behind by making this journey... no more lazy bones... no more excuses for not having the life I want.

Feeling pensive and a bit anxious about whether this process will work. After all, nothing else in my life ever did. Well, actually, everything else has moved and shifted me a tiny bit at a time. But, this could shift my life completely if it works.

Next up: Introspection/Contemplation

November 8, 2013

Card for Pensive/Indifferent

Even though I'm feeling indifferent about whether or not I want to see a clear path and I feel pensive about how slowly the process seems to be moving, I acknowledge that it's possible for me to believe that I am moving forward and that I will experience release from debt and will realize the free-flowing financial abundance that seems to be absent right now. So right now I am OK feeling pensive, and it's okay for me to feel indifferent and feel the expectations that arise from this. It's okay to be right where I am. I am in the process and I'm willing to give it a chance and I believe what Greg is sharing with me and I believe it's possible. And though it seems a long way off, for right now it's okay for me to be right where I am.

Thank you Universe! Thank you for flowing love and acceptance and resources into my life. Thank you for people who believe in me and in the gifts that are flowing into their lives through working and being with me. Thank you for reminding me that although I'm not where I want to be with manifesting the resolution and release from debt, and the free-flowing financial abundance, I will stay the course. Thank you for reminding me that you are infinite, abundant, creative, and anything is possible with you and it is easy for you to manifest the desires of my heart. We are all on the same page with that! And your gracious and generous gifts today remind me of your complete support of my path.

November 10, 2013

Introspection/Contemplation

I am spending time in introspection about this process of transitioning from the more 'negative' emotions up the emotional ladder to where my

263

dreams can become reality.

Contemplating, thinking and ruminating about what can be done that leads to advancement of my financial state and an increase in my financial welfare

Meditating and introspection to allow the voices of the new state of life to make themselves known, giving them freedom to express, to stretch and find space for their awakening.

Thinking and introspection about how my life is shifting and changing over these short few weeks. And the trajectory and flow that has been released to bring growth that results in the eventual fulfillment of my life purpose and dreams.

Next up: Acceptance/Peace

November 12, 2013

Acceptance/Peace

I am feeling acceptance and peace about my path, no matter if some days it does feel like the pace moves slowly, I acknowledge that it's likely for me to move forward now, and that I will experience release from debt and will realize the free-flowing financial abundance that seems to be absent right now. So right now I am OK feeling OK with acceptance and peace. It's okay for me to feel simple acceptance, and feel the expectations that arise from this. It's okay to be right where I am. I am in the process and I'm willing to give it a chance and I believe what Greg is sharing with me and I believe it's possible. And though it seems a long way off, for right now it's okay for me to be right where I am.

Thank you Universe! Thank you for flowing love and acceptance and resources into my life. Thank you for people who believe in me and in the gifts that are flowing into their lives through working and being with me. Thank you for reminding me that although I'm not where I want to be with manifesting the resolution and release from debt, and the free-flowing financial abundance, I will stay the course. Thank you for reminding me that you are infinite, abundant, creative, and anything is possible with you and it is easy for you to manifest the desires of my heart. We are all on the same page with that! And your gracious and generous gifts today remind me of your complete support of my path.

Next up: Interest/Inquisitive

November 14, 2013

Interest/Inquisitive

I am feeling inquisitive about how my path will be revealed, no matter if some days it does feel like the pace moves slowly, I acknowledge that it's likely for me to move forward now, and that I will experience release from debt and will realize the free-flowing financial abundance that seems to be absent right now. So right now I am OK feeling OK with being inquisitive and interested in how the outcome will come about. It's okay for me to feel simple interest, and feel the expectations that arise from this. It's okay to be right where I am. I am in the process and I'm willing to give it a chance and I believe what Greg is sharing with me and I believe it's possible. And though it seems a long way off, for right now it's okay for me to be right where I am.

Thank you Universe! Thank you for flowing love and acceptance and resources into my life. Thank you for people who believe in me and in the gifts that are flowing into their lives through working and being with me. Thank you for reminding me that although I'm not where I want to be with manifesting the resolution and release from debt, and the free-flowing financial abundance, I will stay the course. Thank you for reminding me that you are infinite, abundant, creative, and anything is possible with you and it is easy for you to manifest the desires of my heart. We are all on the same page with that! And your gracious and generous gifts today remind me of your complete support of my path.

Next up: Hopefulness/Optimism

November 25, 2013

Target: Free Flowing Financial Abundance, and living debt free.

Emotionally, this optimism seems tied in with the Quantum Alignment validity and my ability to provide a valid transformational experience for people that they will be willing to pay for.

I feel hopeful and optimistic about the possibilities of Quantum Living Systems and Quantum Success Acceleration!

I had a great call with TB yesterday. The explanation of how the Kuhn/Abrahams Emotional Reference Chart can help him with a very difficult challenge created some excitement for me.

After discussing my take on Voice Dialogue, it becomes even clearer that these techniques provide value and hope for people.

TB gave me deep-felt encouragement about how significantly people's lives will be affected through the Quantum Living Systems program.

People continue to encourage me, and give me blessings and positive expectations of how much happiness this can bring to people.

Another 'partner in crime' stated that I do this (Voice Dialogue) so much better than she. And, that gives me hope that the significance of Quantum Alignment is 'real'

I do have some feeling about 'when will the other shoe drop.' Still, there is significant feedback that allows me to hope and find optimism about the validity of the process.

Knowing how much this has affected different people in my life gives me significant hope that the service is valuable, and that others will pay my asking fees for the service.

Isn't it nice to be in the Optimistic side of the cycle? Well, now the question arises about how to deal with whatever I am dragging with me up the ladder.

The answer is to create Inner Dialog Release cards.

Next up: Enthusiasm/Ambition

November 25, 2013

Hopefulness/Optimism daily card

Target: Free Flowing Financial Abundance, and living debt free.

Emotionally, this optimism seems tied in with the Quantum Living Systems validity and my ability to provide a valid transformational experience for people that they will be willing to pay for.

Hopefulness/Optimism

I am feeling hopeful and optimistic about how my path is being revealed, no matter if it sometimes does feel like I am waiting for the other shoe to drop, I acknowledge that it's likely for me to move forward now, and that I am experiencing release from the worry about the value of Quantum Living Systems. And, that release from debt can be realize with the free-flowing financial abundance, even if they seem to be absent right now.

So right now I am OK feeling OK with being optimistic and hopeful about how the outcome is come about, even while there still can be feelings of anxiety at moments in time. It is okay for me to feel simple optimism, and feel the expectations that arise from this. It's okay to be right where I am. I am in the process and I'm willing to give it a chance and I believe what Greg is sharing with me and I believe it's possible. And though it seems a long way off, for right now it's okay for me to be right where I am.

Thank you Universe! Thank you for flowing love and acceptance and resources into my life. Thank you for people who believe in me and in the gifts that are flowing into their lives through working and being with me. Thank you for reminding me that although I'm not where I want to be with manifesting the resolution and release from debt, and the free-flowing financial abundance, I will stay the course. Thank you for reminding me that you are infinite, abundant, creative, and anything is possible with you and it is easy for you to manifest the desires of my heart. We are all on the same page with that! And your gracious and generous gifts today remind me of your complete support of my path.

And, everything is exactly as it should be. And, everything is OK exactly as it is.

November 26, 2013

Target: Free Flowing Financial Abundance, and living debt free.

Emotionally, this Enthusiasm seems tied in with my ability to provide a valid transformational experience for people that people will be willing to pay for.

Enthusiasm/Ambition

I am beginning to feel ambitious about creating the infrastructure for Quantum Living Systems and Quantum Success Acceleration.

I just discovered that Quantum Success Acceleration is available as a web site. That is very cool. What a sweet gift from the Universe! THAT is creating a little jolt of enthusiasm for me!

I am enthusiastic about the feedback that I am being given from those I know. How cool is that. The work penetrates through and dissolves old barriers to transformation.

Yesterday brought one of the most important Inner Dialog Release Cards.

The aspect of me that wanted to just 'drift away in contented oblivion' got to speak. This is the very earliest personal/child aspect. Wow! It is Mystery when transformed. It can give up on trying to stop 'us' from proceeding with the understanding that it IS the Child that I Love. And, that it is the connection with Spirit and all Other Dimensional energy. The BIG discovery was that IT is not afraid. It was just throwing up 'chaff' of fearful ideas to stop the progress that would eliminate it's fanciful magical-thinking dream of doing nothing in life... the 'trust-fund kid' that just has everything that it wants and can do no wrong with Daddy. Here I was thinking that my 'Child-Self' was terrified. It just was threatened (it's fanciful idea was threatened) by real success that is right here right now.

Time to build the physical tools to go with the mystery Time for some real-life Ambition!

Next Up: Anticipation/Eagerness

November 26, 2013

Enthusiasm/Ambition Daily Card

Target: Free Flowing Financial Abundance, and living debt free. Emotionally, this Enthusiasm seems tied in with my ability to provide a valid transformational experience for people that they will be willing to pay for.

Enthusiasm/Ambition

I am feeling Enthusiastic and beginning to build Ambition about how my path is being revealed, no matter if it sometimes does feel like it. I acknowledge that it's likely for me to move forward now, and that I am experiencing release from the worry about the value of Quantum Living Systems. And, that release from debt can be realized with the free-flowing financial abundance, even if they seem to be absent right now.

So right now I am OK feeling OK with being Enthusiastic and Ambitious and am beginning to work on the physical tasks needed for bringing about the outcome, even while there still can be feelings of anxiety at moments in time. It is okay for me to feel enthusiasm and begin to really make physical headway, and feel the expectations that arise from this. It's okay to be right where I am. I am in the process and I'm willing to give it a chance and I believe what Greg is sharing with me and I believe it's possible. And though it seems a long way off, for right now it's okay for me to be right where I am.

Thank you Universe! Thank you for flowing love and acceptance and resources into my life. Thank you for people who believe in me and in the gifts that are flowing into their lives through working and being with me. Thank you for reminding me that although I'm not where I want to be with manifesting the resolution and release from debt, and the free-flowing financial abundance, I will stay the course. Thank you for reminding me that you are infinite, abundant, creative, and anything is possible with you and it is easy for you to manifest the desires of my heart. We are all on the same page with that! And your gracious and generous gifts today remind me of your complete support of my path.

And, everything is exactly as it should be. And, everything is OK exactly as it is.

December 2, 2013

Target: Free Flowing Financial Abundance, and living debt free

Anticipation/Eagerness

I am anticipating easily moving into this new phase of my life. I look forward two or three years and see an entirely different way of living compared to my previous struggles.

I am eager to finish the infrastructure pieces of the Stop Smoking program. I am looking forward to getting in front of people and speaking about this powerful method of shifting lives.

I can see how corporations could back my working with their people as a Certified Transformational Coach. The work we do is so powerful and allows every participant to experience new breakthroughs in their experience.

Today has been a bit of a setback as there were multiple instances at work with nothing going as I wished. So, my energy level for upgrading my life is rather low. I am anticipating that the energy level is at an ebb due to bronchial infection. When that is gone, I will be back to eagerness and anticipation full bore.

This has been a very difficult week. I have been slowly recovering from bronchitis and low energy. There have been many days of feeling sub-par and out of sorts. Yet, I find my main base-line continues to be

Anticipation and Eagerness about the work.

Next Up: Excitement/Passion

December 31, 2013

Target: Free Flowing Financial Abundance, and living debt free

Excitement & Passion

I am feeling very Passionate about this work that is beginning to flow from me!

I do not know where it leads. I do not know for certain how to move forward, but there are steps that I can take. Like a flower, I do not know. And, like a flower, it does not matter much at all. I am still excited about the unfolding as it is showing up here in 3D space.

Excitement is great. Movement is even better. And, movement is beginning to take shape. Flowing from the inner motivation that excitement and passion creates. The concerns about finances are drifting into a very misty 'nothing' as my Excitement increases about the work that unfolds at my feet.

My session today with a client was a bit challenging. She did allow us to do some interesting and exciting work today. She received the prompting to move into her 'uneasy' state with grace. The work today was quite interesting. I really am passionate about this work. And it so easily takes people into transformative states.

I saw today, that when we cheat, when we who are hearing the calling heart of Spirit wooing us cop out and mimic love from fear, that we cheat Mother Earth GAIA of Her new Human Species. I am passionate about the Human integration of themselves with their inner parts and aspects. All of the voices wish to be heard. I believe that may be all that is necessary to bring a shift and transformational momentum into the world.

I am feeling excited and honored to be allowed on the inside of the mind to observe how it responds to change. I believe that the change we desire is right there at our fingertips. That is exciting to my Soul.

This client is using the Emotional Reference Chart to know where to go (up), and Voice Dialog to allow shifts out of stuck places. She is brave, even fearless, to allow another person such intimate access to her BEing. And, I am passionate about working from a pristine place with her and with each client who chooses this work.

Next up: Confidence & Inspiration

January 1, 2014

Target: Free Flowing Financial Abundance, and living debt free

Confidence & Inspiration

I am feeling confident and inspired about developing a powerful business model that generates free-flowing income. From this base of abundance, I can see how debt-free living is entirely possible. Yay.

Did a 'mental session' with a phone conference call today on introducing people to how we can release ourselves from the things that get us stuck. It was fun. I am confident that I can do the same thing in 'real time' in the near future.

Today was a sad day. I spoke to a friend, or someone that I thought I have been building a friendship with, and I unfortunately was over-the-top enthusiastic. He did not like my domineering pushy attitude. Inspiration can be a two-edged sword, at least for me. So, my confidence is smashed down, feeling low. I am not my feelings. I was being a 'brat' in a way, I wanted him to see the value of my work so very much. I could see him batting away the ideas, not participating early on. But, I wanted him to see the value so much and to share in my enthusiasm. It could have been a significant benefit for his work. Now we may never speak again. And, it was my own doing.

And, other news about a family change that is so disheartening. So, my confidence in moving forward is in a low right now. It is just an emotion. The emotions are not me. And, I choose to release them, and accept what is in the process of showing up in life, for me and others.

Wow, what a confidence booster! I met with two people today for sessions. The work was encouraging and inspiring. And, the feedback is bringing me such amazing joy as I find my inner source of commitment, love, wisdom and courage. Wow.

Next up: Ease/Power

<u>January 22, 2013</u>

Ease/Power

Target:

Free Flowing Financial Abundance, and living debt free

This has been an amazing week of Ease and Power. There has also been learning about not 'leaning too far forward on the surf board' in anticipation.

This experience is NOT about me, though it is my experience.

I got banged around a bit during a group get-together. The time progressed into a couple of sessions, both invited by the 'leaders' in the group. However, what they wanted was not really the deep inner-dialog work that I ended up doing. It was very powerful. However, my sensitivity to their 'real' needs was lacking. So, I got feedback that I was 'pushing too hard'.

After I got over my feeling of disappointment, I came to feel how great a compliment they gave me, such a major change for me from the social phobias of my near past. And, I learned to step back a bit in my power and enthusiasm. And, to be more sensitive to the undercurrent of the REAL messages coming my way.

Went to a networking launch meeting. The people there were absolutely wonderful in their support of my work. Ease and Power. It was very cool. Someday perhaps I will get past feeling so surprised and shocked by the "new me." Right now, it is really a KICK!

Although I have been on Ease and Power for nearly a week, the week has been really amazing! So MANY options are opening up for the financial abundance that I have desired. Two major breakthroughs have occurred related to my restricting fears. One that seems so simple is that the core of my BEing is love. This can be experienced during my Inner Dialog sessions. So, the core of the Highest of ALL beings (some call God) must also be LOVE! And, therefore, God EXPECTS me to prosper. The other is that I am BOTH engaged as a 'Son' in the process of Life, a Son to the Father/Mother of Light with responsibilities and privileges, and ALSO, I can be totally free to WANT what I WANT without guilt or remorse or cowering waiting for the 'fist' to pummel me.

So, I have now created a list of EVERYTHING that I WANT in life, at the deepest levels that I can reach in my conscious state today. After each point that I wrote down, I asked, "Is there ANYTHING ELSE?" And, "If you received EVERYTHING on your list, would that take care of EVERYTHING you could ever want?" THAT was quite an experience.

I think it is time to move to the next rung up the ladder...

Next up: Joy/Elation

January 28, 2014

Joy/Elation

Target:

Free Flowing Financial Abundance, and living debt free

Wow!

It was only weeks ago that I was still not certain that 'this would work.' I mean, even at anticipation and eagerness, I still was not certain. Wow.

Joe Vitale has come along through his books. The impact has been staggering. His 5-step process The Attractor Factor IS one of Ease and Power! And, up until a few weeks ago, I didn't even really find his messages very attractive. So... seeing the light now.

We are going to develop a great e-mail based training program related to Inner Dialog. We can find a very nice audience for this training. Everything really is in place already except for infrastructure things.

How big are we willing to dream? How many people can be found that will be assisted by this new work? We can put the project together in the Quantum Field, and the outcome is beyond our ability to understand from this point in time.

~

I am SO stunned! Joy and Elation, it is true!

Love and Life are pouring out on me in ways that I can no longer even begin to describe here. Every part that we could need has shown itself now. I am no longer hunting. No more feelings of desperation. I am in Awe of the combination of awareness and methods and people that have come together!

In this time, I have finalized two seemingly opposite 'contracts' with

Spirit… This is in addition to the original contract of 40 years ago…. First, Asking for the Work to be completed by the Power of Spirit, I have agreed to put my all into what I am doing. No more passivity and 'hope without hope.' And, I have agreed to be dedicated to the changes in me for the sake of the outcome in the world. Second, within days of more and more agitation, I also struck an agreement that I WILL ask for what I WANT without fear or guilt or remorse or defense of my "why." The original contract still stands. The first new contract stands. The second new contract stands. It cannot be comprehended in my mind. However, after these events, I have felt SO EMPOWERED and freed from the bondage of false guilt that it cannot really be put into words or even understood by my own mind.

The physical form of fulfillment has come as seeds. There are so MANY seeds that all I can do is walk in the path of inspiration and inspired action, and watch and be mindful, noticing what seeds sprout first. There is no doubt whatsoever that these are all wonderful seeds. There are eight business plans. All but one are easy to implement through known methods. Each of these deserves to become LIVE and WHOLE. And, now I am simply loving them all, letting them rest in my open palms, while I do what needs to be done in the moments of the day that I have.

And, at my core, Joy is growing. Happiness. Elation. And, a quiet confidence that all is, and all has been, well in my world. All is exactly as it should be. Thank You spirits, energies, God Essence. You have opened up my awareness to the flow of gifts. And, I am satisfied that the world is as it should be, my Mother & Father of Abundance.

Next up: Love/Ecstasy!

January 30, 2013

Love/Ecstasy!

Target:

Free Flowing Financial Abundance, and living debt free

Can anyone move from total fear of everyone that they ever met to Joy and Love and Ecstasy?

Through a fairly short, but winding road, I have done so. And, now, with the work of shifting my beliefs around money and abundance, life is making openings for me to really live!

What can I say, except that I am truly amazed. Looking for the experience of the tipping point - the out-materialization of the inner joy. What a great and amazing work this has been.

~

This is an amazing time. I am LOVING life, every day now. When I sit in gratitude for this Life, I move into Ecstasy! Heaven is here.

(There went a negative DING! And, now I can say, THAT is not how my mind works any more. Those old thoughts simply remind me of where I know that Spirit resides. Everything that creates Expansion of Spirit is of Spirit. Everything else is not. Simple.)

I have been given 8 different business opportunities. Each of them is amazing. One was just dropped into my mind only moments ago. It can, all by itself, provide me the monthly income base-line that I have requested/ordered up from the Universe! Living in Ecstasy. Not something that I would have even imagined in my wildest dreams only weeks ago.

This trip up the Emotional Reference Chart did, in fact, shift my emotional responses to creating wealth, to the opportunities for getting way beyond my current financial conditions. (Thank you, Thank you, Thank you!)

The underlying experience of my life HAS changed substantially. I am entirely comfortable going to a business networking group launch with 60 people. I became aware that they do not have anything more to offer the world than I do. In fact, I sense that my enthusiasm for my work, and my willingness to experiment and to expand in the Universe may be in the top of the chart. How comforting and inspiring! So, now it is time to build a business system that will rock the world!

Next up... LIVING!

Thank you, Dwight, for allowing us all to share your journey. Please visit Dwight's website to see, firsthand, what he has been inspired by his journey to create. Would you, like Dwight, enjoy sharing how you play "Grow a Greater You" in one of my future books? If so, start playing "Grow a Greater You" right now and then email your story to me at gregkuhn@whyquantumphycisists.com. How much fun would it be for your success story to inspire others as Dwight has done for us all here?

Chapter Twenty

About the Author

Author Greg Kuhn is a professional educator and a futurist, specializing in framing new paradigms for 21st century living. Prior to writing his own book series, he had written primarily with his father, Dr. Clifford Kuhn, M.D., about health, wellness, and productivity.

The other acclaimed books in Greg's series are:

How Quantum Physicists Build New Beliefs

Why Quantum Physicists Do Not Fail

Why Quantum Physicists Don't Get Fat

Why Quantum Physicists Create More Abundance

Why Quantum Physicists Do Not Suffer

Greg Kuhn lives in Louisville, KY, with a wonderful wife and four fantastic sons (one by marriage) whom he couldn't have published this book without. You can read more at Greg's website or Greg's Tweets.

Greg is profoundly grateful for the opportunity to be of value you bestow upon him: "Your decisions to make my books and seminars important and meaningful is something I do not take for granted. Thank you for allowing me to be of service to you and thank you for helping spread the word about our power as the contextual creators of our life experiences. Together we are contextually creating a world where suffering can truly be optional."

Future books in Greg's "Why Quantum Physicists..." series will cover:

- Money
- Romantic relationships
- Parenting
- Blending Families
- Teaching

Greg gives talks and presentations for these topics, tailored for both adult and youth audiences. If you'd like to inquire about his availability, simply contact him via email and/or contact him through the means previously listed. Feel free, also, to suggest additional topics for his "*Why Quantum Physicists...*" series.

Made in the USA
Lexington, KY
08 September 2014